P9-CDH-365

DATE DUE

ILL 9-2-93			
JUN 0 8 1995			
JUL 1 1 2001			

A Tra

DEMCO 38-297

ENCOURAGING COMMUNITY DEVELOPMENT

A Training Guide for Local Workers

WILLIAM W. BIDDLE

with the collaboration of

LOUREIDE J. BIDDLE

HOLT, RINEHART AND WINSTON, INC.
New York   Chicago   San Francisco
Atlanta   Dallas   Montreal
Toronto   London

Preface

This book is a training guide. It is therefore a textbook, but a textbook of an unusual kind. It has been written to meet an unusual challenge in a period of rapid social change and consciously planned development. It offers training for that most important but most neglected contributor to intelligent development, the local worker who will live with people for a time. It is addressed to those who will accept the discipline of planned training.

Conscious development can be planned at many levels, from international to local. This book focuses mainly upon that local improvement which has come to be known as community development. But it begins to relate local programs and processes to larger national and international efforts.

In community development there are several levels of training necessary. We, in this book, are covering one only: training for nonprofessionals or preprofessionals. Training for professionals (social workers, teachers, community development experts, program administrators, social science researchers, and the like) is mentioned only inferentially, if at all. We do not go into training for program sponsors (legislators, boards of trustees, and other approvers of budgets) and we touch only lightly upon publicity to gain public support. Our concern is for the important job of the improver who will live locally with the people who are to participate in development, yet who must relate himself, his neighbor, and the process to the professionals and the big decision-makers.

When people talk or write about improving the social order they usually insert a remark such as, "Of course, human beings will have to be made better." That casually delivered "of course" hides a task of extraordinary difficulty, but of great hope.

This is a book about that humanity-developing task. It tells of some ways in which ordinary citizens can be persuaded to improve themselves. It tells of how encouragers who live and work with them can speed the process.

Some readers will say, "Yes, but this book does not tell how the deep-seated injustices of the past shall be overcome, or how new legislation is to be enacted, or how great programs of social betterment shall be financed and administered." All this is true. The pages that follow have to do with the human change phases of the great programs of improvement.

Some other readers will say, "The descriptions you give of human behavior are overidealistic. People don't act that way." And this will be true also—as long as the critic is talking about the way human beings *are*. It will not be true of human beings *becoming better,* as a result of living through educational processes that can be encouraged. This is a book for those who will do the encouraging.

The text deals with the local and even personal development aspects of large-scale and much-publicised programs. It tells how a new breed of volunteers may make a unique contribution that experts can seldom make, yet which the experts and legislators and planners count upon for success of their efforts.

The argument depends upon, and takes off from, another book, *The Community Development Process.*[1] It is hoped that readers will be familiar with, or will make themselves familiar with, the social scientific thinking of the earlier book. More specifically, references are made to the other book in several of the "Addendum for Social Science Students" sections which close all chapters of this text except the Introduction.

An optimism about human potential for improvement pervades this book. This optimism is based upon three guiding assumptions:

1. That social problems have solutions if human beings will search for these with sufficient persistence, intelligence, and good will.

2. That though the great decisions on solutions will be made by legislators, judges, important executives, planners, and program adminis-

---

[1] William W. Biddle, and Loureide J. Biddle, *The Community Development Process.* (New York: Holt, Rinehart and Winston, Inc., 1965).

trators, the small-scale development of ordinary people can influence the big decision-makers in their search for solutions.

3. That both powerful and less prominent people will be willing to commit themselves to an experimental search for such solutions.

The optimism does not rest upon any formulas for reform now available. It rests upon the expectation that solutions to problems will emerge out of processes of development that can be set up and *tested* for effectiveness. One test of effectiveness will be whether or not people do develop their own workable formulas for improvement.

The optimism, however, should leave no implications that favorable results will come easily. The task is of challenging difficulty. This book makes the challenge specific by giving many typical experiences of encouragers of the process of development. It makes clear that no longer can such workers depend upon their good-hearted enthusiasm alone. It insists that their responsibilities cannot be met by imposing or even telling whatever they believe to be the truth. It describes the more sensitive ethical conduct necessary to help people become competent to contribute to the solving of their problems.

Part of that responsibility is found in the belief in people's good-potentials that encourages those potentials to become real. Favorable characteristics in ordinary people do not seem to develop unless someone of importance to them acts as though he expects the desirable changes to occur. The expectation that encourages is a highly skilled attitude, part of the process. But paradoxically, it must be genuine. It is not just a device to be used for effect. A good encourager must genuinely believe in people's potential for growth. Thus optimism about people, though it must be honestly held, becomes a skilled attitude, subject to testing by results.

The writers recognize that, in this time of turmoil, many processes of fundamental change are going forward. These include social revolutions that attempt to correct long-standing injustices, new laws, great programs of rehabilitation and reform. The book does not deal specifically with these tremendous movements. It does not analyze the many social arrangements that resist such change. Instead, it is devoted to exploration of ways local people can gain the collective strength to influence the changes and cope with the forces of resistance. Volunteer, nonprofessional encouragers can do much that no one else can do to bring about this strengthening of local initiative.

Two warnings are appropriate for readers:

1. The episodes given in the text may sound artificial or contrived. Actually, they are accounts of real life experiences. Details have been changed only to avoid identification of persons.

2. The episodes may be read to sound as though the encourager involved, or his supervisor, knew the "correct" answers to the difficulties that arose. Seldom were either sure about any answers, correct or otherwise. They tried to remain calm because they had confidence that people, when wisely encouraged, would themselves work out good answers. The encouragers were not as self-assured as their exterior manner may have indicated at the time. They were confident in the midst of discouragement because they expected processes of development to have favorable outcomes in people's lives.

We recommend that the book be used to stimulate discussion in pretraining before volunteers go on the job, and that they keep it handy for reference as typical problems arise. The problems, episodes, and principles to guide action, have been arranged to facilitate both uses.

What training programs should use the book? Mainly the universities and colleges to which Peace Corps, VISTA, churches, civic associations, and other volunteer-using agencies normally turn for help. The book has been written to meet the needs of such educational institutions, when they respond to requests for help from employers of the new breed of volunteers. As universities accept responsibility for training nonprofessionals, preprofessionals, and citizens-to-be, they may discover that such training constitutes an excellent introduction to that integration of the social sciences that is essential to a good liberal arts education.

We owe a great debt to dozens of people whose names cannot be given. These anonymous friends, by being participants in development processes, have taught us much about how people can change to become more responsible, more competent. Our debt is especially great when they have proved to be the kind of friends who would reveal inner thoughts that give a little understanding of the processes that changed their outlooks on life.

We can mention one person to whom we are specifically indebted, E. F. Spicer of the Department of Anthropology at the University of Arizona, who read earlier forms of this training book and offered wise suggestions for revision. The text is better because of his helpful recommendations.

Seal Beach, California
October, 1967

W. W. B.
L. J. B.

Contents

ENCOURAGING COMMUNITY DEVELOPMENT

A Training Guide for Local Workers

Introduction

Multitudes of nonprofessional community workers have been asking educators for guidance. Sometimes these citizen workers-with-people ask for help directly. More often their request is conveyed by those who employ or supervise them. Is there some way in which generously motivated nonprofessionals can learn to help people develop better communities? Is some training possible that will harness the good will of eager local workers? We believe there is.

By the thousands they appear, idealistically motivated persons who want to devote some portion of their lives to serving their fellow man. They come not for pay, though some may receive a little. They come not with expectation of a career, though some may eventually enter a helping profession. Their number and visibility have increased as a result of federal enterprises such as Peace Corps, Office of Economic Opportunity, and other developmental programs. But many such people of good will have long given of themselves to religious, civic, and social welfare programs and will continue to do so.

The new multitudes are given many titles, aides, amateur assistants, village-level workers, front-line workers, indigenous leaders, community helpers, to mention a few. But the name which has come to have largest acceptance is volunteers. This term is not very satisfactory until the compound adjective "community development" is added to the word. Such a designation removes some of the stigma of being a servant to a trained expert, and opens the way for a discovery that nonprofessional volunteers can do a unique job. When we speak of volunteers, let it be understood that community development is intended, though not always mentioned.

The volunteers are of various ages, from college undergraduates to the retired. They have a diversity of backgrounds, but it is safe to assume that most are unfamiliar with the social scientific thinking necessary to productive human relations. Their training therefore should give them enough understanding of the social sciences to minimize mistakes and maximize their helpfulness.

They will be working with people in the social situations where these people live. We will refer to this social context as a community. But in using the word, we immediately encounter difficulties. How do workers locate or even delimit the size of a community in the midst of urban sprawls or in rural regions with too few or too many towns?

Controversies between social scientists can add to the worker's confusion, unless he understands their contrasting points of view. Sociologists and political scientists usually define a community as some kind of structure; that is, a collection of people, located at some specific point on the map, with a government, different factions in conflict, and a series of organizations in interrelationship.[1] In contrast, anthropologists and social psychologists are likely to define community as an understanding to be found in people's attitudes and thinking.[2]

While being aware of and appreciating the structural point of view, we prefer the functional definition used by anthropologists and psychologists. We prefer this because it allows more room for change: it is dynamic. It calls upon the community worker to do something, rather than to be satisfied with a description of an already existent structure. Our definition, then, is: Community is whatever sense of the local common good citizens can be helped to achieve.[3] That is, many if not most of the people community development volunteers encounter will likely be only dimly aware of belonging to any community. Sense of community is something that has to be created for most people in modern times. It comes as a result of experiences through which they can progress. Part of the volunteer worker's assignment is to help people go through those experiences.

---

[1] See Winston W. Crouch and Beatrice Dinerman, *Southern California Metropolis* (Berkeley, Calif.: University of California Press, 1963), for an example of the political science emphasis. See Maurice R. Stein, *The Eclipse of Community* (Princeton, N.J.: Princeton University Press, 1960), for a summary of sociological concepts.

[2] See Ward Hunt Goodenough, *Cooperation in Change* (New York: Russell Sage Foundation, 1963), for an anthropological point of view. See Ronald Lippitt, Jeanne Watson, and Bruce Westley, *The Dynamics of Planned Change* (New York: Harcourt, Brace & World, Inc., 1958), for a social psychological interpretation.

[3] William W. Biddle and Loureide J. Biddle, *The Community Development Process* (New York: Holt, Rinehart and Winston, Inc., 1965), p. 77.

How large a group of people should a community worker accept as his area of activity—a city block, a neighborhood, a district in a metropolitan or rural area? If the structural definition is followed, the answer is likely to be rigid in terms of a specific number of persons or a fixed territory. If the functional definition is used, the number and size will depend upon how a community development worker goes about his task.

The most fundamental social unit that such a worker encourages people to form is a primary group, a basic nucleus (described later) which accepts responsibility for a small area of neighbors—a city block, two or three blocks, a district of a hundred or so homes. The larger social unit he seeks to help people create is a representative group, a larger nucleus (also described later). This usually serves something known as a neighborhood. This term too has various meanings from city to city and from city to country. A larger nucleus may grow out of several basic nuclei, or out of a coalition of the different organizations that already serve a neighborhood. There is no preferred size of population for a neighborhood, but a rough rule of thumb would place the numbers somewhere between 10,000 and 40,000. These numbers are given with reluctance, for volunteers will find both smaller and larger areas which local people believe to be neighborhoods. And he had better be guided by their perceptions of their neighborhood.

The answer to the question about the number of people that can achieve sense of community depends then upon the groups of people that can be persuaded to form an active association. The size of the area served is governed by the response people give to a worker's efforts of friendship. By helping people create a basic nucleus and a larger nucleus, a community development worker helps them discover for themselves areas of shared community interest. The geographic area associated with a basic group is smaller, that with a larger nucleus more extensive. Early in the process, community is defined by the people themselves at two levels of size. These first community-creating groups can later come together with other groups from nearby and distant areas to create the even larger representative bodies that will give attention to those problems of wider scope that are found beyond the capability of either basic or larger nuclei. Sense of community is not a static creation. It starts with a small group serving a limited area and expands as people's experience tends to induce them to think in wider and more inclusive terms.

Because a nonprofessional volunteer is in a position to live with people at the beginning stages of community creation, he has the opportunity to start processes that enable them to grow in the dignity of self-confidence. They not only discover community interest; they discover that they can gain some recognition, along with others, to influence the small and then the larger and larger decisions of public importance.

The process that volunteers can help citizens to start is known as community development. Because this is a relatively new term in many people's vocabulary, community development has many meanings. We shall define it as a social process by which human beings can become more competent to live with and gain some control over local aspects of a frustrating and changing world.[4] Because it focuses upon changes in people's lives through the development of increasing skill to cope with the problems that threaten the common good, it is an educational process.

It is important for every volunteer to realize, however, that though he knows his work to be educational, he should not become a schoolmaster. The educational process he helps people to start is one based upon learner-chosen experience and learner self-criticism. He is an educator in a much more fundamental sense then he would be if he relied upon telling people what they should do or believe.

The word "process" needs definition also. "Process" refers to a progression of events that is planned by participants to serve goals they have progressively chosen.[5] The events do not occur in any fixed sequence; the pattern of development is always unique to each group of people in a specific locality. But certain stages can be discerned, as will be seen later. A volunteer is privileged to observe and contribute to certain stages in the process. Seldom, if ever, is he in contact with local people long enough to see any process carried through to a stage of completion. But he needs to be aware that events have occurred before he appeared and other events will occur after he leaves. He needs the humility to know that many processes go on always in people's lives; he is privileged to help with one that promises favorable development.

Development needs definition also, since it is so freely and loosely bandied about. As we shall use the word, development means social and personal change that moves toward consciously chosen goals. The choosing is done by the people who are in process of change. But because a volunteer lives close to the people, he also becomes a participant in the development process. His objectives, his values in life, must enter into the discussions by which local people choose their objectives.

Development is always normative; that is, it moves toward some objectives people desire. When these objectives are distant and can be stated as generalized ideals, they are referred to as values. When they are goals that

---

[4] Biddle and Biddle, p. 78.
[5] Biddle and Biddle, p. 79.

can be accomplished within a short time period, they are next steps in a process that should move toward the values. That is, the values are the standards by which people judge a proposed action to be good or bad, and by which they criticize it and themselves, after the action is completed.

Because a volunteer hopes to help people start a normative process of development, he needs to be aware of the values people believe in and of his own. For he will join in the discussion of next steps to be taken and of the distant values by which these actions are to be judged. The training of volunteers must therefore be both descriptive and prescriptive; it needs both to describe what he does and prescribe what he ought to do. Both emphases will be found in this book.

Any community development volunteer intervenes in the lives of people. He tries to persuade them to start new processes of development or to re-direct those already in progress. He must assume responsibility for whatever interference he attempts. Therefore this book recommends certain types of conduct for such a worker-with-people and advises against others. It gives the reasons for approval or disapproval. The reader may or may not agree with these prescriptions. Questions of purpose and value are always open to debate.

Volunteers in training are urged to discuss the conduct recommended and the values served, to determine their own concept of what ought to be. The book states a point of view in line with the social scientific thinking quoted. This is a scientific thinking that is guided by humane values.

The book is addressed directly to the problems, worries, and ways of thinking a nonprofessional citizen volunteer often encounters. It tries to hold the jargon of academic discourse to a minimum. But each chapter, following this introduction, has a final section for social science students. A few footnotes and these final sections constitute an introduction to selected writers, with special attention given to the need for an integration of the social sciences that will serve human need.

There is no intention of giving the final word. The book is an introduction to a responsibility. It is useful for the beginning of a development process that should occur also in the lives of volunteers. In their experience with people and in their further study they will transcend this beginning.

Chapter 1

The Community Development Volunteer

Anyone who proposes to work with people had best be aware of his own tangled motivations. Especially is this true when the work is to occur in the community context where one's loyalty to persons, factions, or ideas may so readily interfere with the achievement of objectivity. Especially is this true when the worker is motivated by good will; he needs always to be suspicious of his own obviously noble motives.

All humans suffer from ambivalences and contradictions of desires. A community development volunteer is no exception to this statement. In fact, he may be prone to domineering action if he is overly conscious of his own desire to help others. After all, he volunteered to do good. His problem is complicated by the fact that many of his motives are unconscious; others are only dimly conscious; and only a few are those he ordinarily admits to himself.

It will not be possible to give a complete catalogue of probable motives that may complicate a volunteer's work. It will not be possible to examine how all the contradictions can be made conscious in every volunteer's life. We can draw attention only to a few of the conflicts community workers should face and among which they should make a choice.

Patience versus Impatience

An early and obvious conflict that any community worker should discover within himself is the struggle between his patience and his impatience. Injustices will cry out so loudly for correction that he will be inclined immediately to join those who noisily attack the alleged perpetrators of injustice. Yet he will know or learn shortly that changes in people's ways of thinking and behaving, in either victims or beneficiaries of injustice, come slowly. He may even say, "Yes, I know the educational processes that lead to permanent progress take time. But can we wait? There is so much evil to be corrected. And the people who are hurt demand relief now."

We say the worker should discover that he is torn between the impatience that demands immediate action and the patience to seek more permanent improvement; but often he is unaware of any such internal contradiction. He may deny his ambivalence by becoming vigorously active in support of some extreme solution to his conflict.

He may fly to an extreme of impatience by attempting to overthrow some organization believed to have power, the Establishment, or even a particular government or ideology. Such extremism often constitutes the attempt to bring about a revolution. Unfortunately, however, there are numerous of the less extremist impatient who enjoy describing their efforts as revolution, even though they do not advocate violence and bloody seizure of power. The loose use of the word revolution confuses many moderate advocates of reform. Later we offer some suggestions on how to cope with such confusion in the use of the word revolution.

The worker may reach an extreme of patience in refusing to be disturbed by injustice and in giving attention to study and discussion that is never meant to result in any action. These overpatient people often refer to their wordy inaction as education. They wholly ignore the concept of education that makes decisions to act, the action itself, and the criticism of the action, part of the learning process. Many of the pages that follow are devoted to finding the processes that educate while people are making progress to overcome injustice and other problems that plague them.

The position we advocate for community workers lies somewhere between these extremes of either impatience or patience. A volunteer who lives close to people must share some of their frustrations and sympathize with some of their angers. He should not avoid impatience at injustice. On the other hand, he asks people to take the time to think out which solutions to problems are most likely to redress the injustice. He seeks an objectivity to help people understand their problems, in the midst of their and his indignation. He urges them to the solutions that promise permanence because they reconcile conflict. He urges them to discuss and do something about their grievances, but in a manner that solves their problems. He needs social scientific skill to help people experiment with the methods of social change that will prove effective.

A Formula versus a Process

Another conflict that may confuse a volunteer is the question of whether he follows a formula of procedure or places his reliance upon people to work out their own formula. In the latter case he trusts people and the processes he can help them to inaugurate to solve problems.

In a community development project in a large city, a professionally trained social worker was trying to learn some newer methods of dealing with people than those he had been taught at graduate school. (The fact that he was a trained social worker did not disqualify him from becoming a community development volunteer. But it did not qualify him either.). He was a member of a neighborhood committee devoted to discovering and meeting the needs of people in the anonymity of an enormous metropolitan area.

He reported later that he had tried to understand and put into practice the "method of development." Then he discovered to his alarm that this method "did not work." As the days passed by, according to his own account, he came finally to the conclusion that the essence of the method of development was flexibility, that he must modify and adapt in collaboration with members of the committee. He must find ways of approaching people that met their understanding. He must help them find solutions to their problems that made sense to them. Then, he found, "the method worked." He made the discovery that there was no precise formula for success. He also discovered the necessity of using his intelligence to help people find their own answers to their questions.

A Disciplined Good Will

A volunteer's consciousness of the idealistic motives which led him to volunteer can prove a handicap. He needs to discipline that good will. His good will must be genuine, and yet he must view it with a humorous skepticism.

The people he encounters may often draw attention to his supposed nobility, sometimes in admiration, sometimes in mockery. Such remarks about him are hard on the ego.

Some years ago a community developer was describing his work to colleagues at an American university. One of his auditors listened to the expounding with impatience. Finally he blurted out, "Do you know what the real difference between you and me is?"

"Well, I can think of several differences. Which one do you have in mind?"

"You believe in people and I don't."

Before there was a Peace Corps, a group of students worked on a Caribbean Island to help local people create a better life for themselves. They helped to construct a concrete platform that could be used for coffee-drying in season, and for children's games at other times. These visitors, who came from the United States, lived in two abandoned and decrepit barns, braving the tropical heat, the drenching rains, the leaking roofs, the vermin, and the threat of diseases that poor sanitation and an inadequate food supply bred.

A priest from a nearby church came over to observe the students' activities. One day, in a burst of enthusiasm, he said to a faculty supervisor:

"This work that you people are doing is pure altruism."

"No," was the reply. "This is not pure altruism. We are getting something out of it."

"What are you getting out of it? I don't see."

"Why, we are associating with people different from ourselves. We are learning a new language. We are getting a lot of free bananas. And——," trailing off into an embarrassed silence.

"As I was saying," remarked the priest, "this is pure altruism."

At a meal later in the day, the faculty member told the students that the priest regarded their work as pure altruism. The students greeted the statement with a raucous laugh, then changed the subject to something more interesting.

Two or three weekends later, these same students were entertained by a grateful government agency. They were put up for two nights in a luxury hotel, far from the primitive village in which they had been living. They were given the best of food and were driven around the scenic countryside. They bathed at the idyllic beaches and were admired as very important persons. When they returned to the coffee-shed barracks to live in close intimacy again with cockroaches, rats, and lizards, their spontaneous comment was, "Gee, it's good to be back home again."

Any worker-with-people needs the critical self-judgment to doubt his own nobility. Even when unworthy motives cannot be raised to the conscious level, the conviction that some antisocial desires are probably lurking somewhere in him can provide a discipline for good will. It is this conviction that will allow a volunteer to use his intelligence to restrain an overbearing generosity.

A community development volunteer needs resilience to recover from mistakes and discouragement. A graduate student in training used to remark, "Boy, I pulled a boo-boo that time," then would cheerfully go on to correct his mistake. And he turned out to be one of the best. Resilience, together with intelligence, can discipline good will. It grows out of the determination to help people discover better impulses in themselves. A volunteer needs undiscouragable good will toward people, even in the face of poor response on their part and of bad judgment on his part.

Volunteer Becomes Encourager

The term volunteer is not especially flattering and not very precise. We will replace it with another more descriptive and more complimentary term, encourager. We will make the role of encourager explicit as we move along.

As a volunteer becomes an encourager, there are many things he will not become. He needs to have a picture of what he is not in order to make clear what he is. His perception of himself is important to the development process. But even more important is other people's perception of his self-perception, that is, what they think he thinks he is.

He may be entertaining mistaken ideas. He may expect to initiate community action himself. He may think he will be called upon to deal with *the* community (whatever that is) or to cope with community social forces (if he can discover what these are) or to reorganize existing community organizations (again if he can discover them; the ones most significant for development often have to be created). Instead, his idea about himself should be that he deals mainly with people. He deals with organizations, social forces, and communities to the extent that these large social entities influence the development of ordinary human beings. His active concern for people and his close relatedness to them is part of his advantage as an amateur and an encourager, a nonprofessional.

If he thinks of himself too much as a traditional volunteer, he may be handicapped by some of the unflattering interpretations of this role already current. When he operates as an encourager, however, a positive role becomes possible, one which no profession has pre-empted as yet, and one which possibly no profession should assume. As a nonprofessional he is in a position to establish a new dignity for himself and for the role of community developer, even though one day this field of work might become professionalized.

The distinctive role for an encourager becomes possible when a community developer can rid himself of desires to act like some kind of professional. These other concepts of himself constitute conflicting motivations until they are consciously rejected.

An encourager is not a health worker—doctor, nurse, sanitarian, or nutritionist. His responsibility is to refer people who need health services to the appropriate specialist. It may even be his job to conduct the person in need, by hand or by car, to the clinic, doctor's office, hospital, or health center, which a citizen often fears to approach.

He is not a professional social welfare worker. He should not attempt such functions as distributing relief, counseling the disturbed, or caring for unwanted babies and finding homes for them—unless he finds himself in a location where such welfare services are not available. If so, he as an encourager should do what he can in an emergency and seek to persuade citizens to bring service agencies into being. Again, his responsibility is to refer the needy to competent agencies when available, or to help make these available.

But the professional role most difficult for him to avoid is that of community organizer. "Community organization" is now used with at least two meanings. The first of these is the traditional organizing of social work agencies and the financing of these through community chests. This traditional meaning has been broadened to include also publicly financed welfare agencies, civic bodies, even churches and other voluntary associations.

But "community organization" is now used also to describe the organizing of associations primarily for political purposes. Frequently the disinherited (and those who will identify with them) are mobilized against the local power structure. The objective is more organizational and less developmental.

It is possible, sometimes even necessary, to encourage organizational activities and developmental activities at the same time, with the same people. But an encourager had best be wary of his own intentions. If his aims are mainly organizational, it is easy to slip into manipulation of people for political or other (often good) causes. But if his intentions are mainly developmental, he is more likely to help people to become aware of their needs and to develop competence in meeting them, in their own way. They will create the organizations they need.

He is not a teacher, in the sense of someone who tells people what they should know or believe, or how they should act. He is an educator in the deepest sense, but not of the instructing variety. He educates by example, by living the principles he wants people to understand and adopt of their own will. He can and must raise pertinent questions, but he avoids instruction.

He is not a subject-matter expert in agriculture, mechanics, finance, publicity, or any other specialty. He is a "generalist," able to understand enough of many fields to know when experts are needed. He is friendly with representatives of many specialties and can call them in to confer with citizen groups. But because he has relationship to both the community member and the specialist, he can facilitate their meeting. He says to the specialist, "Answer questions directly and simply, but no more. Above all, do not say, 'In order for me to answer that question, you must first understand the theory of . . . .' "

He is not a social scientist, conducting experiments and writing monographs for publication. He should cooperate with social scientists and his encouragement should adopt an experimental approach, but he is too close to people to have a wholly detached objectivity about their welfare. A compassion for them gives guidance to his objectivity. He may encourage them to show compassion in the tasks they undertake and in the experiments in which they take part.

He is not an agitator, not even for good causes. The citizens he encourages may wish to put pressure upon someone or some organization. But he does not stir them into the direct action of attack upon enemies. He is more concerned with helping them find solutions to their problems.

For any with Machiavellian ambitions, an encourager is not a manipulator of power. He never will have the necessary control over people or over the situations in which they live. Many other influences will be stronger than his. So he had best decide he does not want to control people.

He expects to see change in people, but he is not a change agent in the sense that he induces people to accept some improvement he has decided they need. He helps people to expedite the good changes they choose to make within their communities and thereby he expects them to take the initiative in making changes in themselves.

He is not a program administrator, though such necessary officials may back him up. And some volunteers may, in time, become program administrators. He is not a government bureaucrat, if he can avoid the identification, although government planning, participation, and even financing are necessary for effectiveness on a large scale. He may receive some compensation from government sources, but he tries to avoid becoming known as a government employee.

In short, he should become an encourager of processes of self-development. He avoids all these other roles in becoming a practically helpful friend.

The Intermediary Role

The social worker in a community development process whom we have already mentioned gave a name to the encourager's task in a further conversation. He called it the intermediary role. He concluded that he had become a correlator between people and the professional resources which could meet their needs.

The clergyman who was the original encourager of this process had recruited nonprofessional community members to serve within a group that included professionals as "discussant" members. The worker-members became encouragers. These encouragers were the clergyman and the social worker, some other professionals who abandoned their specialist roles and manners, and many nonprofessional citizens. All of them found that their opportunity was "in between." They were close enough to people in need to understand them and interpret their fears and frustrations. They were friendly enough with social workers, health authorities, educators, government officials, and so on to call upon these professionals for help. They could encourage people in need to become articulate in ways that strengthened their dignity. They could encourage specialists to make their wisdom and skill available to the people's self-perception of their needs.

Perhaps the acceptance of an intermediary role will not satisfy all volunteers. They are more likely to be challenged if they can realize that they are to become encouragers of processes of development. They are to become encouragers of:

1. Good impulses even when people do not know they have such impulses.
2. The search for these good impulses.
3. Articulation of these impulses.
4. The initiative to act upon some of these good impulses. Development grows out of thoughtful action. People learn from decisions that are carried out. And then they learn from the action itself.
5. Self-criticism before, during, and especially after action.
6. The building of a scheme of values to be used in self-criticism. An uncriticized action makes only a limited contribution to learning. Criticism must be based upon some standards of merit. People should be encouraged to make these clear to themselves.

In relation to professional specialists, a volunteer is to become an encourager of:

1. An understanding of the real and complicated contexts in which problems arise in people's lives. He helps specialists to see needs as citizens express them, not as these are neatly catalogued in textbooks.
2. Cooperation among specialties that have become separated. Community development calls for an interdisciplinary approach.
3. The recognition on the part of each specialist that he is a human being as well as a specialist. He can relate to ordinary citizens on a human level when they cannot understand his professional jargon. When he is thus related, he often finds ways to restate his specialized knowledge to serve their understanding.

Outside and Indigenous Encouragers

There are several varieties of encouragers which we must recognize despite the generalizations we have been making. First, such a community worker may be of any age from eighteen to eighty, and even beyond. Second, he may bring to his assignment a variety of previous training and experience, from the bare beginnings of an untrained but enthusiastic newcomer to the rich experiences of many years in some particular field of work. An enthusiastic youth will be prone to mistakes attributable to overabundant energy, but people will often forgive him because he obviously means to do the "right thing." An older person of great experience may make mistakes that grow out of faithfulness to accustomed practices. And he may unfortunately demand respect for his gray hairs. But again, people will forgive much if they are convinced an encourager is "for" them.

But by all odds the greatest differences among volunteers is to be found between outside as contrasted with indigenous encouragers. Most college undergraduates will act as outside encouragers, as will volunteers who serve Peace Corps, VISTA, and other programs of local improvement. The indigenous encouragers are local leaders who emerge from the processes of development, on the local scene. The outsiders usually have a limited period of contact with the people, while the indigenous ones continue to live with them indefinitely. Both kinds of encourager need training, but usually the outsider acts as trainer of the other. The clearest evidence that the training has succeeded is that it has become self-perpetuating, carrying appropriate attitudes and skills to new emergent encouragers as the process continues. This book is also intended to be helpful to this on-going training responsibility. It should be a handbook to be passed on as a stimulant for discussion among on-the-job self-developing encouragers.

Each kind of encourager has unique opportunities and unique problems. The outsider can be more objective, but is more likely to be a good-hearted generous person who does not understand the local people or the local situation. He is more prone to offer preconceived ideas as solutions to the problems he thinks he sees. The insider often understands much better, but is tempted to become partisan in a controversy. He also may find difficulty in challenging neighbors to raise their standards beyond prevailing local traditions.

Though this book is addressed to both kinds of encouragers, it is more concerned with those who are not native to the local scene. The responsibility for starting the training which we hope will become self-perpetuating rests primarily with the outsider. It is he usually who persuades citizens to start a process. If he does his work well, the process they start becomes self-generating. It passes out of his hands because he has succeeded in inspiring others, who then train others, and these train others—with some help from encouragers.

A Difficult Role

Perhaps this role we have been describing seems vague, even a little frightening. Who an encourager is has been defined largely in terms of what he is to become. We have not given any list of specific ideas to accept or of skills to acquire. No such neat package will be given in this book. Instead, an encourager-to-be is asked to learn from some characteristic dilemmas he and his citizen friends will be called upon to face. He will be asked to use his best judgment and to call upon them to use theirs to find unique solutions for unique complexities of problems.

All this makes the role of an encourager a difficult one. Several uncertainties in it can be pointed out. First, an encourager has no outline to follow. He is dependent upon his own judgment about which he is probably doubtful, and upon the judgment of his citizen collaborators about which he may be even more doubtful. The need for study to make decisions more trustworthy, is obvious.

Then he is asked to learn a new role not just in theory, but also through on-the-job experience. This book should give him some inspiration and reassurance, especially in discussion with the supervisors of his activities. But, in the end, he will have to work out in detail and adopt the kind of role that is compatible with his personality and is acceptable to the people he encourages. No one can tell him what the unique details of his relationships to people will be.

His learning, as well as that of his friends, will not progress smoothly, nor will it move at a nicely graduated pace. It will have its ups and downs, its moments of great insight and other moments of great discouragement. There will also be periods of dullness, when no progress will be observable. But in time a meaningful process, and his place in it, will become clear.

Finally, he may be unhappy to discover that his success will be measured not by what he does but by what the community members do. The quality of initiative that emerges among the people he encourages is the measuring rod for him. He will be judged by their actions. He will live with a paradox: The only behavior he can hope to control is his own; yet he must look to the behavior of others for evidence that he has worked wisely.

In view of these difficulties, he must be or become a person of deep commitment. The assignment he undertakes will try his patience and devotion. He must continue encouraging in the face of both poor response and response so enthusiastic that the initiative, and the credit, passes beyond him. But there are deep satisfactions in this paradoxical role. He will find genuine pleasure when people discover the good potentials in themselves and respond to them. The satisfactions will come, even though people will often fail to thank him for having helped them.

He will be called upon to develop many skills of human relationships. These are the skills of sensitivity which are learned in cooperative inter-action with people. Classroom instruction can provide an introduction, and textbooks such as this one can offer guidance. But both instruction and book are only aids to the actual learning which comes from experience.

He should learn to be sensitive to the frustrations, fears, and hopes of people. He should be able to recognize various stages of development, so that he can decide which outworn traditions he can wisely challenge. For while certain challenges at one time will expedite the processes of self-change, at other times they will only stiffen resistance.

Whatever knowledges and skills an encourager possesses must be used flexibly. They are to be adapted to his perception of the varieties of need for development human beings exhibit.

ADDENDUM FOR SOCIAL SCIENCE STUDENTS

The purpose of the addendum sections at the end of each chapter is not to present a full-scale discussion of social scientific writings. It is rather to introduce students to selected authors whose writings are related to the point of view of this book. Some substantiate that point of view; others

challenge it. These sections are added in the hope that they may inspire
students to read further in the social sciences.

Though we have stated a definite role for the local worker-with-people,
we must point out that there are vigorous differences of opinion among
competent writers on how a community worker should behave. Some of the
differences reflect the professional backgrounds mentioned in the chapter.
Others reflect social scientific preferences for sociology, or anthropology, or
social psychology, or economics, or psychotherapy, or, more recently,
community psychiatry.

Attempts have been made to list and classify these different approaches
and roles. One of the best treatments, with commentaries upon the
differences, was made by Lippitt, Watson, and Westley,[1] in their book
The Dynamics of Planned Change. This excellent analysis is now somewhat
out of date. A number of the programs discussed and writers quoted have
changed their emphases since the book was published in 1958. A more
contemporary classification can be found in an article by Biddle, "The
'Fuzziness' of Definition of Community Development," published in 1966.[2]

An even more extensive listing of and commentary upon contrasting
programs will be found in Appendix I of the Biddles' book.[3] This compila-
tion includes mention of work carried on by universities, at the time of
writing, 1965, with the involvement of various scientific disciplines.

A comprehensive statement about the encourager's role, which we have
stressed in this chapter, will be found in Chapter 16 of the last-mentioned
book. The statement is given as an ideal, but one compatible with social
scientific self-discipline.

---

[1] Ronald Lippitt, Jeanne Watson, and Bruce Westley, *The Dynamics of Planned
Change* (New York: Harcourt, Brace & World, Inc., 1958).

[2] William W. Biddle, "The 'Fuzziness' of Definition of Community Development,"
Community Development Journal (22 Kingston Road, Didsbury, Manchester 20,
England), April 1966.

[3] William W. Biddle and Loureide J. Biddle, *The Community Development Process*
(New York: Holt, Rinehart and Winston, Inc., 1965), pp. 281–296.

Chapter 2

Who Are the People
To Be Served?

People of all kinds will be served, people who need help. Some
know they need help; others do not. Some have lives truncated
either by circumstances or by their own negative attitudes. Some
believe either that they can do nothing to better conditions or
that the temporary satisfaction of publicity attracted by a noisy protest is all
they can hope for.

It would not be surprising if an encourager concluded that the people
to be served are the poor, the miserable, and the disinherited. Most describ-
ers of community development arrive at some such conclusion. But because
the development is concerned with the total community, attention must be
addressed to the privileged and powerful as well.

An encourager will be concerned with the ignorant but also with the
educated. He may work in the slums, but will need to give thought also to
the comfortable suburbs into which the affluent escape. He may try to help
pathological persons, the diseased, the drug addicts, the delinquents, but any
permanent solutions for these unfortunates will have to involve healthy and
normal persons as well. He may spend time with rootless migrants, but
solution of their problems will involve also the disadvantaged in permanent
residences and the comfortable people who would prefer to ignore the
disinherited.

Community means all the people in a given geographic area. Community
development means the improvement of that area, and of all the inhabitants
of it.

A community developer was lecturing to white community leaders at a

southern university. One of the listeners interrupted to ask if the principles
and methods advocated were applicable to the white population only, or also
to Negroes. The lecturer replied, "I will answer by putting a question to
you. Are the Negroes there, in your community?"

"I see what you mean," said the white leader. "You cannot exclude
anyone."

All-inclusiveness applies even to the complacent and to those who say
they wish no improvement or change. Development cannot be forced upon
the unresponsive and reluctant, but the door should be left open for these
resisters so that they may join the common effort when they are ready.
Refusal to join in programs of improvement may have numerous causes.
Some people are genuinely satisfied with the status quo, but others resist
change even though they hunger and thirst for it. They may resist out of
fear of failure or of ridicule.

Although we point out that many kinds of people are to be considered
in the totality of an emerging community, certain generalizations can be
made about most of them. People of both high and low degree suffer from
frustrations and fears, from disappointment of hopes. They will be ham-
pered by rigid attitudes and habits and will vacillate between clinging to old
ways and an impatience with some aspects of the old order. They will be
accustomed to using only a fraction of their abilities and will often be
astounded to discover they have unexpected intelligence, ability to discuss,
and initiative to decide and act.

Most people, rich or poor, will be inclined at first to overvalue material
possessions and the money that will buy these. They will thus respond to a
cliché of the modern age. But they will not always desire a material thing
for itself; they may sometimes regard possessions (even buildings to meet
in or paved roads or cars to drive on them) as symbols of triumph over
frustrations.

Most will be suffering from certain nonmaterial needs, so much so that
they will often seem to be unaware of the lack, and will even resist attempts
to overcome it. They will have lost the sense of community or the experience
of community, if they ever had either. And they may be so uncomfortable
about this experience missing from their lives that they will be unable to
discuss the lack intelligently. A man in a once autonomous town that has
become a satellite of a spreading metropolis stated it: "Something precious
has been lost. But I don't know what it is." No substitute for the community
of old has yet emerged or been created for him.

There may be an increasing feeling of helplessness, an often expressed
belief that individual citizens can do little or nothing to correct the inevitable march of events in unwelcome directions. Sometimes this feeling

results in the rationalization that doing nothing, noninvolvement is justified. Many people will say, "I don't want to get mixed up in that," whether the matter is politics, an effort to combat crime, or some cooperative endeavor to improve the community.

This spreading malaise, which cannot be corrected by material progress alone, often causes people to lose faith in themselves. An encourager will encounter many people who lack self-confidence, both as individuals and as members of a group. It will be clear that as separate persons they are help-less. But, more distressing to the encourager, they may be unwilling to cooperate enough to discover that a collective effort may accomplish things which an individual effort cannot.

The lack of self-confidence often takes a characteristic twist: there is great tendency to blame someone else for one's own or the community's ills. People may say it is all the fault of the rich, or the government, or some specific supposed enemy, a powerful university, the banks, or popular scapegoats like the Negroes or the Jews or indeed white southerners or gentiles. Sometimes these feelings result only in futile complaining. But sometimes an organization is built, with little developmental purpose, upon wide-spread hatred of supposed enemies.

A popular target of attack, in a period of social restlessness, is "the power structure." Sometimes specific supposed members of this "structure" are identified. Sometimes the term is left vague and undefined; it is then even better for arousing hate. Since "the power structure" to be attacked is always believed to be evil, it can be used to create solidarity among the supposed victims of such power. But the resulting organization of citizens is devoted more to attack than to development of ability to solve problems by the member's own positive efforts.

These all-too-common blockages to development are not mentioned here as an invitation to discouragement. We merely want to indicate the human reality with which an encourager will probably have to contend. There are ways to move beyond such evidence of the malaise of our time. An encourager can discover these ways by understanding the motivations of the people who are to develop, and by giving recognition and strength to the prosocial motivations they can find within themselves.

Human Motivation

Often the question is asked, "How do you motivate people?" The answer is simple: an encourager does not try to attach people's motives to the decisions he has decided they should make. Instead he relies upon people to motivate themselves. He provides the encouragement that makes self-motivation likely. The answer is simple but the encouraging is difficult.

By accepting uncritically certain common assumptions about human beings, an encourager can increase the difficulty of his task to the point of misunderstanding his role. One misleading assumption is that people are so lacking in ideas and initiative that they must be induced to accept some program he or his supervisors have decided would be good for them. He then becomes too much a salesman. His avoidance of salesmanship calls for delicate differentiations of attitude and procedure. Every good encourager is enthusiastic and he counts on some contagion of his enthusiasm to stir people. The method of encouragement does not rule out the making of suggestions with persuasive fervor, but it calls for skill in helping people to discover that they themselves can have ideas and the enthusiasm to carry their ideas into action. The question is not who is to be credited with proposing an idea but whether the people adopt it as their own. They must see for themselves that a proposal, whatever its origin, is one they have freely chosen.

Another assumption that can mislead an encourager is that people are lazy (that is, they have no motivations) or that their motivations are evil. It is necessary therefore for someone to control them. Parents, teachers, and other figures of authority used to discipline the young with such assumptions about themselves. And an uncritical encourager can be tempted to nominate himself as some similar authoritarian figure in dealing with people.

A series of more realistic and psychologically wise assumptions can be made as guide for his work:

1. All people have motivations. They have impulses to do many things. These are both generous and selfish, though many of them are difficult to classify in our age of changing standards. In an historical period when the sense of community is weak in most people's experiences, the selfish or antisocial impulses are likely to be the ones that receive most attention.

2. Some impulses are spontaneously prosocial, even when experience of community has been largely lacking. People apparently aspire to serve a common good even though their unselfish impulses fall short of an encourager's hopes for them.

3. The potentially community-serving motivations are often hidden behind the socially acceptable exteriors that people use as protections. These good motives are frequently so well hidden that the person involved refuses to recognize that he has them. Nonetheless, he can be helped to talk about these prosocial impulses as a starting point for community-creating

activities. An encourager needs to be sensitive to accept minor altruistic proposals as the beginning of aspirations for greater and greater programs that will serve an expanding concept of the common good.

4. All people can be helped to come together in the service of some commonly held altruistic purposes. There are, however, practical limitations to his efforts here. One may lack the skill to reach certain people or his personality may be less acceptable to certain people than another encourager's would be. The assumption is not disproved because any one encourager fails to elicit a cooperative response. Another might succeed later when more skillful, or when the people are more ready.

5. The beginnings of development that grow out of people's own motivations are usually humble and on a small scale. The initial number of responders is likely to be few and the first activities of minor significance. When people are learning to discover and trust their own good impulses, they usually try themselves out with lesser enterprises. The grandiose services to the common good are more likely to come later.

These are some assumptions about human motivation that guide the encouraged process of development. The trouble is that an encourager may have difficulty acting as though he were guided by such principles. He may be blocked by his own fears or by his conscious or unconscious acceptance of the folk wisdom that prevails in the area where he works. The clichés of thought that "everyone knows are true" may tend to undermine his self-assurance.

Those who think they are wise about the people they wish to encourage may say, "These people are beyond redemption. They are no good." Or the people themselves may say, "We tried to do something like that five years ago, and it was a great mistake," or "We can't get together; folks fight each other in rival factions." Or even worse, some will say, "We don't want to get involved in anything."

Some workers-with-people hold to other unfortunate assumptions about motivation by saying, "People will not stir out of apathy except as they face a crisis in some major disaster. They will not respond to an invitation to altruistic public service." All these and many other clichés of cynicism can paralyze a majority of the people in a locality. But worst of all they may paralyze an encourager.

If all their friends make cynical assumptions about them, and the people themselves concur in these uncomplimentary assessments, the possibility of positive development is most unlikely. But if some trusted friend, perhaps just one amid the chorus of derogators, indicates a convincing belief in their higher potentials, a developmental process may begin. An encourager can be that trusted friend with positive persuasiveness.

Starting with the Underprivileged

Experienced community developers agree that there is no population of people, no matter how discouraged, apathetic, or sunk in self-pity, who will not respond to skillful encouragement. There are always some better impulses present that can become a basis for a development process. Not every type of human being, however, nor every kind of social situation, has been tested for developmental potential. Volunteer encouragers will find themselves working with people in many untried situations. They will be able to contribute new knowledge from their contact with the unique processes people work out in untested situations.

The story of one developmental process will illustrate how certain people in a depressed population discovered prosocial impulses that granted them initiative. (This project should not be taken as pattern for imitation even in a similar population.) The locale was a slum area in a small city, a county seat with a population of about 50,000. The inhabitants were low-income people. Some were on relief. They were of many backgrounds; there were Negroes, Mexicans, Greeks, Italians, and Anglo-Saxon native Americans who were largely migrants from southern mountain areas. Though these ethnic groups lived in the same neighborhood, there was little trust or communication among them. The area they inhabited was locally known as the city's most deteriorated slum. It had more than its share of unemployment, poverty, and crime. It had repeatedly been surveyed by the sociology students of a nearby college as an example of urban blight. The people were aware of the area's reputation and tended to be apologetic for living there.

In this case, the encouragers were professors and students from the nearby college. Aware of the unhappy history of the people in the area, the encouragers searched for some common problem or hope that could become a starting point for a process. After talking with the principal of the elementary school, with social workers, and with pastors of numerous churches, they decided that a project in service to youth would be good. It was clear to the would-be encouragers that young people were suffering from delinquency, early departures from school, lack of recreation facilities, and danger to life and limb from heavy factory traffic.

The encouragers would have been wiser to allow the people to choose a beginning project themselves. But there was no organization through which the people could do any choosing. And the encouragers were just learning some of the skills necessary for their role.

Having chosen a starting interest, they were under the necessity of winning support. They approached one of the recognized leaders of the neighborhood, a labor union official who had been elected to the city council, but found that he opposed any program, saying that his constituents were hopeless. "Nothing will happen here," he said, "unless it is started by the 'big bugs'." When quizzed as to who the "big bugs" were, he was very vague. They seemed to be some shadowy figures behind the scenes who pulled strings that made mayor, city council, business interests, and church-men dance. Other recognized leaders in schools, churches, and social agencies all wished the proposed program well, but none of them offered help until an organization was well started.

Encouragers visited all the churches in the area, attempting to stir up interest and inviting people to attend a mass meeting to be held in the elementary school. They persuaded the school authorities to send out notices of this meeting through the children. They put notices of the pro-posed project and the mass meeting which was supposed to launch it, in the city newspaper and on the radio. They set up arrangements for the meeting in the school gymnasium, hanging posters, and providing refreshments.

The would-be encouragers, who were learning their role, were acting too much like salesmen. To obtain the advance approval of established leaders, known to some community developers as gatekeepers, was good. But to expect these gatekeepers to be persuaded to take the initiative for a new process was unwise. Then to promote an encourager-chosen interest by publicity and mass meeting was to repeat the sales methods these people had long resisted from various good-hearted promoters of the past. The process, however, moved ahead in spite of the salesmanship.

The great opening night came. The encouragers turned out in force; there were about ten of them. Three local people appeared: a white factory worker, a Negro worker, and a white housewife. Hastily, more than half the student encouragers were sent home, so that they would not seem to overwhelm the small turnout. Those remaining waited for more local people to appear, carrying on cheerful conversations meanwhile. But when no more came, one encourager recommended that the three go ahead to form an organization. They thereupon elected themselves president, vice-president, and secretary-treasurer of a community neighborhood council. And although the beginnings were inauspicious enough, the real development process had begun.

The three people who were all the officers and the total membership of the newly formed council began immediately to recruit friends and neigh-bors. Meeting once a week, with encouragers present, they gradually built up the membership to a dozen. The appeal they used was, "Let's do some-thing for our young people." They extended this invitation to both those who became members of the central group and those who served on sub-committees. Later, the same appeal obtained participation of scores, then hundreds, and ultimately two or three thousand. Whether the efforts of the encouragers had been wise or blundering, more and more people of the community were discovering a motivation that broke enough barriers of misunderstanding to unite them. This motivation was the common concern for the welfare of their young people. The motivation was their own, and they built an active organization upon it.

Their first project was to obtain the use of a former city dump as a playground. It had to be cleaned up and leveled, then turned into baseball diamonds, volleyball courts, a picnic area, and an area for small children with swings, slides, and sandboxes. The group raised money to purchase equipment and employ recreation directors. It came perilously close to becoming a recreation agency in the effort to employ some workers. Later the employment responsibility was turned over to an established social welfare agency and to the public school. At first the people appealed successfully to the local community chest for financial help. Later they decided to raise the necessary money themselves. They launched all kinds of enterprises to accomplish this purpose, from rummage and baked-goods sales to a horse show that attracted paying customers from many miles away.

The neighborhood council continued to be active for five years, affecting the lives of hundreds, who either served on the council (whose membership rotated) or participated in the myriad activities undertaken. Throughout, the program was interracial, included people of all religious persuasions or of none, and was nonpartisan politically. The initiative and leadership came from the neighborhood, but the activity also involved people from the more affluent sections of the city. Some contributed money, others helped in projects, and still others started efforts to improve the entire city, when they saw what these less favored people could do. A city-wide human relations council was formed later to bring about better relations among races and other factions in conflict. Several people from the slums who had demonstrated leadership in the neighborhood became active in the city-wide council. Others came to serve on boards of directors of social welfare agencies. One of these agencies, which had been located in another part of the city, moved to the slum neighborhood, took a new lease on life, and when last observed, was carrying on the work that had been inaugurated by the neighborhood council. Among the accomplishments that are now permanent are recreational and educational programs, the latter especially for learners with academic difficulties, work for better schools, improvement of housing, job training and job placement, and active participation in the city-wide human relations council.

Obtaining Cooperation
of the Privileged

Sometimes a development process may start with the main initiative coming from a privileged person. Some would-be encouragers sought the initiative of the principal of a consolidated high school in a small town. The school served a large rural area, bringing students in by bus every day. Under the principal's leadership, the school had confined its efforts to academic work, neglecting the recreational needs of the young people. The delinquency rate was high among the widely scattered students, and no center had been found to provide for an alternative prosocial activity. The encouragers approached the principal in the hope of making the high school building available for a recreation program.

They made the mistake, however, of talking first with the assistant principal and had succeeded in stirring his interest. This proved to be a mistake because there was rivalry between principal and his assistant; if one approved an idea, the other was likely to oppose it. The principal, when he was approached, raised every possible objection to the proposal to use the school gymnasium, locker rooms, and adjacent classrooms for recreational and hobby-type activities. He pointed out that students would have to come from far away for evening activities, that bills would increase for light and heat, that lively students might break windows, injure the plumbing, and ruin the gymnasium floor. But the final crusher was that the janitor-custodian would surely not cooperate since there was no budget to pay him for overtime work.

Instead of meeting and disposing of each point in the argument, the encouragers sat and listened, occasionally sympathizing with the principal's predicaments. Finally one expressed regret that the young people would continue to be deprived of certain healthful opportunities. The one-sided discussion continued until about lunch time. Then the principal indicated a first shifting of point of view by inviting his visitors to stay for lunch. During the meal, he began to go back over his objections, one by one, and wondered aloud whether there might not be some way to meet the difficulties. The encouragers said nothing. After lunch, he invited them to his office again. There he called in the janitor-custodian to ask if he would be interested in donating his services to an enterprise for the young people. This man proved enthusiastic. He promised to cooperate for an indefinite time. The principal then reexamined his budget and found funds to carry the program (with the volunteered help of students from a nearby college) and soon discovered ways to meet every other obstacle. Throughout all this, the encouragers said little, offering only their enthusiastic agreement with his ideas.

After the interview, one of the encouragers said in bewilderment, "Phew, what happened? First he was all opposed. Then he not only agreed, but he took over the whole program and is now going to run it. I wonder what happened to change him."

Another said, "He changed himself. We didn't change him. In fact, I didn't know what to say."

A third pointed out, "We didn't outargue him."

Finally they all agreed that he had convinced himself that the idea of serving young people in his school had met some of his own basic motivations. He had adopted the ideas as his own, especially in view of the promise of outside help. The proposal now was his.

Subsequent events proved this conclusion to be correct. The principal was responsible for the evening use of the school facilities for years, gradually expanding it to include many of his teachers and even the vice-principal. He asked for help from the college students, then turned increasingly to adults within the school district. They ultimately formed an association to serve young people in the widespread community. Under the influence of this association, many new activities became part of the permanent program of the school.

Those who are cynical about human motivation often insist that the privileged and powerful never willingly surrender any of their advantages; they must be forced to do so. It is assumed that these people do not or cannot find the altruistic impulses to share with the less fortunate. The following account is typical of numerous privileged individuals whose behavior contradicts this assumption.

This man was one of a town's rich men, prominent in politics, a member of a leading church, head of a successful business, and member of a luncheon club that "ran the town." He learned of a community development project in a nearby county and went over to meet the encouragers. He confessed to them that he was interested in a depressed section of his own county where people had lived in endemic poverty for generations. Having been born in this area, he wanted its apathetic inhabitants to help themselves. He did not know how to start but was willing to cooperate with the encouragers, who accepted his invitation to start a new project. During a period of six years, he and his wife became deeply involved in every phase of an active development process, from money-raising to actual physical labor in the hot summer sun.

They became close friends with the depressed people of this pocket of poverty and with the encouragers, including a succession of young people in training for community development. His participation apparently did something favorable to his outlook upon life. At one point, he said to one of the encouragers, "You know, I've been learning from you. You don't get excited when things go wrong. You remain calm, and problems work themselves out; or maybe the people work them out." (He did not know that this same encourager had confessed to others that though he maintained an exterior calm, he fretted inwardly and had to remind himself to remain calm.) "You know," he added, "I am the ulcer type. But now that I can see things develop in their own way when you do your best and wait for people to take the initiative, the ulcers are not as frequent."

One of his greatest triumphs was to win over the support of the luncheon service club. The club agreed to help with the work in many ways. Individual members, however, teased him about his "hobby" and insisted that they supported it only because he pressured them into doing so. But they gave money, entertained the encouragers, and obtained help from government, church, and other holders of power. One fellow member asked him once, "What's the matter with you? Are you going crazy?" when he learned that his man was arising before business hours to work among his depressed friends and devoting hours after business as well. But the club members admired his devotion and even gave of their own time to work on the project, often a bit shamefacedly.

One interesting aspect of this participation by holders of power and privilege was that they did not act as "ladies bountiful." They genuinely sought to increase the decision-making initiative of the depressed people and were pleased when a growing responsibility among local people took the project away from their control. A more detailed description of this growing responsibility among these formerly helpless people will be found in the next chapter.

Several years later, after the organization of local citizens had taken over the process completely and both club members and encouragers had withdrawn, the businessman reminisced to friends, "You know, those were the happiest years of my life. I wish I could live them over again."

Conclusions about People

What generalizations can an encourager make about the people to be served? First, he should regard most skeptically some old wives tales about human nature, such as: the poor are poor because they lack ability;

the rich are rich because they have deserving qualities; human beings will always compete; and it is human nature to seek one's own advantage always.

Second, he should be doubtful about classifications that put human beings into categories, make them members of particular racial or national groupings or divide them into the underprivileged and the privileged. As far as racial and national categories are concerned, the differences among individuals within any one classification are greater than the differences from one category to another. And people are seldom clearly privileged or underprivileged; each falls somewhere along a great scale of privilege that ranges from high to low, with most people in the middle. But most important of all, human beings should be accepted each for his or her uniqueness, not for the type or category.

People should be accepted too, not just for what they *are,* but more for what they might *become,* especially if they are encouraged into development processes. In order to expedite such a process, someone who is trusted as a significant friend needs to believe in the good impulses, and needs to act accordingly. A belief in people will often prevail, even when an encourager exhibits poor methods of work.

The method of encouragement starts by asking people for their prosocial ideas and listening to what they say. It continues by helping them to find some ideas good enough to be put into action. Self-confidence begins to grow when they find a cooperative activity which serves their awakening concept of the good of everyone on the local scene. As they work together they find that they bring to actuality many abilities they had not suspected were potential in them. An encourager can do much to expedite this growth, by sharing in the discussion, in the deciding, and in the work as an interested friend.

Can an encourager make any generalizations in advance about the purposes of the people he expects to serve? It would be unwise to do so. They are likely to be unclear about what impulses move them; those they express in conversation or in answering questionnaires will probably not be the most important ones for them. Furthermore, motivations can be expected to change as the process of development continues. Usually people will start with a fairly immediate goal, for example, a playground for their young people. It will only be later that they will respond to the deeper implications of service to the future, through youth. Even greater changes in motivation will occur as new cooperative tasks are undertaken.

It is well for an encourager to realize that his purposes and theirs will not be the same, at the outset. But the two will tend to move toward each other as the process continues. He should approach people with respect for the favorable potentialities of their and his becoming.

ADDENDUM FOR SOCIAL SCIENCE STUDENTS

Various psychological writers have taken mutually contradictory positions with regard to man's potential for improvement. Years ago, the philosopher-psychologist John Dewey challenged the gloomy view of human beings that grew out of earlier theological conclusions about original sin, in his classic work, *Human Nature and Conduct*.[1] This stated the theoretical position for human malleability and opened the way for conscious improvement.

Later, the behaviorist psychologists, assuming an infinite malleability and leaning heavily upon the work of physiologist Ivan Pavlov, concluded that human beings could be conditioned to a limitless array of behaviors. Their conclusions rest more upon experiments with dogs, rats, monkeys and even pigeons, however, than upon experience with people, especially people in the situation of actual living. Having concluded that men and women could be conditioned to almost any behavior pattern, they were tempted to try to control them. The most eloquent spokesman for this point of view is B. F. Skinner. His book, *Walden Two*,[2] presents a behaviorists psychologist's utopia in which the inhabitants are busy, happy, and useful, because they have been conditioned to be that way. No doubts or desires for revolt ever assail them. And as for impulses toward improvement, these are found only in Skinner's benevolent director of the utopian colony.

Posed against this school of thought is the more recently identified humanistic psychology which accepts human malleability but points to impulses toward generous and prosocial motivations. Most writers of this persuasion rest their case upon findings from clinical psychology. Probably the most eloquent spokesman for this point of view is Carl R. Rogers who, in 1955, debated with Skinner before the American Psychological Association. Like most debates, the outcome was rather inconclusive. Rogers has stated his position much more clearly and convincingly in a recent book, *On Becoming a Person*.[3]

Humanistic psychology has many other spokesmen: Abraham Maslow, Gordon W. Allport, Clark Moustakas, J. F. T. Bugental, to name a few. These writers, although taking different emphases within the general point of

---

[1] John Dewey, *Human Nature and Conduct* (New York: Holt, Rinehart and Winston, Inc., 1922).

[2] B. F. Skinner, *Walden Two* (New York: Crowell-Collier and Macmillan, Inc., 1948).

[3] Carl R. Rogers, *On Becoming a Person* (Boston: Houghton Mifflin Company, 1961).

view, all agree upon the necessity for ethical values to guide the experiments and influences which shall encourage emergence of prosocial impulses.

For a more general statement of the possibilities for favorable change in man, see Gardner Murphy's book, *Human Potentialities*.[4] This presents an informed and mature summary of much current thinking. Murphy's position lies somewhere between the behaviorists and the humanists, but he is closer to the humanists. He writes first of an original human nature and second to a socially formed human nature. Then he goes on to examine the possibilities for moving beyond the limitations of both, especially when people are persuaded to cooperate in their own improvement. He points to the enormous potentials for favorable growth that lie dormant in most human beings, once these same human beings have discovered the creative means for releasing these potentials.

---

[4] Gardner Murphy, *Human Potentialities* (New York: Basic Books, Inc., 1958).

Chapter 3

What Is the Process?

Why do we refer to an encourager's responsibility with people as community development? Why not call it community action, or leadership development, or community education, or social planning? We could add other terms. All of these terms, together with community organization, which we have already mentioned, have been defined by professionals in ways that make them less useful for an encourager. But the more important reason is that the work he is to do is concerned with a process in people's lives. More clearly than any of these other fields of work, community development is centered upon a process of human growth.

The Concept of Process

Community improvers were slow to formulate a concept of a process that results in human self-improvement. First, they were overwhelmed by the fact that the people they hoped to stir were so discouraged and seemed so incompetent. It was clear that the people to be helped were both victims of and contributors to their miseries. Consequently, certain would-be improvers gave up the struggle and contented themselves with describing how terrible social conditions are and how unwilling people are to better themselves.

Then other improvers sought development by providing better facilities for living, increased income, better housing, and so on, only to discover that the people served still did not develop in ways to match the environmental improvement. They carried the attitudes and habits of their former existence into the better facilities.

Then various improvers called for an effort to educate people to adapt to their bettered environment. But they discovered that these people were often unresponsive or even resistant to teaching. Only when the improvers came to live with the people and shared their often inarticulate hopes did they conceive the possibility of a learner-motivated educational process. They discovered that people can be encouraged to solve some of their own problems and can thus contribute to their own educational growth.

The process that enlightened improvers now seek is not one that produces final solutions to problems; it is one that develops people to become competent problem-solvers. People learn to search for answers to the immediate problems in order to cultivate the ability to cope with the unpredicted problems of the future.

An encourager is called upon to expedite such a process, so that people may become responsible for improvements in their communities and in themselves. He is expected to bring into being abilities which do not yet exist, or exist only potentially.

To say that a process of favorable change is possible is not to say that only one such process is possible. The precise outline to be followed depends upon local conditions and local people. We will describe more than one process. But we will try to make clear an idea of sequence that can be outlined in such a way as to allow for variety.

An Outlineable Sequence

Some Spanish-speaking people were living in an isolated valley in the tropics. About sixty percent of them were illiterate. As victims of centuries of discrimination and exploitation, they were thought hopeless by certain authorities connected with the near-by university. These warned the encouragers who undertook to start a process that their time and energy would be wasted. These disadvantaged people were deemed hopeless by reason of illiteracy, disease, poor nutrition, and low economic status, but most of all by reason of the apathy that had been their inheritance for generations. They were often referred to as "peasants," and they seemed to look upon themselves as such. "We are so poor," they would say, apparently meaning poor in ambition as well as in money.

The encouragers were outsiders who had to be invited into the situation by someone. They had to have sponsors. The invitation came from the mayor of the municipio (a political subdivision corresponding roughly to a county in American local government), and from the businessman mentioned in the previous chapter. The people themselves were too far sunk in hopelessness to invite anyone, even to think that improvement was possible or to be able to define what their problems were.

Shepherded by the mayor, the encouragers came into the valley of despair for a visit. There was a road that came through a pass (locally known as "The Gates of Hell") which petered out after extending half a mile or so into the valley. Thereafter, even the mayor's four-wheel-drive jeep stuck in the mud, and the trip continued on foot. Their good will certified by the mayor's introduction, the encouragers, in their poor Spanish, talked with the residents. They drank coffee in shack after shack (praying that their typhoid immunizations were still effective). They made the first advances toward friendship and were encouraged to believe that they would be welcome.

These encouragers were a little wiser than some already discussed. Instead of deciding for the people which activity was desirable for a start, they listened to hear what the people talked about. They heard certain vague hopes for improvement expressed, but one specific need was mentioned again and again: a road. This need loomed larger in conversations than a number of other improvements the encouragers thought more immediate, such as needs for better health, a school for children, and increased income.

There was a recognized local leader in the valley who seemed quite affable and remained so throughout the years of the process. He promised to help but never lifted a finger. Ordinary people promised to work together, with help from the government and students, in the construction of a road. Most of the promisers did work but they followed an irregular and unpredictable time schedule. Various agencies and government offices that might have helped were interested only in wishing the project well. The people were thus thrown back upon their own energies and upon the faith and determination of the encouragers.

The public health authorities were approached by the encouragers. They said they could not help because construction of a road had nothing to do with health. Yet a road was necessary to get sick people out and doctors and nurses in. The recreation agency said it would be glad to help when the project needed baseballs and bats, but a road was beyond their scope of action. The same was true for public school people, for agricultural extension agents, and so on. They were all mistaken; the people were right! The key to progress was the road. These other resources of help became cooperative later as the process proceeded and their specialized services were needed.

With the occasional help of a bulldozer borrowed, with driver, from the mayor, with tools assembled by the businessman, with sand and cement and culverts from private donors and local government, the road was begun. The work really became energetic when encouragers took up temporary residence and established a daily work schedule. At the same time the encouragers began to call residents together into a new experience, a public meeting. These inarticulate people had to learn how to speak up in a meeting and how to be attentive when someone else was speaking, how to be a chairman and how to respond to a chairman, how to appoint committees and how to persuade committees to carry out their assignments and report back to the meeting.

After the first year, given over largely to work on the road, visits in homes, and the first meetings, a research team from the university was sent out to evaluate the early stages of the project. Investigators, unknown to the encouragers, went from shack to shack in the valley to collect opinions about the outsiders who had come to live and work with the people. The investigators reported an almost universal response: "They're crazy to come and live in this mess and work with us without pay." However, another comment almost always followed: "But then, they are so nice that we just have to cooperate with them. What else can we do?" This was accompanied by an eloquent shrug.

The appreciation of encouragers who came to share hardship, work, and flickering hope, helped these despairing people to begin a process of self-change. Often this sharing is the most significant contribution a community developer can make.

The encouragers called the first meeting. It convened on a grassy hilltop, well supplied with "mimis" (small gnats whose every bite produced a welt). The men, drunk enough to be free from their usual inhibitions, came into the center of the meeting, but the women hung back on the fringes. A businessman and some of his friends from his luncheon club acted as chairmen. Several local citizens took the opportunity to unburden themselves of grievances, condemning the government, the rich, the church, all who could have helped, yet had not, according to the speakers. The only people unscathed by the attack were the encouragers, who were referred to as angels. One speaker, with characteristic Spanish eloquence, gave thanks that these angels had come through the "gates of Hell" to help them. This unintended witticism, delivered with great solemnity, produced gales of laughter that contributed to the good feeling and friendliness of the meeting.

Such an unloading of grievances and hopes, which is known to social scientists as a catharsis, was apparently a necessary experience for these people, who had been burdened by generations of repression and failure. Only after several episodes of such verbal relief were they able to begin acquiring more positive attitudes and habits. Yet even in catharsis, they were learning how to put their thoughts into words that made sense and to organize their thoughts so that words could express them. Through the meetings they were becoming articulate.

The first officers chosen failed to appear at the next meeting. The first committees appointed to carry out certain assignments never met and never were asked to report. But the encouragers kept urging the people to choose new officers and new committees, and then tried to help each achieve some self-discipline of responsibility.

After completion of the road (completion is too final a word; the road had to be worked on by the people and government for years) interest turned to other activities. Gradually the habits of responsibility increased in the meetings; new activities were discussed, adopted or rejected, and planned. Some activities were carried on by individual citizens, such as helping with the construction of a school and the building of two churches, Catholic and Protestant. Others came about by decisions of the meeting, such as construction of a milk and food station for children and a community center where meetings could be held. A series of more traditional educational activities was undertaken, including classes in literacy, nutrition, farming practices, and recreation. Help for these was requested from the proper authorities by action of the meeting. Eventually committees were appointed to raise money, at first principally by making and selling such things as clothes and food, but later also by going out of the valley to appeal to the government or to private donors selected by the friendly businessmen.

The people decided for themselves (without lectures on temperance from encouragers or anyone else) that drunkenness was not acceptable at the meetings. Two sergeants-at-arms were appointed to remove anyone who was obviously drunk or drinking. On one occassion, these two men seemed to enjoy ejecting a government official who came to a meeting unwisely liquored.

During these gradual changes, various improvements were adopted. Requests for classes in literacy are a case in point. Since the entire country was industrializing, it had become apparent that factory employment was open only to people who knew how to read and write, and handle some arithmetic. Many persons were imprisoned by their rural poverty unless they could qualify for training in factory jobs. And such training could not begin until a person was literate. This individual lack was made poignant when illiterate people would come to an encourager with a political handbill, home-instruction leaflet, or announcement of a job available, and ask, "What does this say?" The encourager, who often had to turn the paper right-side up, would read it and avoid any lecture on the advantages of literacy. He would not wish to make his friends unhappy by calling attention to their educational inferiority.

Eventually one person, then another and another, asked the encouragers to start literacy classes, promising to come and to bring their neighbors. The encouragers turned to the public school authorities, asking them to start the classes. They provided a teacher on specified evenings, and the literacy classes became a permanent contribution to the process.

Changes in farming and nutritional practices, on the other hand, were brought about by decision of the meeting, which invited experts to attend and join the discussion. As a result, farmers were persuaded to lime their soil, use fertilizers, terrace their crops, and plant more productive coffee bushes and banana trees. They also agreed to raise rabbits for meat. The diet was woefullly deficient in proteins, and an earlier attempt to introduce chickens had failed. Chickens were raised primarily for cock fights, not for eggs or meat, hence the rabbits.

More and more visitors, government officials, public school people, professors from the university, businessmen, and others came to see what was going on. The people became accustomed to welcoming various representatives of privilege, wealth, and power as equals. They also began to use their road for making trips out of the valley to meet important organizations they had once condemned in their frustration. They had achieved enough self-discipline and self-dignity to meet the powerful as man to man, without apology, without cringing, without condemnation.

After six years of the process, the encouragers concluded that these people had gained enough self-direction to allow them to withdraw. They talked this over with the people. The people agreed, although they expressed great affection for their encouraging friends. The mayor and the businessman agreed. The encouragers were thus able to turn their attention to other processes elsewhere, asking that these people and their community organization deal directly thereafter with Agricultural Extension, the Department of Health, the public schools, the office of recreation, and other authorities who could help them and their community to continue to develop.

Could the process have reached this point in less time than six years? Probably. We believe now that good results can be obtained within three to four years. An awareness of how the process works and of how it can be expedited helps. The encouragers in this instance grew a little wiser from their experience.

Several of the gains made by the people can be summarized. In six years, the average family income in the community had risen some four hundred percent. (The percentage of increase is always greater at the lower end of the economic scale. As living standards rise the percentage of increase cannot be expected to remain as large.) New and better homes had been built. Children were better clothed and wore shoes, which are very important in a tropical climate where hookworm is rampant. Diet had improved; more people were chlorinating their drinking water; sick people were being treated by doctors either at home or in a hospital in the nearby town. Farming practices had improved, and the people were in constant contact with agricultural experts. The educational level had risen, for children and adults; classes for both were a part of community life. Two churches were thriving. A central area for community life had been developed, including a permanent building which the people themselves had constructed late in the process without help from the encouragers. The central area also included one of the churches, the school, a store, a playground, and a garden. All of this was maintained by the now permanent community organization, with the help of various outside agencies and government services.

During the later stages of the process, some social scientists from the university called an evaluational meeting that included some of the participants, but not the encouragers. The businessman who had been closest to the entire sequence of events was present. During the meeting, a skeptical sociologist said, "Now, I will grant you that tremendous changes have taken place, greater improvements than I ever thought possible. But can you prove to me that these people (the encouragers) brought these changes about?"

The businessman replied, "No, I can't prove any such thing. But I will point out several things to you. First, the favorable changes did take place. Second, they took place here. Third, they did not take place anywhere else." (We cannot vouch for the accuracy of this statement.) "And finally, they took place while these people were 'hanging around'."

The businessman had drawn attention to a very important aspect of an encourager's role. An encourager is someone who "hangs around" and lives with people to share their troubles and their development processes. It is difficult to spell out in detail what an encourager does while he "hangs around." Let it be said that he establishes himself as a friend, even if this makes him seem a little odd. He convinces people that he is devoted to them and to their development. He shares their lot in life in order to be present to help them develop as they choose to develop.

Basic-Nucleus Outline

Again, it is appropriate *to warn against making the process described here a pattern for universal adoption.* The process is always an indigenous sequence of experiences that is formulated and lived by the local people, usually with an encourager's help. It is produced by the people's perception of need and growing awareness of possible ways to meet that need.

The process is always unique to each specific social situation, and is not repeatable in other situations. Certain basic principles are transferable, however. An encourager is wise when he is flexible enough to follow the leads that the people and their situation make available. He must be willing to experiment, but in a self-disciplined fashion, to carry on a research into the ways of realizing human potential for growth. The basic principles are related to his responsibility as an experimenter.

These principles can be stated in terms of certain stages that can be discerned in this and other community processes. The stages that follow are appropriate to a process that starts with a small community, either rural or urban. We will talk later about stages appropriate to an effort that begins with a large, usually metropolitan community, and works down to small groups.

EXPLORATORY STAGE   An encourager's job is to make friends and to convince people that he likes them, believes in them, wants to be with them. His skills are those that encourage conversation. He asks questions that do not alarm or put people on the defensive. He listens to them and makes use of a good idea when one is offered. A student of community development once said to an encourager he had observed, "I was watching you listening to those people. Then I saw you pounce like a cat upon their idea. You sure pounced." Perhaps the cat analogy is not the most complimentary one, but the important point is the encourager's alertness to the constructive proposal.

DISCUSSIONAL STAGE   An encourager's responsibility is to keep the conversation going so that it does not bog down in an argument, pro and con, about one proposal only, and so that it tends to move eventually toward a specific decision for something to be done by a group. He should help people express themselves clearly, examine many alternative ideas, and arrive at some proposed next steps to be taken. Discussion involves also the collecting of information from experts, from books, from city halls, from surveys conducted by the group. The pertinent information obtained is digested in discussion.

ORGANIZATIONAL STAGE   An encourager's job is to help the people form some social instrument with which to work. Such an instrument is frequently an informal discussion group in the beginning, but it usually evolves into a committee, a council, or some other organized association with officers, regular meetings, and some structure of subcommittees. Certain responsibilities within the organization are delegated to specific persons.

ACTIVITY STAGE   An encourager's job is to help the group carry out its decision to serve the common good. He provides some of the confidence, muscle, and organizational know-how that makes cooperative work possible. People will often continue to discuss indefinitely unless the encourager convinces them that they can do something, and helps them to find the means for doing it. His influence is important both for the decision to act and for the action that follows.

EVALUATIONAL STAGE   An encourager's responsibility is to elicit from the people self-criticism of their activities and even of their discussions. He himself does not criticize the people or their work. But he encourages them to accept self-evaluation as a necessary part of the process. Evaluation can occur before, during, and after an activity, but it is especially important after. The encourager also helps people to make articulate the values by which they judge an action good or bad. He encourages them to revise these standards from time to time, as the process moves on.

CONTINUATION STAGE   An encourager's responsibility is to recommend that the process be nonterminal, even though he himself may eventually withdraw. He encourages people to form an organization that allows for rotation of members and officers, and for continuation of the developmental process through many decisions, actions, and evaluations.

It must be clear that although we have separated these stages from each other and have put them in an order that may imply sequence, they often occur simultaneously and interweave. Furthermore, action may precede organization, or vice versa. There is not an approved sequence, except that exploration precedes, and continuation obviously follows, all the rest. The encourager's responsibilities are related to whichever stage seems most important at any given time.

The Purposes of the Process

Because a community development process is dynamic, it must have direction, as has already been pointed out. It must serve some values which an encourager and the people involved have chosen. The people often start with some very specific immediate purpose (for example, a road to be constructed) but are most vague about ultimate purposes. Only gradually and with an encourager's help will they make articulate their ultimate aims. But an encourager had best make clear, at least to himself, what his values and distant purposes are.

In stating purposes, it is easy to fall into the use of time-honored phrases about democracy, the common man, and the good life. Community itself is a term we all love, without either definition or understanding. And development is equally to be admired, as long as it proceeds toward a goal the admirer approves. Let us see if we can be more precise.

The overriding purpose of the process is to seek a cooperative life that serves the interests of all people on the local scene. This purpose rests upon the assumption, or even the faith, that a good life which benefits everyone is discoverable. It repudiates the contrasting assumption that a needy person or faction can benefit only by taking position, power, or wealth away from those who hold these privileges. According to much modern economic theory, benefits can actually be shared by all. But this much too complicated a matter to go into here. We therefore list the idea as an article of faith that should guide an encourager's aspirations.

Stated in other words, the purpose of the process is to develop in people the ability to create a cooperative community of mutual benefit. Such a community (part of a cooperative society) implies two underlying agreements. First is the agreement that such a community will be built cooperatively. It cannot be imposed. The decisions and actions that bring it into being will be made jointly by local people, by experts, and by encouragers. All of them live in a society that is, but can help create a society that is to be.

Second is an agreement that the form of the community-to-be cannot be predicted. A new community will not be created in a pattern chosen in advance, not by an encourager, not by any theorist, not by any authority. The welfare of the people, which they themselves must judge to be worth pursuing, is the criterion by which they will create the community of the future. Circumstances beyond their control will always limit their choosing but they can contribute much more to their future than they have been doing.

The second agreement rests upon another assumption that an encourager should make. This is that the people he deals with want ultimately to be ethical, according to their best understanding (which may be faulty). He holds to this assumption in spite of people's obvious shortcomings. He may find people stupid, selfish, wrongheaded, and stubborn in their wrongheadedness. But it is his job to try to help a few, and then a few more, and a few more to uncover and respond to ethical impulses that are meaningful to them.

The belief in ethical impulses in people applies also to deliquents, criminals and gangsters, bigots, and people who adhere to unethical ideologies. There are, however, practical considerations that limit one's ability to encourage the emergence of the ethical in all these people. With hardened evildoers, an encourager will probably not have the time or patience or skill to bring out the better impulse. He will have to leave that assignment to the experts—and even they do not agree amongst themselves.

The task of discovering and strengthening these ethical impulses in ordinary people will tax the ability of any normal encourager. Even with them, he will require the patience to accept both progress and backsliding. He will have to develop means of dealing with people who sometimes ignore him, sometimes appreciate him, and sometimes resent him for his contribution to the pain of their development. His purposes for the process will tend to be colored by the response people give to him.

Whatever the reactions toward himself, an encourager should continue to believe in the unrealized yet potential good in people. By giving them the benefit of his belief in them, he makes a process possible in which they may grow toward their idea of prosocial goals. He does not condemn them to a life of wrongdoing by acting as though they were beyond redemption.

All of this points to a final purpose for the process. It is to provide a means by which ordinary people can become articulate, especially in spheres of social influence. They are so often inarticulate and voiceless. A major purpose of community development is to provide a social instrument through which the people may be heard, through which they may contribute to the unending dialogue by which men seek to plan their future.

ADDENDUM FOR SOCIAL SCIENCE STUDENTS

For a more exacting analysis see the Biddles *Community Development Process,*[1] Chapter 6, "The Basic Nucleus." This chapter discusses the ways in which apathy, in ordinary people, can be overcome and a process inaugurated that points toward participation in the life of the larger community. Chapter 8, "Research Design," fits the experimental method into the process. Chapter 12, "Scientific Relatedness," brings the whole within the scope of social scientific discipline.

These chapters and other sections of the book deal with the question of

---

[1] William W. Biddle and Loureide Biddle, *The Community Development Process* (New York: Holt, Rinehart and Winston, Inc., 1965).

how schemes of value are formulated and changed by feedback from research. For further consideration of feedback in social research methods, see a book edited by Festinger and Katz, *Research Methods in the Behavioral Sciences.*[2] The whole book should be studied, but Chapter 13, "The Utilization of Social Science," as particularly helpful. This chapter, written by Rensis Lickert and Ronald Lippitt, tells how participants in a development process can utilize feedback to expedite the process.

Students who wish to pursue the economics of a society that no longer needs to take away from those who have in order to benefit those who have not should see J. M. Keynes' *Essays in Persuasion.*[3] He insists that as far as absolute needs are concerned, the economic problem can be solved. It is when the need to triumph over rivals becomes so important that human beings compete and cannot cooperate. A cooperative community, or society, or world, might thus become possible once human beings persuade themselves it is possible and seek to create such a social order. The search for cooperative community in thousands of places makes a contribution towards self-persuasion in favor of cooperation.

John K. Galbraith, in *The Affluent Society,*[4] brings the argument up to date. In the main he agrees with the Keynesian position, but goes on to point out numerous difficulties moderns (Americans especially) face because an economy of abundance has replaced the old economy of scarcity. Belief that the latter still exists has led reformers to recommend that the "have-nots" sieze from the "haves." The problem, in the nations that know abundance, is to learn how to live with affluence by sharing in cooperative living. Learning how to do this can begin within local communities.

---

[2] Leon Festinger and Daniel Katz, *Research Methods in the Behavioral Sciences* (New York: Holt, Rinehart and Winston, Inc., 1953).

[3] J. M. Keynes, *Essays in Persuasion, Economic Possibilities for Our Grandchildren* (London: Collier-Macmillan, Ltd., 1931).

[4] John Kenneth Galbraith, *The Affluent Society* (Boston: Houghton Mifflin Company, 1958).

Chapter 4

Forming a Larger Working Group

Some process such as the one outlined in Chapter 3 is basic to group life when people come together and cooperate, face to face, to accomplish some common purpose. We call this the basic-nucleus process.

There are other procedures that we refer to as the larger-nucleus process. Sometimes these grow out of the basic experience, as they do in several of the examples in this book. But sometimes community developers start with the larger group and omit the basic stages. It is possible to start a development process in a wider area, usually called a neighborhood, and yet benefit from the basic experience.

The Initiators

When an encourager begins to develop a larger working group, he depends more upon selected individuals we will call initiators. He has a hand in searching for and selecting these people, but to an extent they select themselves by their response. What are the characteristics to be sought in an initiator? Formal education is an uncertain criterion, although poorly educated people usually have comparatively less skill in group operation. But this is not always true. And graduate degrees are no guarantee of the ability to work with others.

It might be helpful to ask the following questions about prospective initiators. Can they conduct a meeting according to democratic procedures?

Do they know how to choose a chairman? Do they know how a chairman should act, giving the floor to every contending point of view equally while keeping the meeting in order to hear whatever is presented? Do they know that the chairman, or someone else, should summarize discussion and press for a decision? Are they articulate? Do they understand that listening to an opponent with attention and respect is as important as expressing their own convictions? Can they listen to an opponent without condemning him as dishonest, unintelligent, or evil? Can they believe that an opponent can be sincere and well informed, even though he differs with them? Are they willing to place the welfare and continuity of the group above the triumph of their own favorite ideas? Are they willing to search for a common (community) good, beyond their loyalty to a special interest?

An encourager will seldom be able to give a positive answer to all these questions for any one prospective initiator. Furthermore, most of his answers will have to be based upon his best guess. And he may make the wrong guess. There is no way to avoid this difficulty. He must make his best guess as to how familiar persons are with social skills but also as to how rapidly they can be helped to acquire these skills. And he must be prepared to correct his guesses when he finds them wrong. With experience, he will find that his guessing will become more accurate. But he will never be entirely free from faulty estimates of people's capabilities.

Before an approach to the process is selected, the encourager will need to inform himself about the local situation. The initiators, whose level of sophistication he must estimate, need to be representative of that local situation. Their skills in group operation will preferably be similar to those of most of the local people. The social skills may be a little above the prevailing level, but not very much higher.

If initiators are too far advanced beyond the citizens they represent, there is danger of loss of contact; people will fail to identify with the development process they initiate. But, even worse, the initiators may become self-conscious about their superiority and be tempted to manipulate the people they regard as inferior, in order to accomplish whatever they have decided is good.

The decision as to which approach to development is best will be made by the initiators with an encourager's advice. But the decision as to whether the process will serve political or developmental objectives primarily must be made by an encourager, even before he starts searching for initiators. He cannot escape this responsibility. For his decision about the objective of the process will determine the kind of initiators he will seek and the invitations he extends to recruit their interest. He will be stymied unless he can clarify his own thinking about his objectives.

Political versus
Developmental Objectives

Many community workers who *say* they are devoted to development cling to methods that contradict the developmental purpose they espouse. There is no way to overcome the confusion for them but to make clear to them that they are pursuing two contrasting objectives. In the service of one objective a community group is organized to promote a cause. The cause is more important than the fate of the members of the group, and certainly more important than the fate of the group's opponents. In the service of the other objective, a group is organized to bring about development of citizens, and through them of their community. The fate of the people, all of them, is deemed to be more important than any cause they serve.

The two objectives are based upon two separate schemes of value. One is political and relies upon the methods of competitive pressure. The other is developmental and relies more upon education. The confusion for community workers grows out of the fact that though the ultimate objectives of these two points of view are different, in actual practice the two methods of forming community groups look somewhat alike. Educational groups dabble in politics but keep developmental objectives foremost. Political groups use educational experiences that serve political ends.

Political and developmental activities are interrelated. Political achievements are not likely to be made unless there is some development of persons. And in order for people to develop, certain experiences which sooner or later include attention to politics, are necessary. Nevertheless, the criteria for judging the success of a politically motivated group are far different from those used to judge a developmental group.

The political point of view emphasizes controversy. A community group is set up, or activated, to fight for a particular cause—a political party, a candidate for public office, some piece of legislation, or a category of people in the total population. It competes with rival interests. The skills to be learned, and the experiences out of which these grow are combative.

Such competition between rival points of view and programs is a healthy thing in a democracy. It sharpens differences (when it is working properly) and it draws alternatives sharply to the attention of citizens. Voters are then free to choose between the alternatives in hard-fought elections. In a community group that serves this competitive purpose, however, it is easy for initiators to be so eager for victory that they forget the needs for development of fellow members and especially of opponents.

In the developmental point of view, on the other hand, the values served grow out of cooperation. A community group is set up to reconcile competing points of view, in the hope of enhancing the total good of all. The skills to be learned are those of understanding and consideration for the needs and feelings of others. Initiators set out to increase their, and other people's, ability to deal with controversy in a manner that will benefit and develop everyone.

This reconciling cooperation is also necessary to a democracy. But the skills of reconciliation have not had anywhere near as much cultivation as the skills of competition. Experiences that develop cooperative skills are not much emphasized because they lack the fire and excitement of battle. Even a people as experienced in democratic ways as we, are still prone to respond to controversy as if it were a battle between the "good guys" (ourselves) and the "bad guys" (our opponents).

Both promotion of controversy and reconciliation to resolve conflict are necessary in the communities of an open society. The groups devoted to each kind of objective complement each other. Reconciliation is not possible until there are rival points of view to reconcile. And political controversy should ever remain a part of our democratic society. But development of skills to understand complicated rival interest and to seek mutually beneficial agreement are also necessary.

As a worker with people in communities, an encourager cannot seek to promote both controversy and cooperation simultaneously. He will be understood as an advocate of one or the other or he will not be understood at all. So he will have to make up his mind about which set of values he is serving at a given time.

Most believers in democracy have advanced to the point of admiring controversy and stopped there. They are fighters for what they deem to be righteous. Some have advanced further to an admiration of compromise but the compromise they have in mind usually means a yielding of some demands when opponents will also yield a few—a type of horse-trading. Only a few have advanced to an appreciation of creative reconciliation, in which new and undreamed of solutions to problems arise out of cooperative thinking and working together. Here is the great need and opportunity in an age of increasingly complex problems and interdependent solutions. An encourager belongs in the company of the creative reconcilers.

By accepting developmental goals, he does not reject political controversy. He merely leaves this necessary activity to someone else. His job is not to encourage attack upon rivals but to strengthen people's abilities to find creative solutions to conflict. He is not a political controversialist. He is a reconciler of conflict, to the end that people may become more competent to create their own solutions to problems.

In one city, part of a vast metropolitan complex, a young clergyman undertook encouragement of a civic betterment association. He enlisted the interest of several highly sophisticated initiators from his own and other congregations. These were people with a history of activity in organizations like the League of Women Voters, the YWCA, various mayor's commissions, the chamber of commerce, labor unions, minority ethnic associations, and so on. These initiators were willing to try out a cooperative approach to their city's problems, in spite of the experience of fighting for righteous causes some had known in the past. But the clergyman himself never was able to abandon his desires to propagandize for the "correct" solution to problems. He never quite accepted the objective search for new solutions to be created by the group, as will be seen later.

The initiators and the encourager together found a chairman for the group who accepted the objectives of cooperative reconciliation. During his two-year chairmanship, much was accomplished. The group caught the attention of the local newspaper, which was intrigued by the idea of a civic association that was not seeking to promote the interest of any one political faction. It appealed to candidates for mayor and city council in a forthcoming election to take a position on a selected list of important problems. After the election the group cooperated with the municipal government to obtain a new bus system for the city, to make some progress with cleaning up slum housing, to obtain better recreation for children, and so on. But the group retained enough independence to criticize the government and to make the school board uncomfortable by recommending improvements at numerous meetings of the board.

When the first chairman, a young businessman, moved away from the city, another person was found to take his place. This man, who was prominent in a minority ethnic group, was chosen by the group with the endorsement of the encourager, largely because of his ethnic affiliation. Within the year, the new chairman publicly announced his support of one of the candidates for governor of the state. He did this without consulting the group, but since he was chairman, his partisan stand was generally accepted as the position of the entire group.

The chairman's action dealt the group a serious blow, which was made even worse when the endorsed candidate lost the election. Public confidence was diminished and the group and its members were accused of seeking political advantage. Some members dropped out, saying they did not want to be associated with such an organization. After some time, a few initiators brought the group back to life, without the offending chairman, but it has never regained its influence in the city.

The difficulty grew out of the failure of the encourager to make clear—to himself and to group members—the distinction between political and developmental objectives. He allowed the two contrasting schemes of value to become confused in the thinking of people who might have participated in a process of development. He never gave up his love for political controversy and later accepted an assignment in a church propaganda office, working to promote the civil liberties movement. He does well in this work and is happy and convincing with it. Perhaps he had always felt ill at ease in the role of encourager.

If an encourager wishes to become a political propagandist, he should not try to combine that role with his responsibility as an encourager. He cannot be both at once. He is a developer of people and of their life together. He is not a controversialist. He should leave the propaganda job to someone else.

Significance of the Basic Process

In sociological language, a basic nucleus is a primary group. It is an association of friends who have intimate contacts in pursuit of commonly chosen goals. They see each other often and interact with one another. But they are also close in trust of each other, despite possible disputes and differences of opinion.

The primary group is preeminently the social instrument for bringing about favorable changes in people, especially when it grapples with real problems and when it tries to seek solutions that serve the members' concept of the common (community) good. Its possibilities have just begun to be explored in social scientific research. There is much more to learn.

A primary group such as a basic nucleus provides experiences in which a person can learn and benefit from friendship. Here each member of the group can receive the personal recognition he needs to build up his own self-esteem; yet he can be disciplined when he becomes overbearing. Service to (the member's concept of) the community good is the criterion of criticism to be used by the group as a whole when one member's ego becomes domineering. The friendliness learned within the group can be extended by analogy to people outside the group. The job of helping people carry over some aspects of friendship from primary group experience to nonmembers is the encourager's.

The basic-nucleus process is recommended when the number of people involved is small, as in a rural area or in a part of a city neighborhood and especially when the initiators are at the lower end of the scale of sophistication. It is useful in helping disadvantaged people to develop. But the experience to be found in these small face-to-face groups is so valuable that it ought to be made available to the privileged and the prominent, and to middle-class people, also. All up and down American society we find people who suffer from frustration, uncertainty about their own selfhood, and ideals they have been unable to put into practice.

So valuable is basic-nucleus experience that we consider it essential to all training in human relations. An encourager needs this experience in order to become competent. Initiators of community groups need it and should have it before they attempt to initiate a larger nucleus. One of the causes of failure of large community organizations is that many of the initiators have lost or never discovered the friendly human touch. Experience in a basic nucleus provides opportunity for learning this human sensitivity.

In an Appalachian community, the work began with the formation of a basic nucleus. The people were functionally illiterate and among the most disadvantaged of the nation. The initiators were a miner's wife and the minister of a small struggling church, together with a partly unemployed man who wanted something better for his children. Their achievement in forming a group was remarkable in an area where development of community spirit had been blocked by loyalty to the hollow in which families lived. The initiators succeeded in forming a group by enlisting many families to work together on flood walls that would protect the main creek into which surplus water spilled from several hollows. Although the people from each hollow were suspicious of "strangers" from the next, and even more of outside encouragers, the initiators finally persuaded them to join forces against the flood that hurt them all.

After some experience of friendliness in discussing, planning, and working together on flood control, the group went on to many other cooperative activities: painting and rehabilitating their once rival churches, setting up recreation for their young people, obtaining roads and bridges from the county and state governments, bringing in electric lights and telephones, starting several small handwork industries, making a beginning of a tourist trade.

Throughout all these achievements, the members of the nucleus were learning how to cooperate, not only with each other, but also with government officials, agricultural extension people, representatives from the university, and businessmen in two cities to which people were able to drive over the new roads. The original nucleus inspired the formation of another and another nucleus, and all were invited to send representatives to chambers of commerce in the cities and to take part in planning activities started by the university and state government. A process that started with the face-to-face intimacy of a basic nucleus tended to move into the activities of a larger nucleus, while the friendship of the original groups continued to serve local people.

The basic-nucleus approach is preferable when the social situation is simpler. But it would be a mistake to conclude that this approach should therefore be limited to simple, uncomplicated social situations. Many of the frustrated and often rootless citizens of great metropolitan complexes will not be able to find their dignity as persons unless they take part in similar small primary group experiences. It is an encourager's responsibility to help the larger process produce a multitude of basic nuclei, when he finds himself working in the complexity of metropolitan life.

Larger-Nucleus Approach

When an encourager is faced with the dismaying complications of city life, the larger-nucleus approach is a good starting method. This approach is often referred to as community organization, but we prefer not to use this term at this point, first, because of the many conflicting definitions, but even more because its use usually misleads the initiators. They are too prone to be satisfied when they have organized the social forces or agencies or clubs and associations of a city without pressing the process on to the creation of basic nuclei that reach the needs of ordinary people. Initiators need encouragement to create basic nuclei. These smaller groups, however, may come and go; they are likely to be less permanent than the larger nucleus. They serve the entire community best by working through the larger association.

In a metropolis an encourager is likely to find privileged people whose background of education and organizational experience leads them to think in city-wide or larger-area terms. It is possible for the encourager to ignore these would-be initiators and turn his attention to the underprivileged; some people start community action programs this way. But the result usually is that an organization is built to fight the privileged and powerful, one that too easily turns to politics instead of development. A process more committed to cooperation can be worked out by selecting initiators from among the most flexible and altruistic privileged people and encouraging them to associate with ordinary underprivileged people to build up a neighborhood organization.

If an encourager decides to work with the underprivileged exclusively, the basic nucleus approach can be used in the beginning, with initiators found in smaller areas. Such underprivileged initiators, who will form small nuclei within sections of a neighborhood, often city blocks, can be discovered. But an encourager needs to avoid forcing a block organization on people. He should listen to the initiators. They will often tell him what small territories in a neighborhood represent meaningful areas for nucleus formation. But even as he encourages small nuclei, he should also give attention to the formation of a larger nucleus through initiators who think in terms of an entire neighborhood or even city.

Sophisticated initiators (some of whom will be found among the under-privileged) will already possess some of the skills needed to organize and operate a larger, representative group. But many of the skills and attitudes they bring may prove incompatible with the process being encouraged. They may insist upon being competitive and working for special interests. Or they may be overburdened by rules of parliamentary procedure or may speak too often of their formal education. Furthermore, any initiators may too easily slip into a role of dominance over the less sophisticated and less articulate. Part of an encourager's job is to help initiators overcome in-appropriate habits and attitudes and to guard against becoming self-appointed leaders who tell people what to do. The best way of helping them is to draw their attention continually to the needs and frustrations of other people—to see what they can do to help these others grow in competence.

In one city, a neighborhood was in process of transition from a middle-class, racially integrated area to a low-income, all-Negro ghetto. When the community development process began, a number of blocks had already been taken over by the low-income invaders as white families fled. It seemed likely that the tide of slum encroachment would shortly sweep over the whole area and beyond.

A group of ten initiators started the process (five married couples, three white and two Negro). All of them were professional people, old residents of the neighborhood who wished to preserve its pleasant residential charac-ter. The men were educators, social workers, church employees, and a doctor. Their wives either were professionally employed or could point to years of experience of working with such organizations as women's clubs and the YWCA. One of the couples had asked for help from an encourager, after he had spoken to many people and agencies in the city to let them know that he and his colleagues would welcome an invitation. Following an encourager's recommendation, one initiator called the other four couples into the first meeting with the encouragers to get the process started.

The first ten initiators succeeded in forming a neighborhood council (a larger nucleus). They invited friends, and friends of friends, to attend dis-cussions of problems of the area and of ways of protecting the integrity of the neighborhood, as a pleasant, racially integrated residential area. In addi-tion to friendship as a criterion for selecting members of the neighborhood council, the initiators sought representation of all organizations and interests that were important in the area—all churches, schools, a university (which was part of the neighborhood), and racial and economic groups.

A difficulty lay in the fact that all of the initiators were affiliated with city-wide organizations that had no neighborhood branches. In many ways, it would have been easier for them to form a city-wide council, but such a council would not have provided an instrument for meeting the problems of the particular neighborhood. They would furthermore have found it much more difficult to touch personal lives of their neighbors. And finally, there were already city-wide community organizations: a social welfare council, a federation of churches, a Jewish and a Catholic welfare organization. The need was for a larger nucleus that could represent neighborhood interests in relationship to the city as a whole while it reached the people of the area.

The five initiator couples succeeded in starting the process, but ironically, all but one of the original couples dropped out, each for a different reason. And the one couple that stayed on was absent during the crucial second year, returning later. The expectation of a rotation in council membership was built into the process from the beginning, however, as well as a rotation of officerships.

Over a period of years, the neighborhood council carried on activities of increasing complexity. It saved a small block-sized park from being turned into a parking lot and established a recreation program on it, handled problems of zoning-law violations (by appealing to the civic conscience of violators), learned how to deal with racial clashes and local violence (by working with the offenders), and set up a welcoming procedure and tactful instruction in the niceties of city living for newcomers to the neighborhood. The Negroes have increased in number, but they have become good neighbors. Many white families have stayed on, and others have moved back into what they now consider a desirable neighborhood. The council has learned to cooperate with the city and county planning commissions, with school authorities (to find an education better adapted to preparing the youth of a minority group for jobs), with city recreation authorities, with the mayor's committee on human relations, and so on. Today it is still in existence and continues to train its members in competence.

In order to carry out these and many other activities, some suborganizations became necessary. Without them, ordinary people could not be reached. Several forms of smaller group were tried. One was a temporary subcommittee appointed to do some special job such as a survey of the area, preparation for a large-scale open meeting, advising a citizen who needed to learn how to become a good neighbor. Later, more permanent committees were set up, one on preparation of large meetings, another on welcoming newcomers, another on neighborhood beautification, another on the improving of schools. Finally, the whole area was subdivided into districts and committees were formed in each district. Each committee met with an indigenous encourager who was assigned by the neighborhood council. These district groups became basic nuclei, concerned with their own immediate problems but conscious of the larger body that received communications from them and helped each of them when necessary. Sometimes the districts corresponded to city blocks; sometimes they included several blocks. The size in each case depended upon the wishes of the residents and upon the analysis of the situations made by the council.

The neighborhood council and it subgroups have worked so well that the pattern they developed has become a prototype for the entire city. The newspapers, the city government, the privately supported agencies and organizations look to it for ideas and guidance. Not all the problems are solved. But a means has been set up for training people in competence and for helping them to think constructively about the solution of problems.

An Outline of the Larger-Nucleus Approach

It is now possible to outline a typical sequence of events of a larger-nucleus approach. The process starts with several initiators who enlist the interest of others. These people should represent as much as possible all churches, schools, organizations, agencies, and factions. As a result of several meetings with this gradually expanding company, a city or neighborhood council (a larger nucleus) is formed.

It is wise to agree upon a number of items when the association is formed. (1) All who set it up should make a commitment to stay with the organization through thick and thin, knowing that there will be disappointments, conflicts, and setbacks. (2) An agreement should be reached to hold the door of welcome open for any representation or faction that does not come in at the time of formation, or for any new organization that might appear in the future. (3) Membership and officership should rotate; this implies a further commitment to search constantly for new recruits. (4) While representation of all points of view is important, the best criteria for selection of new members are the commitment of the individual, his potential understanding of the job to be done, and his willingness to work; these are more important than his representation of a particular faction in the population.

Shortly after its formation, the group as a whole has several other decisions to make. (1) An area of service should be selected. A city neighborhood seldom has a separate identity or clear-cut boundaries. The group will have to decide what area it proposes to serve, and then be prepared to revise the boundaries it sets, as it works along. (2) It should make some outline of the probable steps to be followed for the first two or three years. This gives some order to the process, even though it is subject to revisions with experience. (3) It should set up the beginnings of a research design, mainly in the form of records of meetings and actions taken, to be fed back into the process of further deciding and planning.

The group then goes to work to study the area of service, the people in it, their problems, their frustrations, their aspirations. It can be helped in this study by some training in the methods of understanding and working with people. This training has been arranged for by an encourager. He can invite trainers from many places—universities, social work agencies, churches—when he is sure the specialist he chooses has some idea of the process to be carried on. He himself can join in on some of the training, but should not allow himself to drift into the position of becoming an instructor. His friendship with members of the group is of a different quality from that of teacher to learner.

As a result of study and training, group members usually become more aware of the people of need, the disadvantaged minorities. A minority group given attention may be defined by race, by age (the very young or the very old), or by a handicap (the blind, the diseased, the delinquent, the jobless) or other characteristic. With our current concern with overcoming poverty, the very poor are especially to be given attention. Out of the group's awareness of the disadvantaged people comes a decision to work with selected groups of the needy.

If the study and training have gone well, various members of the larger nucleus, or new recruits to it, will volunteer to work with subgroups formed among the people of need. The process of forming and reforming these subgroups goes on indefinitely; new basic nuclei are formed from time to time by local volunteers who have been trained to become indigenous encouragers by larger-nucleus members. These smaller nuclei meet, report their problems and requests to the larger body, and are helped by this neighborhood group to do whatever jobs they undertake. These local groups also become places of recruitment for the larger-neighborhood nucleus.

There is a further training, in which an encourager can be the trainer. This is training in the interpretation of on-going experience for participants. It is on-the-job training in development that can be carried on only by someone close to the participants and to the process. Skill in this day-by-day educational process is a matter of restraint and maintaining silence, quite as much as of eloquence. Above all, it calls for judgment on an encourager's part as to which will help the participants most at any given time.

Ideally, a larger nucleus becomes a permanent body that addresses its most sensitive thinking to the problems of the people in the area of service, creates and serves basic nuclei as local needs change, and relates itself also to the larger city-wide, state-wide, and national organizations and programs. It becomes a nonpartisan conscience of the area, forever searching for solutions to problems that will benefit everyone.

Some Generalizations

A few questions and tentative answers can be listed about the formation of working groups:

1. When forming basic nuclei, does an encourager use existing groups or form new ones? New ones are preferable, since many existing groups represent special and even selfish interests. With new groups, an encourager is in a position to help members set purposes in terms of service to their present and growing idea of community. In addition, a proliferation of many local groups is good, even though they may come and go. The benefit from the experience remains.

2. When forming a larger nucleus, does an encourager use an already existing body, a federation of churches, a chamber of commerce, a women's association, a council of social agencies, a labor federation? It is a good idea to use one of these organizations in a small city; but in a metropolitan area, most of these groups will serve too large an area to make an effective larger nucleus. In addition, organizations like these do not serve well unless they are willing to change their special purposes to serve the whole community and unless they are willing to open their membership to factions and groups not yet represented.

In view of these difficulties, it is usually better to form a new group for a larger nucleus. There is this warning, however: an encourager should avoid making the new association a rival of existing organizations. They should be included by representation. The advantage of a new larger nucleus is that it can be developed on a nonpartisan basis, without obligation to any faction, church, denomination, social class, political party, or cause to be promoted. It can then gain the strength of being known as a free searcher for the community good.

3. Can a neighborhood or other larger organization do the community development job without use of small local groups? No, the importance of basic nuclei cannot be overstressed. Every community needs more of these than it already has. But these small groups fail in their purpose unless they seek to serve a community beyond their own intimate circle. They can effectively serve the broader community when they relate themselves to a larger nucleus, which in turn relates itself to even larger units of decision-making and planning.

ADDENDUM FOR SOCIAL SCIENCE STUDENTS

When research is made an essential part of the community development process, it can become an applied social science. The research methodology used is one introduced by social psychologist Kurt Lewin, action research. A discussion of this methodology will be found in Lewin's book *Resolving Social Conflict*.[1] The method researches the process while it is going on. Characteristically, it calls upon participants to choose objectives, observe the actions, and evaluate the results according to the objectives chosen. Ordinary citizens of a community are called upon to become researchers to the extent of which they are capable. And that capability can be increased by the experience of the process.

In pursuit of this same line of thinking, the student is urged to look into group dynamics, a related sociopsychological field of research. A brief but informative book to start with is *Introduction to Group Dynamics* by Malcolm and Hulda Knowles.[2] It opens up the different approaches to the study of groups and presents several annotated bibliographies for further study. For the student who wants to dig deeper and more laboriously into this field, *Group Dynamics* by Dorwin Cartwright and Alvin Zander [3] is recommended. This book presents papers written by many of the important contributors to the 1953 edition. A more recent anthology has been edited by A. Paul Hare, *Handbook of Small Group Research*.[4]

All these are valuable presentations of research into group behavior, but the emphasis in all of them is on the group in a laboratory setting or other controlled social situation. The study of group behavior in the *situ* of community living has yet to be perfected. Researchers who go into this more difficult kind of study should be guided by the findings from controlled small group research. But they should be prepared also to venture into a kind of action research in community, where controls of the process are not available.

Because communities are so uncontrollable, the field of community organization is filled with controversy. One of the best summaries of tradi-

---

[1] Kurt Lewin, *Resolving Social Conflict* (New York: Harper & Row, Publishers, Inc., 1948).

[2] Malcolm and Hulda Knowles, *Introduction to Group Dynamics* (New York: Association Press, 1959).

[3] Dorwin Cartwright and Alvin Zander (editors), *Group Dynamics* (New York: Harper & Row, Publishers, 1953).

[4] A. Paul Hare, Ed., *Handbook of Small Group Research* (New York: The Free Press of Glencoe, Inc., 1963).

tional thinking in this field is found in a book by Dunham and Harper, *Community Organization in Action.*[5] Another writer, Murray G. Ross,[6] presents a classic of the more conventional point of view. But Lyle E. Schaller, in his *Community Organization: Conflict and Reconciliation* [7] deals with the controversies that whirl about in more recent times.

---

[5] Arthur Dunham and Ernest B. Harper, Eds., *Community Organization in Action* (New York: Association Press, 1959).

[6] Murray G. Ross, *Community Organization* (New York: Harper & Row, Publishers, 1955).

[7] Lyle E. Schaller, *Community Organization: Conflict and Reconciliation* (Nashville, Tenn.: Abingdon Press, 1966).

Chapter 5

The Increase
of Sensitivity

Encouragement of people to develop themselves while they improve their communities calls for sensitivity to subtle human changes. When new abilities or prosocial points of view emerge they are often timidly expressed. They may even be unrecognized by the person in whom they appear until an encourager draws attention to them.

These favorable changes are delicate growths, appearing in the midst of bad habits, fears of failure, and other encumbrances that can paralyze the will to develop. In order to cultivate favorable growth, an encourager needs to understand, but be free from condemnation of, the undesirable characteristics people exhibit. Condemnation creates resistance against self-change.

He needs to be sensitive to very complicated human reactions—to conscious, dimly conscious, and unconscious motivations. He can be helped in this by an awareness of the equally complicated and changing balance of conflicting motivations that operates within himself. Out of these understandings of others and of self, he can hope to help those he influences to tolerate him and to deal with each other in patience.

One of the great problems he will have to contend with in himself is the intolerance of the reformer. A belief in people, which he should have, can easily turn to cynicism when people fall short of his expectations for them. He can blame them or excuse himself by pointing to that old bugaboo, human nature. He can conclude that he has failed because an evil human nature stubbornly resisted his best efforts. (Note that the intolerance of the reformer allows him to be sensitive to his own feelings, not to what is happening to the people to be reformed.)

History is strewn with the wreckage of utopias that failed allegedly because of recalcitrant human nature. A reformer dreams up a utopia on paper, or he even sets up a social order, or a colony of ideal living, according to his heart's desire. He then is dismayed to discover that people refuse to accept the "blessings" he offers them, either in prospect or in actuality. In pursuit of ideals or even in the midst of ideal living, people fight amongst themselves. Or they resist the discipline which any living together requires. The reformer turns sour or becomes a dictator, in order to force people to "cooperate" (that is, to obey his rules). And once again uncooperative human beings are blamed by the idealistic reformer for the failure.

An encourager can easily slip into the intolerance of the reformer, even though he dreams up no utopia, creates no colony of idealistic living. He still will have aspirations for people to become better. And if these people he trusts fail to behave in the fashion he thinks they should, he may become cynical about them or about the human nature that would not "cooperate" with him.

The best guarantee he can have against the cynicism of the frustrated reformer is a sensitivity to people in the process of favorable becoming. With that he is less likely to demand immediately the behavior he hopes will emerge. His trust is placed less in people as they are than in people in the process of becoming. He then can more easily realize that their becoming may be expedited by processes he can help to set in motion. He can contribute to their becoming.

The sensitivity needed, the kind that tends to increase sensitivity in associates, is one that is based upon the expectation of process rather than the expectation of conformity. It is guided by compassion for human beings who strive to develop beyond their presently observable human nature.

For Outside Encouragers

An outside encourager is inescapably identified as a spokesman for strange social customs. These strange customs will arouse varying degrees of defensiveness, some so strong as to call for a rejection of the encourager, personally. He should not be surprised if the process he hopes to encourage gets off to a bad start.

In the early days of the project in the Spanish-speaking tropics, girl students insisted upon swinging picks and shovels along with the men and thereby created a crisis. The men of the community objected; such hard work was not for women. Furthermore, for women to indulge in hard physical labor made their own work look feminine. They were losing their masculinity by sharing labor with women—or even worse, with girls!

When the matter was discussed among the encouragers, the girls insisted upon their right to work. This decision was conveyed to the men of the area, who, although they were uneasy about the matter, seemed willing to allow some change. After all, they did want the road. And they were willing to put up with some nonsense in order to get it. Nonetheless, they looked upon such changes in the role of women with misgiving. No good could come of it. "Why, first thing you know, our own girls will be leaving home to work out in the sun." Their dire predictions proved well founded; before long their own women began to flee the confinement of home duties. But this was just the beginning. Many more changes, some even more disturbing, were to come about.

The next tradition to be challenged was the matter of feminine clothing. In the community, women and girls were supposed to wear dresses. But the feminine outsiders wore pants—blue jeans—when they worked. Shortly local girls, then older women, began to appear in blue jeans despite the protests of their menfolk. The pants began to be worn at home, on the road, in stores, and when going into town.

Soon slacks appeared, also introduced by students, but these were limited to a few permissible colors. When after two years, a college girl began wearing bright scarlet slacks, the tolerance of the men (and possibly of the women too) broke. To them, pants of that shade of red meant that the wearer was a "fallen woman." They objected so strenuously that again the matter was discussed at length among the encouragers. Both boys and girls finally decided that although they saw no moral issue in scarlet slacks, they did not wish to offend their citizen friends so much as to hinder the process of change to modern ways. So the offending girl folded her slacks away in her bag and wore them no more. The local people eventually accepted such attire, but only after two or three years more had passed. The students learned some self-restraint from their achieving sensitivity toward their friends. They decided not to force changes upon their friends too quickly.

But the students in this project did not always behave sensitively, or even sensibly. Early in the process a boy and girl in the midst of a romance were allowed to join the group of outsiders. (To allow them to come was an error. Young people in love are typically more concerned with their own inner bliss and agony than with the impression they make upon others.) These two people were in each other's company constantly and insisted upon kissing and caressing in public. Their behavior offended the local people. Yet when their offense was pointed out to them, they could see nothing wrong with their conduct. After all, this sort of behavior was wholly acceptable on the campus. Why not here?

When the couple refused to comply with the customs of the community, they became the objects of increasing gossip. Finally word began to pass around that the visiting girls (all of them) were overly permissive. Boys of reputedly low character began to invade the secluded valley, to enjoy the companionship of these girls, especially for dances and other social events. Their invasion alarmed the other student girls and even more the local people.

Pressure from the other students did not persuade the couple to behave differently. It was only when they were threatened by immediate expulsion, to be sent home, that they finally agreed to respect local custom. Even so, the dances had to be terminated in order to cut off the flow of unfortunate characters into the valley. Gradually, however, the gossip died down.

Two postscripts can be added to the story. The couple broke up shortly after this episode and ultimately they expressed gratitude for the intervention that forced change in their conduct. And in time, the local standards governing behavior between the sexes have shifted toward greater freedom. Whether this change is to be credited to the episode we recount here and whether the revised standards represent progress are left to the reader's judgment. Our best guess is that many traditional standards, here as elsewhere, are being modernized as part of the total deterioration and rebuilding in an era of rapid social change. There are certain current changes in human behavior that are admirable and to be adopted. Others are questionable. The moral standards for judging these behaviors good or bad are in the process of revision in many communities.

An outside encourager is a disturber of tradition—an irritant, although, hopefully, a kindly one. He cannot avoid introducing unaccustomed ways of doing things. He must be sensitive to the disturbance he causes so that he can introduce the new only as fast as it will contribute to processes of citizen-chosen change. But his sensitivity to others will enable him to help the people he disturbs to create their own new moral standards.

Changing standards are not observed only in relations between the sexes. An encourager needs to be sensitive to reactions to many kinds of conduct. During this same project in the Spanish-speaking population, some of the young male encouragers decided to grow beards. Local people looked upon such facial decorations as an insult to their dignity. Apparently, incipient beards, especially at the early stubble stage when a face looks unwashed, were interpreted by these people as evidence of deterioration in contact with people visitors regarded as inferior. But the boys insisted upon their right to decorate their faces as they saw fit. Apparently beards had become for them a symbol of youthful masculine revolt. Indeed beards did become a conventional way to reject conventionality among young men, especially in the society from which the boys came.

But the crucial question for sensitive encouragers was how these boys should conduct themselves and use their faces in such a way as to contribute most to the people's development. It became apparent that they needed to curtail their expression of revolt in order to meet the needs of the people they had come to serve. The boys were reluctant to accept this conclusion, especially when they discovered that the girls in the group of visitors had joined in the chorus of disapproval. Eventually, however, the boys returned to their razors, postponing the beard revolt for a more appreciative audience. And this crisis passed.

The young people's self-discipline for the sake of others operated more positively in another instance. This had to do with the consumption of alcoholic beverages. From the beginning they concluded, after conferences with knowledgeable sponsors of the project, that drunkeness was one of the great problems of the area. Money that might have bought food or clothing for children was spent on drink that made the heads of household less able to earn. Although several of the encouragers themselves drank, they decided not to indulge while they were with the people of the valley. Each new batch of students discussed this question and voted to impose the same discipline upon all resident encouragers.

After numerous refusals to accept alcoholic refreshment, word got around that "these people don't drink." Apparently as a result, the consumption of liquor among the people of the valley diminished. When encouragers were invited to indulge they chose a soft drink. Noticing that their new friends tended to follow suit, they wondered whether, if they chose a healthful drink like tomato juice, their friends would again follow suit. They tried it and soon found that consumption of certain vitamin-rich beverages in the community increased considerably.

The encouragers' apparent preference for nonalcoholic drinks became a matter of much conversation among these people whose country boasted of rum as a major product. At first the peculiarity was considered as a mild madness, but later the visitors were admired for being faithful to their principles. And because they were admired on other grounds also, the local people began to imitate them. Consumption of intoxicating beverages diminished, and as we have already noted, the community meeting ruled that no drunken person could remain during discussion of serious business.

One of the older encouragers in the party encountered a moral dilemma. He was torn between obligations to students and to citizens of the community. He had no personal objection to drinking. When he was entertained in homes, away from the young people, he was urged to accept rum drinks. What was he to do? Finally, he pointed out that, as a member of the group of encouragers, he was bound by the group decision, even though he was not a teetotaler. His friends accepted this explanation. But he went further to ask for and sing the praises of coffee (also a product of the tropical climate). His assertion that he loved coffee came to be truer, as time went on. And he was relieved of the necessity of violating the group-imposed discipline.

Every community developer should realize that he faces the moral dilemma of the person who chooses to intervene in other people's lives. An outside encourager comes from the confining world of his own background into the probably equally narrow world of those he would help. He is obliged to discipline his behavior, not in terms of his needs, but in terms of the meaning of what he does to those he hopes to serve. He should control his words and actions in such a way as to contribute most to their choosing of the growth that is prosocial for them.

Unfortunately, no rule can be laid down for being sensitive to the people he encourages. He must learn through experience. He must try to understand the people he serves and to sympathize with local custom, even though he may not accept it. He should listen for reactions to whatever he says or does. He would be wise to find some sympathetic local person (or several) who will guide and caution him. And when he makes mistakes, he should apologize for them and appropriately modify his conduct.

But all these recommendations do not answer the question of how far and how fast he should go in introducing new ideas. He introduces different standards by his words, but even more, by his conduct. He believes his standards are superior; after all, they are his. But do the people he works with regard them as superior? Will they adopt these ideas as they observe them in him? The more likely outcome is that they will adopt some composite of his ideas and theirs. His sensitivity should allow room for some such unspecific goal of development. There is no rule of sensitivity he can depend upon, except eternal attentiveness to reactions from people, to sympathetic interpretation of their understandings. There is this one consolation: if people come to trust him they will excuse many mistakes and will tolerate many peculiar ways. They will even come to adopt some of his ideas, because they like him.

For Indigenous Encouragers

An indigenous encourager's ideas are less likely to be criticized as alien. The people will often concoct ingenious explanations as to why a native of these parts should endorse new and strange proposals. Sometimes they will blame his peculiarities upon an outside encourager. Typically, however, the blame is laid upon influences farther away, perhaps upon the university or government bureau that sponsors a community program.

In the project in the southern Appalachians, the indigenous encourager who eventually took over was claimed as cousin by most of the people, and his name showed local origin. But during an absence of several years while he attended college, he had picked up ideas his people thought odd.

For a time he acted as minister of a small church, although he made his living principally as a teacher. The people liked him as a person but did not seem to care for him as a preacher. They would accept his leadership as long as he did not make himself too prominent. They accepted his invitations to attend meetings for planning community improvements, but refused his invitations to attend church. He was acceptable as an encourager, but not as a sermonizer from the pulpit. Eventually, he was invited to resign from the church, but he then gained stature as a community leader. He came to discover greater satisfaction acting as secretary of community councils, a less prominent role, but more influential. He became more effective as an encourager. As his sensitivity to people's needs grew, his preaching diminished and his skill at expediting a process increased.

One might think an indigenous encourager would be more sensitive to the local people than his outside counterpart, but this is not necessarily the case. Familiarity with local tradition and people may lead to impatience with both. Among his own people, an encourager may become hypercritical. This fault is not fatal, however, if the encourager is aware of the tendency in himself and if he learns to restrain his impatience.

A community project in one large American city is serving Mexican people and other ethnic populations in a crowded area. One indigenous encourager became convinced that some of the leaders who had emerged in the process were perpetuating low standards of speech in the use of English, especially among the children. Not all local leaders and certainly not she were to be thus criticized. She did not publicize her opinion among her compatriots but she did work to bring numerous other people with better standards of speech, and even of politeness, into frequent association with the project. She promoted bus caravans that took children and important adults on cultural trips. Each bus has one or more high school or college student aboard to converse with the children and with their leaders. This enterprise proved to be the beginning, in this city, of a Project Head Start for culturally deprived children.

This indigenous encourager proved sensitive enough to her compatriots to avoid making them feel inferior because of their limited cultural background. And in the process she started a type of program for the culturally deprived of an entire city.

The point is that sensitivity can never be taken for granted; it is an attitude and kind of behavior that must be cultivated. Every person who would speed processes of development needs to be attentive to his own motives (irritations, impatiences, and so on) and to his probable impact upon others. He needs to adapt that impact to the peculiarities of the people he hopes to see benefit by the processes of becoming.

In this same city, another indigenous encourager has had remarkable success in working with boys who have dropped out of school. He had been a dropout himself. Even more, he was known to have had a brush with the police some years before. Probably his record helped to make him acceptable to the boys. Since they thought of themselves as rejects by respectable society, they were suspicious of any older person who seemed too much in league with the authorities. But this man, a few years older than they were, had suffered rejections similar to their own. They could trust him to be an indigenous encourager.

After a few years of maturation following his misadventures and after contact with the minister of a church (an outside encourager), he accepted the responsibility of working with the dropouts. He tried all kinds of activities to interest them, parties with refreshments, movies, games, puzzles, trips to points of interest. None of these elicited more than a passing interest.

He studied the boys and kept studying them. What activity would reach them? What would penetrate beyond their disillusion with society, their resistance to everyone in authority, their self-doubt? After many trials and errors (mostly errors, to judge by the disappointing responses), he finally fell upon an activity that was greeted with enthusiasm: tutoring. He discovered that though these boys all had records of school failure, they were hungering and thirsting for book-learning.

With the backing of a community council which had recruited him in the first place, he enlisted the participation of undergraduates from a nearby college. Enough students, both men and women, volunteered to act as tutors that the ratio of tutors to pupils was maintained at one to one. The students enjoyed the experience, and received college credit for field work. The boys enjoyed the individual attention they were given and made rapid progress in such basic skills as reading for comprehension and mathematics. Some went on to study auto repair and electronics. The tutoring continued for a time, but as the boys gained confidence, they were gradually persuaded to return to school. Relying upon occasional tutoring to help them over difficulties, they continue to progress.

Who would have predicted that tutoring in school subjects would be the activity to which these dropouts would respond? Very few persons are as yet wise enough to make any such predictions. Yet this man who was peculiarly qualified by a background that made him acceptable to the boys, discovered an activity that was meaningful to them.

For Citizens in Process

Citizen sensitivity grows largely out of experiences in the process. It comes as a gradual accumulation of insights into what is happening to them and to their friends. Although encouragers can expedite this gaining of perspective, they need to choose the occasions for interpretation with care. Sometimes people welcome interpretations; sometimes they reject them. A wise encourager makes his best guess as to their probable readiness, and then is prepared to correct himself if he has guessed badly.

Often it is better to remain silent and wait while people exchange ideas and insights. Especially when they are trying to understand the meaning of changes in themselves, it is usually wise to do no more than ask questions. It is even wiser to wait for citizens to ask questions. Interpretation that leads to new insights comes best when people ask for it.

To remain silent is often most difficult, especially if things are going wrong. The temptation to step in and set things straight is often overwhelming. But when growth of people's sensitivity is the predominant objective, it is better for an encourager to restrain himself.

The chairman of an urban human relations council was a lawyer. He was an able and eloquent advocate, as a lawyer should be. He could organize his case well, marshalling facts and arguments in logical and convincing fashion. But he did not convince a majority of the members of his community group.

He was prone to introduce a topic to the attention of the meeting, then to proceed immediately with his solution to the problem. When he had finished a well-thought-out presentation, a deadly silence would ensue. Often no action was taken, or his proposal would be voted down, or if it was supported, there was noticeable lack of enthusiasm.

Sitting in on a meeting, an encourager became aware of grumblings of discontent. He later asked some of the grumblers what was wrong and why they did not speak up. "Oh no, we couldn't oppose him." Why not? "Because we can't stand up to his arguments. After all he is a lawyer and a good one. He would make us look foolish. Why he might even cross-examine us the way he does witnesses in court."

The encourager faced a dilemma: the group was gradually becoming paralyzed. Should he intervene in a meeting or with the chairman in personal conversation? If he did either, would the chairman resent the interference enough to cause him to resign? Having confidence in the man's essentially good motivations, the encourager decided to wait to see if growing uneasiness would cause the chairman to ask questions.

This procedure proved wise. After several unproductive meetings the chairman asked, "What's wrong with our meetings? People won't talk." The encourager gave his interpretation of the situation. "Do you mean to say that they won't talk because I talk first? Why I was just leading off to get them started. They ought to argue against me."

"Yes," said the encourager, "but they are scared of your eloquence. They are not trained to present a convincing case as you are. If they speak, they will be thinking out loud, trying to formulate their ideas. And they are afraid they will look foolish compared with you."

"Okay then. What do I do?"

"Why don't you just state what the problem is, then quiet down to see what will happen." This prescription worked. It brought the meeting back to life and action. And the lawyer chairman gained some needed sensitivity to members of the meeting.

In the same city, a neighborhood citizens' council had been organized on an interracial basis. At the time of the first election of officers, an encourager recommended that the offices be divided among Negroes and whites equally. At the organization meeting, the suggestion was rejected. Several speakers of both races argued that they wished to choose the best qualified person irrespective of race because they wanted to get some serious work done. The encourager had proved less wise than the citizens, and he learned that he needed to become more sensitive to their scheme of values.

After several years during which the two races worked cooperatively, the chairman of the group, a white factory worker, one day reminisced with an encourager in the presence of a student from a cooperating college. The chairman pointed out that his wife had changed her attitudes toward Negroes over the years of the project. She had originally been suspicious, even afraid of them, because she had thought they were aggressive, smelled bad, and carried razors to use on anyone who opposed them.

But for months she had associated with them in shared work. She had been in their kitchens and they in hers, preparing cakes and pies for bake sales. They had all worked together to provide playgrounds for youngsters of both races. She knew them now as persons and called them by their first names. They knew her and addressed her too by her first name.

Of course the speaker was describing himself quite as much as (or more than) his wife. This became apparent when he next spontaneously burst out with:

"Say, have you been workin' on us to get us to change in this way?"

The encourager was in an uncomfortable spot. Not knowing what to reply, and feeling tense because a student was present, he sought refuge in the truth:

"Yes, I have been hoping you would change along this line. But if we have been working on you, as you say, more important, you have been working on yourselves."

There was a thoughtful pause, followed by, "Say, that's right. We have been workin' on ourselves." More thought, then, "You know, we're all better off this way. Now we trust each other. Now we are friends."

An insight had come to him, aided by an interpretation from an encourager, given in response to his question. He had become aware that a process had taken place, and was still going on, that increased his sensitivity towards his neighbors, towards his wife, and towards his own changing motivations.

Some Conclusions

The sensitivity that expedites development can grow as a result of living and sharing with people. But it grows only as there is increased understanding of others and of one's self. It grows in sympathy for the problems and complications other people face, but also in the willingness to recognize similar difficulties in one's self. An encourager can expedite this growth, in others and in himself, by quiet words of friendliness, by occasional questions and interpretations when these are requested, and by willingness to learn along with people.

There is a paradox in the understanding that is part of sensitivity. One becomes aware of both the severe limitations that plague people and of the enormous potential for development beyond these limitations. This awareness of paradox applies also to an encourager's interpretation of himself. He also has both serious limitations and unrealized potentials.

Certain suggestions might help him to attain the kind of sensitivity he will need. He should always seek to clear up a misunderstanding. Any dispute that is unresolved tends to rankle and become exaggerated.

In clearing up a misunderstanding, he should be as direct as the other person can accept. Frankness is good, but it must be adapted to the maturity level of the other person.

An encourager should realize that he cannot start a process of development for people. They do this for themselves. He can urge them on, he can help them discover the insights that grow out of the experiences in the process.

He should constantly seek to make clear to himself the motivations, conflicts, and complexities in people's lives. He will never reach the end of this seeking. It is a life-long responsibility.

He should constantly raise questions in his mind about how his words, actions (or lack of actions), and attitudes may be interpreted by those with whom he associates.

He should try to help people be patient with others, especially with their opponents, those who seek goals in conflict with theirs. By helping others to patience and understanding, he tends to increase these qualities in himself.

In seeking the kind of sensitivity necessary to a good encourager, he denies to himself the satisfaction of extreme emotional expression. He does not talk all the time, nor does he remain silent all the time. He does not indulge in displays of either great approval or great disapproval. He governs his speech and conduct in terms of his assessment of the developmental needs of others. This is part of his never-ending search for sensitivity.

The ideal of sensitivity goes far beyond awareness of one's own and the other fellow's limitations and sufferings. It calls even more for the conscious effort to say and do the thing that will contribute most to the other fellow's favorable growth. This is an ideal striven after, but seldom reached. Too often one's own emotional needs and self-serving efforts deflect from the ideal. Still, if one is a good encourager, one keeps trying to approximate this effort to promote the best growth in others.

ADDENDUM FOR SOCIAL SCIENCE STUDENTS

Anthropologists have long recognized that an insensitive introducer of social change can do immeasurable harm. They have sought to discover the attitudes and skills that will make community developers sensitive to people's needs for self-change. Edward H. Spicer edited a book of case studies [1] of programs of introduced change, some successful, others not. Another anthropologist, Ward Hunt Goodenough, wrote *Cooperation In Change* [2] to examine the training needed to bring into being a profession of community developers who would be skillful in obtaining cooperation from those who were to change themselves.

---

[1] Edward H. Spicer (editor), *Human Problems in Technological Change* (New York: Russell Sage Foundation, 1952).

[2] Ward Hunt Goodenough, *Cooperation In Change* (New York: Russell Sage Foundation, 1963).

Sensitivity training has been the central core of the work of the National Training Laboratories.[3] This organization for research in the behavioral sciences, which is not directly affiliated with any university or scientific foundation, has served hundreds of social scientists in many institutions. It has produced a great number of research studies in its own publications and in books and various social scientific journals. The most comprehensive single book is probably one entitled *T-group Theory and Laboratory Method*.[4]

As is implied in the name of the organization, its study of the growth of sensitivity is carried on in laboratory situations set up for training purposes. These are known as T-Groups ("T" for training). Such groups bring together for a limited period of time, usually two to three weeks, persons who have (a) enough sophistication to know about and appreciate such research and training, (b) enough free time to make a trip to the place where the laboratory is to be held (a number of centers throughout the nation have been used in addition to Bethel Academy in Maine) and to stay for the prescribed time period, and (c) enough money to pay the costs. Such requirements mean that the people who benefit by the training are a highly selected, largely self-chosen lot.

During the T-Group experience, participants live together, sharing meals, social events, and conversations. They attend lectures and take part in discussions that supplement the T-Group experience. But this experience remains the heart of the training. The selected persons assemble daily for two hours or so, without agenda, organization, or assigned task, in the presence of a trainer who remains largely silent after a brief and nondirective introduction. The experience of sitting in a room together, around a table, and looking at each other, without program or assignment, proves disturbing and even frustrating to participants at first. They may make attempts to organize the amorphous assemblage of people to do something. Whether these attempts succeed or fail, the participants usually work themselves around to pointing out each other's unpleasant peculiarities. The experience usually illuminates for each participant his own weaknesses and increases his understanding of those peculiarities in other members that can appear in the limited time period. The hope is that the sensitivity thus acquired will be carried back to the employment situations, community environments, and the like, to which the participants return.

---

[3] National Training Laboratories (Bethel Academy, Bethel, Maine) and the National Education Association (1201 Sixteenth Street, N.W., Washington, D.C. 20036).

[4] Leland P. Bradford, Jack R. Gibb, and Kenneth D. Benne, *T-Group Theory and Laboratory Method* (New York: John Wiley and Sons, Inc., 1963).

This training in sensitivity falls within the scope of the process we have been describing in this chapter. The highly compressed time together proves to be a memorable experience for many participants, one which changes their insights into self and others.

Such sensitivity learned in a laboratory setting is analogous to that needed in the complications of community change. Community developers can benefit from both T-Group experience and anthropological studies. But these workers-with-people on the local scene must develop their own adaptations of skills learned in another context.

Chapter 6

Learning
Leadership

Much of the thinking about leadership has long been burdened with ideas that "everyone" accepted, though they were erroneous and often mutually contradictory. It is important that an encourager rid himself of most of these. Otherwise, he will find it difficult to contribute to cultivation of leadership on the local scene.

As a beginning, let us challenge the widely held idea that leadership is demonstrated by a large followership—that someone is proven to be a leader by the fact that numerous people do as he says. This concept of the leader-follower relationship reminds one of the feudal past or of the dictatorships of modern times. We are seeking a leadership that is much more fundamental—an inner quality that can grow within persons, an accumulation of habits and attitudes that makes a person independent and self-assured, yet responsible. When people exhibit this inner-directed confidence, they are likely to be accepted as leaders, but their usefulness is not dependent upon such recognition. We will concentrate upon the attainment of this responsible self-confidence rather than upon the ability to give orders and be obeyed.

Leadership thus defined is open to many people in all communities. No one can know precisely how many might become such leaders until more honest efforts are made to cultivate this quality. Growth of the ability is not dependent upon a few strong persons developing in ways to triumph over rivals. The skills such growing leaders seek are not those of domination, but those of cooperation. That an individual has become strong in his or her own right is demonstrated by independence that knows how to work in a team relationship with other strong persons. We shall call this quality to be developed in people cooperative responsibility.

Exorcizing Some Misconceptions

We will list several more mistaken ideas about leadership. Each of these will be followed by a substitute assumption that has some scientific support and also offers positive possibilities for people's growth.

First is the often repeated maxim that one must learn to be a follower before he can become a leader. This is an assurance given to the young to persuade them to accept orders they might otherwise reject. It is often extended also to adults who become obstreperous. The statement is most likely untrue, even within the leadership-followership type of thinking: leaders who dominate more often come to their positions by accident, by selection based upon privilege, or after some experience of reaction against authority. A more likely statement is that the skills of leadership understood as cooperative responsibility are learned through a growth of dignity for one's self and respect for others. These are acquired in the process of choosing to take responsibility, and carrying out commitments made in the face of both success and failure, through both criticism and approval.

Then there is the assumption that there are natural leaders. Certain social workers and sociologists accept this idea and believe that community developers should work through these people. But the assumption is predicated on a desire to bring the people in a community into line in order to gain some political triumph or the acceptance of action that someone in authority wants. The idea that there are natural leaders who can be used to gain some desired end implies that only a few people are qualified for leadership. Others in a community cannot be expected to become leaders. A more useful term is emergent leader, which assumes that many people not yet in leadership roles may grow into them in cooperative responsibility.

Related to the natural leader concept is the idea that these scarce and unusual persons possess a charismatic quality, a magic or God-given or even hypnotic ability. Those who hold most enthusiastically to charisma as necessary to leadership believe that it is inborn and tell tales of miraculous events surrounding a leader's birth or evidence of future greatness appearing in early childhood. A more realistic interpretation is that leadership is usually a by-product of social experience that calls it into being. That is, leaders may be expected to emerge as a part of the process of community development. An encourager should expect to contribute to this emergence.

Sociologists and psychologists have largely abandoned the notion that traits can be listed as part of the inherent personality of a leader. They look instead to specific behavior that appears in persons when reacting to particular and often complex social situations. Leadership ability is open to cultivation in individuals as a result of the social experiences through which they may grow to become more competent persons.

A widely held assumption which contradicts the charismatic idea of leadership is that leadership can be taught in classes. Such classes present knowledges and skills to be acquired in a logical organization. Some courses go further to include practice in public speaking, parliamentary law, discussion leadership, salesmanship, and so on.

So widely popular is the idea that leadership can be learned and so much is this idea in line with social scientific thinking that this point of view cannot be dismissed as unfounded. The problem here has to do with the how of learning. Does it come primarily as a result of systematic teaching or as a result of experience in which the learner is deeply committed to some cooperative accomplishment?

The learning that results from formal teaching to which the learner has given only acquiescence is unproductive. The learning is genuine when it is acquired from a process that involves the whole person, his hopes and fears, and especially his aspirations for a better community life. When such a learner-guided process is the central experience of the learning, episodes of formal teaching can be introduced constructively. These are best introduced at the request of the learners, after an encourager has recommended these. And the final assessment of the usefulness of the formal instruction must be made by the learners. They extend the invitation, and pass judgment on the usefulness of the teaching.

Classes in such specific skills as public speaking, discussion leadership, and poise and self-confidence are available in or near most communities. Instructors of these skills can often be invited to provide a number of learning sessions for citizen groups. And courses are available in the discussion of great books and great ideas, and of international problems. These courses often require people to register and to attend class regularly. Brief courses are sometimes offered at university centers of continuing education. All these instructional resources are usually classified as adult education. Whether they will prove useful to the central process of citizen-guided leadership learning must be decided by the citizen group with the help of an encourager.

These instructional procedures are no more than professional aids to the citizen-motivated learning process which can be encouraged. But there is one identifiable educational process an encourager can use without violating his role. This is sociodrama or, as it is called by some, psychodrama.

Members of the group are asked to take part in improvised dramatic sketches in order to increase their ability to cope with other people or points of view. They are asked to play the role of some person, often an opponent, in a characteristic episode—a mother lecturing her daughter, a timid citizen asking help from a rule-bound bureaucrat, and so on. After a brief playing of the parts, sometimes no more than five minutes, an appointed member of the group can ask that the acting stop. Then each actor is quizzed as to how he or she felt. The acting and the way of handling such conflicts can become a matter for discussion by the entire group.

Such sociodrama can be introduced and started by an encourager, but the method seems to work best when it is taken over by other members of the group who assign parts to be played, call a halt, and take part in the discussion of the episode dramatized.

In one human relations group in a city, discrimination against Negroes in employment was being discussed. Finally someone suggested a sociodrama episode. A Negro man, an attorney and active advocate of minority rights, was asked to play the part of a white employment manager in a factory. A white member of the group, who had little sympathy for minority sufferings, consented to act the part of a Negro job applicant. The applicant came to ask for a job, cringing and hat in hand. The employment manager was haughty and arrogant. Then each made an effort to understand the other. But the applicant proved unqualified, and the employer was inflexible in his devotion to employment tests and company rules. After the acting, the Negro expressed considerable illumination about the plight of the employer who was bent upon maintaining the level of efficiency in his plant. And the white man insisted that he had become more understanding of the plight of the minority applicant who fears he is going to be rejected even before he applies for a job.

Leadership Potential Is Widespread

Another limitation of most formal instruction for leadership learning is that it is addressed mainly to people with a good background of formal education. However, some formal instruction for the disadvantaged is being made available in job training. Whether this will prove helpful for cultivation of emergent leadership is not known as yet.

To make leadership training available to the educated only is to close the door of leadership to the disadvantaged. The list of the individuals or classifications of persons who do not qualify because "everybody knows" they cannot grow, or are not to be allowed to grow, is long. Sometimes these people are from "bad" families or from "the wrong side of the tracks," or they may have records of delinquency or of undesirable associations. Such people are often condemned to inferiority by their neighbors' opinions.

But the most serious closing of the door to growth is that which shuts out whole categories of people. Prejudice that assigns Negroes to an inferior status is familiar enough. So is prejudice that hampers Jews, Puerto Ricans, Mexicans, American Indians, and other ethnic populations. Various bigoted arguments attempt to prove that all people within a condemned classification are inferior. Even when a few from such a category rise to recognized leadership, their success represents "the exception that proves the rule." We are not pausing to prove that prejudice against racial, nationality, or lower-status groups is unfounded. An encourager should not need such proof. The point is to find ways to open doors to leadership growth that have been closed against people condemned by prejudice.

The finding of scapegoats who are believed to be incapable of growth is an almost universal human tendency, to be found in every community. In one small city, some encouragers found people referring in a sneering tone of voice to the Islanders. So-and-so was an Islander and therefore no good could be expected of him. The encouragers asked who these condemned people were. Citizens were reluctant to make reply, though the sneering continued.

At length the story came out. Years ago there had been a slum section known as The Island. It was located at what was then the city limits, surrounded by a railroad yard, a warehouse area, and a city dump, and people who lived there received the opprobrium that was attached to their place of residence. Since then, however, the whole area had been rebuilt in an urban renewal improvement and the people had all moved elsewhere in the city. But they were still known as Islanders, classified so low on the scale of worth as to be believed incapable of development. The condemnation outlasted the condition that had produced it.

In many small cities and towns immediately north of the Ohio River, there are older inhabitants who condemn new neighbors as Kentuckians. The Kentuckians thus designated are low-income, poorly educated white people who may have originated in any of four or five southern states. Frequently they are former mountaineers from the Appalachian highlands. But their condemners are likely also to be people of low income. They too are often alleged to have little potential for self improvement by those who feel superior to them.

A similar migration of the Okies and the Arkies (poor farm people forced out of Oklahoma and Arkansas produced a condemned population in California. Their plight was celebrated in John Steinbeck's novel *The Grapes of Wrath*. They were given much attention in the early years of the Roosevelt's New Deal. These people were hopeless human beings until the economic expansion of the Second World War brought them employment and they were able to fade into the surrounding population. They were able to do so when improved income allowed them to look like their neighbors.

Sometimes the populations condemned by prejudice are newcomers to a community. Sometimes they are natives who live under the shadow of a deeply held conviction that they are inferior. Sometimes they are migrants, who move about from community to community following crops or hope of jobs. Or in certain other countries there are more or less permanent enclaves of refugees. All these unfortunates may suffer from the combination of their own and other people's belief in their inferiority.

Wholesale condemnation of categories of people imply that the condemners themselves suffer from conscious or unconscious feelings of inferiority. They enhance their own egos by pointing a rejecting finger at some classification of people to which they can feel superior. Such condemnation hurts the condemner; it diminishes his capacity to meet other people as persons. Yet all of us suffer, to some extent, from this projection of our own feelings of inferiority.

But the rejection hurts the people rejected even more. They can become convinced that they are inferior and stop trying to improve. Such self-distrust can paralyze people. Or it can produce a fury of revolt against those who can be blamed for the indignities they suffer. Often this fury is a necessary stage through which the victims of discrimination must pass; it is their means of drawing attention to the injustice of their lot in life. But this stage can be no more than an emotional explosion if no process of growth toward responsible cooperation is cultivated.

Worst of all, a community developer too may believe that people of a certain category are condemned to permanent inferiority. If so, he will forfeit his role of encourager. He may regain this by starting processes of development that are based upon the expectation that the rejected people may be persuaded to develop to become leaders.

As part of the encouraged process, he should advise the disinherited as to the most effective means of raising their voices, either in protest or in cooperative planning. But all activities of people rising from a condemned status should be thought of in the perspective of the total process. An encourager's responsibility is not complete with protest or with giving voice to the voiceless. His obligation is to help those who are assumed to be disqualified to achieve the leadership of cooperative responsibility. He has an obligation also to help the leaders already in power to welcome the rising disinherited. But more of this in later chapters.

Emergent Leadership

Varying amounts and kinds of leadership ability can be expected to emerge among people breaking out of inferiority. There is no one correct form that the process must take. And not all participants will become the kind of leaders an encourager thinks they might be.

A story of community improvement can be told in terms of growth of individual leadership ability. A village of population about 1200 is located in a midwestern state. It had once been prosperous but had become poor from soil erosion and loss of transportation and industry. Since the farming **was poor, most** of the residents were employed in factories, offices, and stores in cities miles away. The income level was low and the town, which serves an outlying area as well as its own people, was down at the heel and the people were discouraged at the time when encouragers were first invited into the situation.

There were two major elements in the population, old-line families left over from earlier days of prosperity—and newcomer Kentuckians, one group as poor as the other. The older families were generally looked upon as ambitionless people who had not had energy enough to leave. They, in turn, looked down upon the newcomers. Failure of the two factions to cooperate contributed to the lack of initiative for improvement. But the community was further split by seven feeble little rival churches, each of which was constantly stealing members from the others.

At the time of first contact, an enormous list of worrisome problems was thrust upon the encouragers. How could they straighten out the tangled mess of town finances? How could they obtain a fire department? What could be done to prop up or replace the town water tower which threatened to collapse at any time? How could the people obtain telephone services? (The only company available had refused to install telephones. The people were too poor.) How could they replace the decrepit old high school? (It had no inside toilets and no gymnasium for basketball, an ultimate admission of degradation in that state.) Could they do anything to improve health? (There were no sewers and no sewage disposal plant.) How could they entice some good stores into the town? And so on.

The encouragers replied that they had no solutions for any of these problems, but they would be happy to work with them to help find answers. In short, they recommended that a long-term process of development, which might in time cope with all these problems and more, be undertaken. The people were not too happy about the process approach; many of them wanted quick answers. But they did agree to work together at simple tasks first, then gradually to undertake the overwhelming problems.

The process, which went through triumphs and disappointments, through periods of great activity and of quiescence, may be summed up by an account of the changes occurring in the treasurer of the community association. He was a very conservative man, so opposed to innovation that he refused to spend seventy-five cents to purchase an account book until the meeting had voted its authorization. His initial attitude was, "We can't do anything." After some time of cooperative work, however, he was saying, "We've got to make this thing go." Then when discussion moved on to the building of a new high school, he said, "We've got to figure out some way to pay for this."

He then became more active and less verbal. He met with lawyers, architects, and representatives of the state office of education to work out plans in the company of other citizens. Then he watched over the construction work by a contractor and later joined crews of his neighbors to lay floor tiles, paint, and install desks. Finally, his comment was, "Oh, of course, we did it."

The treasurer belonged to one of the old-line families, but the Kentuckians progressed also. One of them was a handyman who worked at odd jobs, repairing fences and broken steps and the like. In one of the early activities, a cleanup of two small parks, he showed himself adept at assembling tools and lumber for construction. As a result, he was put in charge of the work squad that built picnic tables for the parks. Later, he led crews that labored to finish the high school. In the process, other people forgot, and he forgot too, that he belonged to a group condemned as inferior. He became an active and respected member of an improving community.

Ethical attitudes changed. The town had a reputation for being inhospitable to strangers, especially those of another race. The encouragers had heard the boast that no Negro had ever stayed overnight in their town. But during some of the active work periods, the encouragers wished to introduce nonwhite and foreign-born students. They asked a town councilman, himself a migrant from the south, if a Negro student would be welcome in a general work period. "Oh sure, let him come," was the reply. "After all we're not that far south." The boy came, worked hard, enjoyed himself, ate with everyone else, and was accepted. Said the councilman, "I've been watching that boy. He's a good worker. He's a nice fellow. I'd like to have him live in our town."

Emboldened by such results, the encouragers introduced other Negro students as well as Orientals and people from the Near East in subsequent work periods. The town began to be proud of welcoming nonwhite and foreign visitors. The outsiders were invited to attend meetings of the community association and even to address the meeting as honored guests.

The chairman of the community association himself demonstrated the characteristic changes from timidity to self-confidence. He was a farmer and a factory worker, a poorly educated man who had never before been chairman of any group, had never handled organizational matters. He had been reluctant to become chairman, but had been pressed into the position by neighbors who trusted him. He was not sure how to conduct a meeting and appealed often to the encouragers for guidance. The encouragers gave him the requested advice, no more. Then they placed simple outlines of parliamentary procedure in his hands for study. He eventually became an excellent chairman, by learning on the job.

When it was decided to build a school, it became necessary to acquire a piece of property. A foundation created by the association was to solicit money, purchase property, and handle the legal and financial details of construction and repayment of debts. The chairman found himself in the middle of these complicated negotiations, guiding the decisions of specialists so that the future needs of children and of the community would be met. Although he was not a specialist himself, he learned to cope with the experts in a dignified manner.

Money-raising became necessary. The inexperienced chairman became the principal organizer of a large social affair held at the old high school for the purpose of soliciting pledges. There were many booths for selling food and other items, but also an emotion-stirring meeting was planned to obtain pledges for contributions. The chairman conducted all this with a fine flair. On discovering that promises for more than four thousand dollars had been obtained, he crowed with triumph. He said to an encourager,

"We are so grateful for what you are doing for us."

"Oh don't give me credit," said the encourager, "I am not doing it. You are."

"Yes, yes, I know. But we wouldn't be doing it if you hadn't got us started."

After the big evening, the officers of the association and the foundation met together to enjoy their triumph. No one had realized that as much as four thousand dollars was available in the town. The encourager took it upon himself to warn the chairman and the other officers that their triumph might be followed at any time by a setback, but they were too happy to pay heed.

Within a week the setback came. The owners of the property they sought, a fraternal society, had learned of the money-raising triumph and boosted their price. They refused to negotiate for a more reasonable figure. The chairman and his officers were as downcast as they had been elated a week earlier. They then insisted the encourager was a prophet for having foreseen the disaster. The encourager denied this and urged them to seek other property. Finally the chairman took the lead in finding a new and better property for a reasonable price. He and his officers thus learned that leadership includes the ability to recover from disappointment as well as to score a triumph.

Ultimately, the chairman's dependence upon the encouragers diminished. In time, he and other members of the association and foundation came to stand on their own feet. They then forgot to give the encouragers credit for their having "got us started." But this outcome is as it should be. The leadership had been achieved and self-confidence established. They still like the encouragers and welcome them into the community, however.

In a project in a city slum, another emergent leader gained self-confidence. This man was a Negro truck driver who was friendly and cheerful but had never thought of himself as having any outstanding ability. Certainly, he had never aspired to be a leader. But he became involved in a community improvement program, the first effort of which was to construct and operate a neighborhood playground.

A bachelor himself, he had not been thought of as a likely recruit for a neighborhood council that was setting up facilities for children. His truck and also his cheerful manner were sought, however, when cooperative work began on the former city dump, which was to be transformed into baseball diamonds, volleyball courts, and other play and picnic areas. His strong back was needed to help shovel up debris and his truck to haul it away. He also hauled in dirt for leveling the ground and stayed to help construct baseball backstops, picnic tables, and so on. He became so interested and found so much pleasure in working with others that he shortly was invited to join the council which was planning further progress.

Since he was unaccustomed to serious discussion or study, he contributed little beyond his presence and attention at first. Then it became necessary to raise more money for purchasing playground equipment and employing supervisors. The council began to work out plans for a fair at which various items would be sold to visitors on the partially completed playground. Someone thought of approaching local retail merchants for small gifts which could be sold (the store making the gift would be given credit). The proposal became specific: why not obtain one watermelon which could be cut into slices and sold for five cents a slice?

The idea was adopted as a good one, and a grocery store was selected to which the request should be made. Who should go to the manager and ask for the gift? Every member of the council except the truck driver had already accepted some individual assignment. When the others looked at him hopefully, he fidgeted uncomfortably in his chair. Finally, they asked him outright if he would go and see the manager of the store. The reply he gave was the characteristic alibi heard again and again in the early stages of emergent leadership: "Oh, I couldn't possibly do it. Why, I've never done anything like that in my life." The others just looked at him. He fidgeted and protested further, but when the others continued to look at him hopefully and silently, he finally said, "Well, all right, I'll try."

At the next meeting he returned, his eyes shining. He had the promise of not one watermelon, but a dozen. In view of his success, his fellow members asked him to obtain a case of soft drinks from another store. "Sure," he said, "I'll see what I can do." He came back with ten cases, explaining that both merchants were happy to contribute to such a worthy community effort.

His career as a money-raiser had begun with a dozen watermelons and ten cases of soft drinks. The truck driver shortly became the council's chief agent for obtaining support from many sources—neighborhood stores, department stores in the central shopping center, factories, businessmen, and offices of the local community chest and of the municipal government. The man turned out to have a positive genius for persuading people to give goods, money, interest, and even attendance at meetings and other affairs. He was so successful that an encourager, who was a poor money-raiser, asked him in awe, "How do you do it?"

"Oh, I just ask 'em and they give it to me," was his not very enlightening reply. Apparently something of his friendliness, sincerity, and conviction that his work was helping the young people was transmitted by his words, smile, and gestures. The donors not only gave but were grateful for the opportunity to give. And the truckdriver money-raiser was wise enough never to ask too often or to press too hard.

Such talent could not be allowed to be wasted on one community enterprise only. After a time, he was elected to the board of trustees of a settlement house, along with a number of the most influential citizens of the city. Then he was appointed to the mayor's committee on human relations. He became known as a knowledgeable person in an endeavor that is necessary to all public service in the United States, the gaining of voluntary contributions and support. Yet, when last seen he was still a truckdriver and a cheerful friend of other people's children.

Anyone inclined to doubt that such ability represents leadership has only to ask himself why certain men are chosen as presidents of colleges and universities.

Some Conclusions

So confused is much thinking about leadership that encouragers must be wary of accepting all the ideas that "everyone knows" are correct. It is not enough to disbelieve the many false ideas. An encourager should substitute new ideas to replace the abandoned ones. Then it is even more necessary to discover people in the process of becoming emergent leaders. One of the paradoxes of his role as an encourager is that he will never really abandon his disbelief in people's potential for leadership until he sees one or two or more unpromising persons become so competent that they surprise themselves. And he is not likely to see this unless he can act as though he expected it to occur.

An encourager must be wary of concluding that people will always be as he sees them now, that they will always respond as poorly to his best efforts as they do now. Like the weather, they will change. He must also be wary of thinking that the first responses of emergent leadership are the final ones, or even worse, that the first emergent leaders who appear are the only ones who will appear. As long as the process continues, there is always room for the unexpected favorable development in people's lives.

In order to ease the paradox and speed the process, several generalizations can be made. Leadership can be broken into many different responsibilities that can be learned, one by one. Few people will become good at all of them. One person may become a public speaker, another an organizer of work periods, another a chairman, another a recruiter of volunteers. Each of these tasks can bring the dignity of confidence to the person.

Separate responsibilities can be arranged somewhat in an order of increasing difficulty. Arranged this way and accepted in the order of increasing complexity, the emerging leader grows in confidence, even though he may be quite surprised at himself. He gradually comes to feel confident partly because he identifies with the group of whose accomplishments he is proud. He reaches the point where he can stand up to people of big reputation without cringing or defiance. He comes to know that he and his group have much that deserves recognition.

The ability to meet the powerful and prominent with confidence is important in an era when individuals are overwhelmed by the complexity of the problems that effect their lives. So many solutions to problems must be nationwide and comprehensive. Community groups must learn to relate their thinking and actions to the great planners, the great program makers, the sources of financial help on a national scale. Federal authorities are often waiting to welcome emergent leadership as rapidly as it will develop to meet their planning.

No one is in as favorable a position to cultivate emergent leadership as is an encourager of the community development process. His has a key function, both in building up the dignity of local people and in helping develop that local leadership which is essential to comprehensive programs of reform.

ADDENDUM FOR SOCIAL SCIENCE STUDENTS

The persons who become community leaders, as we have described them, become self-directed independent persons. The sociologist David Riesman calls this type of individual an inner-directed person as contrasted with other-directed persons.[1] He concludes that a majority of people in modern times are dominated by the crowd, by the current behavior of the particular group with which they are associated. They are thus lost in a lonely crowd of conformity. But he recognizes, without amplifying, the possibility of developing an inner-directedness by which individuals can become self-moving.

The psychologists Adorno and Frenkel-Brunswick explored the phenomenon of conformity even further in *The Authoritarian Personality*.[2] They were concerned with isolating those characteristics in people which led them to become followers of an authoritarian leader or ideology. By omission, they describe the kind of leader we have been discussing; they open the possibility for independent personalities by listing the characteristics to be avoided. They suggest but do not develop the idea of how people shall learn to lose their love for conformity and become democratically cooperative personalities.

Many social scientists with a sense of history recognize that modern man suffers from a malaise that makes mass conformity and surrender to

---

[1] David Riesman, *The Lonely Crowd* (New Haven, Conn.: Yale University Press, 1950).

[2] T. W. Adorno, E. Frenkel-Brunswick, and R. N. Sanford, *The Authoritarian Personality* (New York: Harper & Row, Publishers, 1950).

authority easy. Sociologists call this anomie. Psychologists and psychiatrists refer to it as alienation. This malaise in turn makes popular concepts of personality that downgrade the importance of individual persons. Psychiatrists point to the general weakening of self-awareness and self-respect in the population.

When the possibility for alienated people to learn leadership is opened, more helpful concepts of man appear, new leads for research are discovered. Psychologist A. H. Maslow has carried on research into human potentials and their actualization. He has made studies of self-motivated, creative people. For a summary of his evidence and thinking see his *Motivation and Personality*.[3] Another book that brings together contributions by Maslow and others is *The Self,* edited by Clark E. Moustakas.[4]

The psychiatrist Erich Fromm has developed much theory concerning the developmental possibilities of man when immersed in a social atmosphere that encourages his ethical independence. Fromm started his writings in commentary upon the flight to authoritarianism found in acceptance of such totaliatarian regimes as Nazism. But he has developed much theory for research in the achievement of democracy. His *Sane Society* [5] gives his positive contribution succinctly in a single book, although a number of others precede and follow this one.

For some small-scale beginnings of practical experimentation in the learning of leadership, see Biddle's book, *The Cultivation of Community Leaders*.[6] Chapter 1 and 4 suggest some immediate beginning leads.

---

[3] Abraham H. Maslow, *Motivation and Personality* (New York: Harper & Row, Publishers, 1954).

[4] Clark E. Moustakas, (editor), *The Self* (New York: Harper & Row, Publishers, 1956).

[5] Erich Fromm, *The Sane Society* (New York: Holt, Rinehart and Winston, Inc., 1955).

[6] William W. Biddle, *The Cultivation of Community Leaders* (New York: Harper & Row, Publishers, 1953).

Chapter 7

Establishing Friendship that Encourages

Ordinarily, friendship is looked upon as an intimate relationship that arises spontaneously between persons who have much in common. The friendship that is used to encourage development is different. It is consciously sought, usually by an encourager. It can be cultivated between persons who begin with little or no common experience.

Friendship is the lubricant of human development. It allows the wheels of process to keep turning, even when blundering encouragers have slowed them down. The people with whom they work will forgive many errors if they know they can count upon encouragers as true friends.

In order to become a friend to people, an encourager trusts them. He cultivates a faith in them in order that they may find the energy and good sense to make a process of development work. He indicates by word, manner, and deed that he believes in them. As a result, they will learn to trust him, often in spite of his peculiarities. They will believe that he had good motives, that is, that he means well, and this compensates, in their thinking, for his many oddities.

An encourager who cultivates friendship does not have to agree with the ideas and prejudices of his friends-to-be. Trust is not dependent upon conformity. It is possible for him to believe in people with whom he differs and for them to accept unusual things in him. But such sophistication of trust is an achievement, a reward of effort. Without the effort, people tend to trust only those who resemble themselves.

The achievement of mutual trust despite differences is in itself a process.

It can be started by an encourager. It can begin with an exhibition of trust on the part of an encourager and continue with a persistence of it in spite of suspicion, misinterpretation, and even rejection of his cordiality. The responsibility to create friendship is his. This is usually one-sided before it becomes mutual.

All this means that he takes steps to establish friendship without ceasing to be himself. He learns how to hold to his own beliefs and loyalties in ways that do not threaten the people he wants to encourage into favorable self-change. The problem is to be himself without being obnoxious. He must learn to be faithful to his own point of view and yet be a friend to those who do not necessarily accept that point of view.

Sharing People's Ways of Life

The people with whom he wants to establish friendship will often be suspicious at first. If he is an outside encourager, they may reject him because they will believe he does not understand them. If he is an indigenous encourager, they will be suspicious because he has nominated himself to become a leader over them. Friendship can be built in spite of these obstacles, however, through shared experience.

He begins by going to them. But going to them is a delicate matter. He does not interfere with their affairs or tell them how to behave. He tries to obtain some kind of invitation to come, or he seeks an introduction by a mutual friend. He tries to find some legitimate reason (legitimate in their eyes) for being there. And in spite of all legitimacy and proper introduction, he should not be surprised if they still are not sure they can trust him.

He goes to them to listen to whatever they want to talk about. He should expect to share whatever interests them, but must be genuinely interested. His offer to share a worry or an enthusiasm cannot be an act, put on for effect.

One encourager wished to be friendly with some inhabitants of an isolated village in the southern Rocky Mountains, where people spoke Spanish and were strongly Roman Catholic. In the windows of many houses were signs saying that anyone not Catholic was unwelcome. The would-be encourager was known to be a Protestant. How was he to extend his friendship?

A prominent citizen of the village was a wood carver, a descendent of a long line of *santo*makers. (The religious figurines found in churches are locally known as *santos,* that is, saints.) This present descendent of the family had branched out beyond carving church saints to become an artist in wood. The encourager happened also to enjoy wood carving. He asked the only person available to provide an introduction to the *santo*maker. But the introduction got off to a bad start, since the introducer was a Protestant minister, known to the villagers but not trusted, since he as a representative of the "wrong" religion.

The *santo*maker spoke little English and the would-be encourager little Spanish. But somehow they communicated their mutual enthusiasm. Shortly, they were comparing notes on the intricacies of wood carving, despite the language barrier. Eventually, the encourager learned some secrets of the art and came away with gifts, not of carvings, which would have been evidence of perfunctory friendship only, but with pieces of wood which he could carve later. The basis for friendship was found in a common enthusiasm.

An encourager goes to people to share the same kind of housing, food, diseases, problems, and worries they have. One of the failures of religious missions has been that missionaries have lived among people to be served, but have not shared their way of life. They have lived in better and more sanitary homes, normally in a compound where food, education, and general conditions were superior. Diplomatic missions have also suffered from being isolated from the general population. Representatives of one nation have lived in the security of an embassy which is deemed to be the territory of another. An encourager is less likely to be burdened by the "compound-itis" of the religious missionary or the "embassitis" of the diplomat. He is free to take his chances in sharing the people's way of life.

In taking his chances, he anticipates both pleasant and unpleasant experiences. When a group of encouragers moved into a decrepit old coffee barn among people they came to befriend, some of the people gave them gifts. But others kept them awake at night by showering rocks on the corrugated iron roof.

When he wishes to establish friendship with underprivileged people, an encourager must take his chances in the matter of health. When he goes to live in city slums or in an underdeveloped rural area, he prepares himself with innoculations against the prevalent diseases. But there are no innoculations against unsanitary or spoiled food. Yet the initiative for friendship demands that he eat and drink something when refreshment is offered.

It has been said that it is more blessed to give than to receive, but it is certainly blessed to receive also. The gestures of generosity which people make are often the first response to friendliness. The encouragers who lived in the decrepit barn often visited the shacks of their friends, where coffee, the almost universal drink of hospitality in that country, was offered. Sometimes there was but one cup to serve all members of the family as well as the guests. The single cup of friendship was passed to each person present, starting with the oldest and working down to the youngest. Between servings it would be dipped in the nearby rain barrel for washing. The encouragers drank with appreciation, and with a silent prayer that their typhoid innoculations were still effective. But dysentery was an ever-present possibility that sometimes became an actuality.

An encourager takes his chances also with rats, cockroaches, lizards, and other vermin. He may run the risk of fire in poor structures, of violence in some city neighborhoods, and of other hazards that are part of the way of life he has come to share.

He shares the hazards, but also the work. There is no better solvent of misunderstanding than the experience of working with others towards a common goal. It may be sweaty work that leaves sore muscles, or it may be mental work with papers, words, and statistics that runs far into the night. An encourager does not do the whole job, nor does he direct it. He does not need to be present at every work period. But he should do enough to establish a friendship out of serving a mutual hope.

He also shares worry. An encourager will find that one of the best ways of showing his friendship is to be genuinely concerned about whatever bothers people. They will often praise his helpfulness when he did no more than share their worry. It is not necessary to endorse their hates or adopt their proposals. Sometimes he will want to challenge prejudiced judgment. Sometimes he will remain silent. His attitude in each instance should be governed by his assessment of their needs at the current stage of development. The essential thing, however, is to indicate that he understands their problems and finds them serious even though he is optimistic about their finding eventual solutions.

In all this sharing of their way of life, he will remain himself. He cannot become absorbed into their background. He cannot deny his own. He has his own unique peculiarities whether he is perceived as an outsider or an insider. He must recognize that his peculiarities can be threatening, especially to people who are insecure. He cannot avoid being a separate person with his own ideas. He learns to live with the peculiarities of others, and they learn to live with his and with each other's. He can expedite the achievement of mutual tolerance by increasing the number of mutually experienced episodes of discussion, worry, decision, and work.

If he tries to lose himself in another way of life, he will be disappointed. But if he should succeed in part, he will deny the people he is helping the experienced of trusting someone who is different. They may think him strange but he should be able to help them achieve the maturity of trusting someone different from themselves. His job is not to take on their habits and loyalties, but to help them learn to trust him and to accept his and other people's uniqueness.

Misinterpreted Friendship

Much has been made of the mistakes of representatives of a rich nation who carry their affluent standards into a poorer culture and of middle-class people who try to help the underprivileged. The error is obvious enough, but it is stated in a much oversimplified form. The fact of the matter is that everyone is limited by his background. And we all tend to see other people's problems in terms of our own needs, not theirs.

In a group of encouragers-in-training (all were Americans living and working with less affluent Latin Americans) was a generously motivated young man. He had the best of intentions toward the less privileged people of another culture. But he also had a healthy appetite that was not adequately appeased by the camp food provided in the training program.

On a Sunday (a day off from work but not from responsibility as an encourager) he spent some time in the town plaza. There he met an attractive girl. After some friendly chit chat, she invited him to her home for Sunday dinner. He accepted with enthusiasm. Later in the day, he reappeared in camp to boast to his fellow encouragers about the fabulous food he had enjoyed.

Another Sunday was impending, and the girl sent a note inviting him for a second meal. He accepted in writing, having visions of more good food. In a day or so, an interested supporter of the process asked another encourager, "How soon will he announce his engagement to the girl?" It seemed that by local custom, two acceptances of invitations to visit a girl and her family were tantamount to an engagement to marry. This information was conveyed to the young man, who was immediately horrified.

"Oh gosh," he said. "This is awful. I had no idea . . . How do I get out of this one?"

The matter was discussed in the group of encouragers. The general consensus was that the boy had allowed his appetite to interfere with his obligation to understand local custom. Now, faced with a crisis, it was up to him to break the relationship with as little hurt to the girl as possible and with a minimum of encouragement to local gossip.

The boy sent another note, apologizing because he would not be able to come after all since some important work had been assigned to him for that day. This ended the almost engagement. But the girl blamed the boy for jilting her, and spread the story about. His usefulness as encourager was impaired by such a breach of friendship.

In another instance, a girl allowed herself to become persona non grata by drifting into a misinterpreted friendship. Again the people among whom she had come to work had a way of life quite alien to her background. She was a recent college graduate. She accepted an assignment to work among southern mountaineers. But her altruism led her to misconstrue their behavior toward her.

She concluded that the great need for these people was formal education. And since the older people were resistant to such instruction, she concentrated upon the youth. The teen-age boys were of particular interest, because she thought she might fire them with ambition. She spent a great deal of time counselling these boys (at least she thought she was counselling them).

She was a pretty girl, so that the local teen-age boys enjoyed the personal attention. The counselling occurred during walks down the road or on trails through the woods, a form of boy-girl association frowned upon by local custom. She urged them to seek more education and they enjoyed the attention, no matter what she said. Shortly various boys boasted of how they were "making progress" with the new girl. Public observation of the walks served to give substance to the boast. The girls found herself overwhelmed with more boys eager to enjoy the benefits of her counselling. She really thought she was exhibiting her skill at working with youth, which had been taught to her in psychology classes at college.

As the walks increased in number with more boys, these contacts became a matter of public gossip. The walks were innocent enough, according to the standards of her background. But they violated local ideas of proper relationships. And some of the boys of the area were only too happy to take advantage of the situation. Even though nothing of a scandalous nature ever occurred, the principal of the school that employed her concluded that public comment had reached such a pitch that it would be better for the girl to leave.

In both of these instances, of the boy who went out for dinner and of the girl who counselled unwisely, the community development processes went on to make genuine progress. These two were casualties of misinterpreted friendship. Some persons who misinterpreted were hurt, but not fatally. The two were unable to continue as effective encouragers because they could not escape from their own backgrounds. They were unable to interpret their behavior as the people in another culture would. Other encouragers, their compatriots, rescued the situations. Ultimately the two were forgiven (after their departures) but mainly because other encouragers picked up the task of building friendship.

It was easier for compatriots to rescue the processes because both of the offending persons were recognized as outsiders. It is easier to excuse mistakes made by an outsider. Also, it is easier to forgive the mistakes of the young and inexperienced. But an encourager should not count upon either strangeness or youth or compatriots to get him out of difficulties. He had best plan to figure out some way to correct misunderstandings and misinterpretations of friendship himself.

His problem becomes even greater when he is perceived to be indigenous to the local way of life. His local friends will tend to assume that he agrees with them in all things, unless he makes an issue of disagreeing. What should he do when friends or acquaintances express opinions that "everyone believes" and he differs? If he gives voice to disapproval, his words may be regarded as threatening to their security. That is, his challenge to hitherto unchallenged ideas may be misinterpreted as an attack upon the individuals who believe that friendship is possible only among the like-minded.

Should he tell them he thinks they are wrong? Should he say that he holds to another point of view? Should he say nothing? The problem is to be true to his own convictions, yet be trusted as a friend. There is no easy solution to this dilemma. He will have to search for solutions. He will make progress in his search when he concentrates less upon defending his beliefs and more upon helping other persons to challenge their points of view and to correct them in their own way. The fact that he holds to contradictory views will expedite this self-challenge, provided the bonds of friendship have not been broken.

Friendship that Encourages

When an encourager concentrates upon the maximum favorable development of all participants in the process, he can put friendship to positive use. Especially is this true if the differences that ordinarily separate people are openly admitted with a cheerful good humor.

In the small American municipality that constructed a new high school, the contractor had completed the building, but had left some jobs for citizen volunteers to complete. One of these jobs for citizens was the painting of the cement block northern wall of the new building before the winter rain and freezing arrived. A day was set aside for many citizens to cooperate in completing the painting, in one day, if possible.

To this painting enterprise, the encouragers brought several outside helpers. Among these visitors was a man from a Middle Eastern nation who was studying community development in this country. He came along willingly, but quite unprepared to join the work crew. In fact, he was wholly unfamiliar with hand labor. He came from the educated aristocracy of a nation in which hard physical work was assigned to peasants. Not being aware of this difference in attitude about physical work, local citizens invited him to join in on the painting. He refused at first, pointing out that he had no suitable clothes for such a dirty job. That difficulty did not deter his friends-to-be. They offered to provide him with a coverall that would protect him from splattered paint. He accepted the offer with reluctance.

He retired to remove his coat and climb into the coverall. But this entailed major difficulties. He had never encountered such a garment before. After several attempts, he finally got it on, but backwards, of course. When he emerged to work, he was greeted with howls of laughter in which he finally joined. In his laughing explanations and rearrangement of the garment, he established himself as a good fellow to be accepted, no matter what his foreign background. Shortly he was found atop a ladder splattering paint on the wall, on himself, and on his new friends and having a wonderful time. He was remembered long after his visit as "that nice fellow" who came from a foreign land.

Another team of encouragers was living among friends whose ideas of sanitation were very primitive. Not being sure how far they could go in recommending better practices, they said nothing about sanitation, while they worked with local people upon improvement activities. They took various steps to protect their own health, but did not try to force any such practices upon the people. Local citizens, however, seeing the encouragers chlorinating containers of drinking water and then covering these against contamination by dust, asked what this procedure was all about. The encouragers explained that they were purifying the water.

"Why?" was the question. "In order to avoid such water-borne diseases as typhoid fever," was the reply.

"You mean, if we put that stuff in our water, we wouldn't get typhoid?" said one local citizen. "Why, my father died of typhoid."

"You can't guarantee freedom from typhoid," was the reply. "But if you chlorinate your water this way, and protect it afterward, you will reduce the chances of getting it."

"Will you show me how to do that?"

In response to this request, a few simple rules for household treatment of drinking water were worked out. These were put into practice by one family after another, with citizen after citizen asking for help in deciding what kind of and how much chlorine to use and how to select proper vessels as containers. In time, the practice of protecting the water spread throughout the area.

By a similar process, sanitary privies were introduced. These had been offered free for years by the local government, if citizens would install them according to mimeographed instructions. But local people showed no interest at all until the encouragers erected two on the school grounds to serve their own needs.

The encouragers requested the two structures, one for women and one for men, from a nearby government office and installed them at a convenient location. The government office made an exception in granting only two; they pointed out that they were in the habit of shipping no fewer than a dozen at a time and demanded bulk quantities for any future orders.

A few days after the privies had been installed, people began to stop by and inquire what "these things were good for." The encouragers explained their use, putting in several words of argument in favor of sanitation. The usual response was "Oh. Well such luxuries are all right for people like you. But as for me and my family, we will continue with the ways of the past. Those are satisfactory for us."

One day, however, a widow came by to inquire if she might obtain such a structure to be erected in her back yard which might serve her children. The encouragers said yes, these were available free from the government. But the widow was reluctant to call at an office of "bureaucrats." Would the encouragers order one for her? Taking a chance, they ordered the dozen minimum. By the time the unassembled parts for these had been delivered, there were half a dozen requests on hand. The encouragers installed the sanitary privy for the widow, then insisted that other people must come to get the parts and do the job for themselves. Within a week more, all the unassembled privies had been claimed and people were busy erecting them on their property.

It was the children mainly who demanded the change from old ways. They wanted something for their homes which they saw in use at the school. In addition, they took pride in having the outhouses as part of their homes.

It should be admitted that the structures were eye-catching. Made of corrugated aluminum, they flashed in the sun under the trees. The children built up local appreciation so that the privies came to be regarded as things of beauty and items of prestige. Eventually every family in the area came to demand these of the government. After the first three were installed by the encouragers, all the rest were erected by local residents, with encouragers acting only as advisers on location and proper installation. As in the case of the water, the demand for improvement came from local people, after they had observed different ideas brought in by outside friends.

The same appeal to friendship worked also in asking the community meeting to make decisions for change. For years, these people had resisted the help of the agricultural extension agents from the state university, saying they did not need any instruction from theoretical "young whippersnappers." The encouragers asked them to invite these same extension agents to their meetings, because these agents were friends of theirs. The meeting extended the invitation several times, just because citizens liked and trusted the encouragers. Eventually, they came to accept the extension agents as friends also. And major changes in agricultural, nutritional, and sanitation practices came about as these agents learned to associate with the people.

All these changes, and many others, were brought about by the local people in response to the nonthreatening influence of outside encouragers they had come to trust. The bonds of friendship were not broken by insistence upon change. People came to accept new practices by their own decision when new ideas had been brought to their attention by friends they liked and trusted.

Progress toward favorable change is more difficult to make when the encouragers are indigenous to the local scene. In a city where they were long-time residents, some encouragers hoped to see ingrained anti-Negro attitudes replaced by attitudes of friendship for people of another race. The indigenous encouragers were already accepted as friends in many circles. How could they throw their weight on the side of acceptance of Negroes as equals in citizenship, in public services, in employment, in choice of homes, in social relations? How could they do this without breaking the bonds of friendship that can encourage change?

The encouragers formed a city-wide interracial association to seek better recognition for minorities. The association sought more and better jobs for Negroes, better education opportunities to qualify Negroes for jobs, elimination of discrimination in theaters, restaurants and barber shops, better housing. Shortly the encouragers found themselves described as "nigger-lovers." This designation was all the more applied when pictures were published in the only city newspaper showing them meeting with Negro members of the association.

During the months while the activities of the interracial association were being reported, the encouragers were active also in such all-white organizations as churches, service clubs, and women's clubs. There they were regarded as being at least a bit queer. But because they were otherwise accepted in these white circles, the condemnatory judgment gradually shifted to one of sneaking admiration, then later of open approval of the position taken. This approval applied to the behavior of the encouragers long before it was copied by other white people. That is, these others would say they admired the encouragers, would even vote financial help for enterprises of the interracial association, long before they would associate in work or social contact with Negroes.

Some of the numerous episodes which contributed to the process of change in racial attitudes will be recounted in later chapters. The point to be noted here is that indigenous encouragers can make progress in a situation where they belong as residents, but they often do so at some penalty of condemnation to themselves. If they are sensitive, however, to the needs of both the underprivileged and the privileged, they can utilize friendship to help both kinds of people bring about favorable changes in themselves. That they suffer from condemnatory name-calling is just an incident of the process.

Over a period of years, the atmosphere of the entire city shifted in the direction of greater acceptance of Negroes as equals. To ascribe the improvement to the encouragers alone would be inaccurate. Many other events and forces were working to change attitudes. But the encouragers can be credited with some contribution to changes in which the norm of majority opinion became favorable to racial equality, and only a small minority of the prejudiced held out against such progress.

Again, the bonds of friendship with white people were not broken while friendship was extended to people of another race, who had been victims of discrimination. The nonthreatening character of new ideas was emphasized by working with the disadvantaged people first, and by cheerfully bearing the onus of condemnation for such activity. Then the talking about the need for change of attitudes could come later in such a way as to minimize resistance to people's choosing to improve their attitudes.

Some Conclusions
about Positive Friendship

There is no nicely outlined set of rules that will guide an encourager in the positive utilization of friendship. He, as either an outside or as indigenous encourager, will have to try out many experiences and then watch for reactions from his friends, or from those he hopes to make into friends. There are, however, some principles to guide his tryout of the experiences of friendship.

1. He should cultivate friendship, not conformity. His friends-to-be are not expected to resemble him, and he should not expect to be absorbed into their way of life. Instead he should seek a mutual appreciation that welcomes variety.

2. Such appreciation of others grows out of new shared experiences, in which he sees people as persons, and each of them sees him as a person.

3. Sharing must be genuine. He should plunge into it, enjoy it. And he should accept the discomforts and the possible negative reactions with as much cheerfulness as possible.

4. The failures of friendship are often due to encouragers who make the mistake of being more concerned with their own needs than with finding the experiences that will speed the process by which the other persons choose to develop.

5. No one is wise enough to know for certain the correct way of behaving in complicated situations of too much or too little or the wrong kind of friendship. An encourager will need to try out ways of being himself without threatening the (often tenuous) security of his friends.

6. The sharing of interests and worries and the accumulation of new mutual experiences allow him to become a friend, even though he may be looked upon as odd. Though people start out to condemn his strange ideas, they may gradually come to accept some, then more, and eventually to imitate his behavior, provided there is a warmth of shared experience. This shared experience becomes part of a newly created background for him and for his friends.

7. There is no need for him to flaunt his differences. He can mention them quietly, often in action better than in eloquent speeches. The action is more acceptable if its obvious intent is kindly.

8. Sometimes people conclude that an encourager has taken advantage of their friendship. It is important for him to avoid doing anything that would give substance to such a conclusion, even though they may take advantage of him. He may cheerfully protest a misinterpretation of himself, but should provide the example of tolerant understanding for them.

ADDENDUM FOR SOCIAL SCIENCE STUDENTS

The personal relationship that encourages individuals into favorable change is known to psychotherapists as rapport. Rapport is deliberately cultivated by psychiatrists and clinical psychologists as a means for encouraging self-change in patients being counselled.

In the early practice and theories of Sigmund Freud, rapport took a very intensive form. It was referred to as a transference; the patient transferred his emotional dependence from his father (or even his God) to the psychiatrist He even "fell in love" with the therapist. This emotional dependence was thought of as necessary for personality change. When the person to be helped had revised his concept of himself sufficiently, it was then necessary to break the transference by becoming obviously indifferent to further pleas for attention and help.

The later Freudians and numerous other psychiatrists and psychotherapists have given a revised definition to rapport. It is no longer thought necessary or desirable to reduce the person to be changed to such emotional subservience. There is more attention given to building up self-respect and conviction of one's own competence, from the outset. Rapport refers more to a friendly relationship that builds the person up in his own self-esteem.

Among the writers who discuss this revised concept of rapport, is Psychotherapist Carl Rogers. His book, already mentioned, *On Becoming a Person*,[1] gives an excellent statement of his point of view, Rogers stresses the necessity for warm acceptance of the person. In addition to warmth he mentions safety, "the safety of being liked." The entire book develops how such a relationship can help individuals to grow into becoming unique and competent persons. It is well worth study for its application to an encourager's work in the context of community improvement.

Noteworthy also is Roger's treatment of the concept of process. His Part III deals with processes in people's lives. This concept can be applied to development of people in community experience. The encouraging relationship uses rapport but in a context of ordinary, day-by-day living.

Another psychotherapist, J. F. T. Bugental, goes deeply into the relationship of rapport in his *The Search for Authenticity*.[2] Bugental redefines the concept of transference in terms of the existential situation in the psychotherapeutic encounter. He also analyzes the attitudes and personal feelings of the therapist, as an essential part of the process for the patient. This analysis is of great significance to an encourager who should realize that his own thinking and emotions contribute to the growth of people in the process.

One further writer is psychiatrist Karl Menninger. In Chapter XV of his *The Vital Balance*,[3] he tells of the intangible relationship between doctor and patient. There is much wisdom in this for the relationship of encourager and citizen.

It is wise, however, to caution every encourager once more. He is not and should not try to become a psychiatrist, psychotherapist, or psychiatric social worker. His behavior must exhibit psychological wisdom, but not the manner of the therapist.

---

[1] Carl R. Rogers, *On Becoming A Person* (Boston: Houghton Mifflin Company, 1961).

[2] H. F. T. Bugental, *The Search For Authenticity* (New York: Holt, Rinehart and Winston, Inc., 1965).

[3] Karl Menninger, *The Vital Balance* (New York: The Viking Press, 1963).

Chapter 8

How People Build a Sense of Community

In order to help citizen initiators start processes of development among their fellow citizens, an encourager needs to increase understanding of these people. He and his collaborators, with his help, need to understand people's present limitations as a starting point. Then development beyond limitations can be anticipated as a result of experiences in search of community. For economy of effort, people can be grouped according to similarities of limitations.

Our purpose here is not to give a definitive or final listing. Any listing or classification will change—and rapidly in our time, even without an encourager's efforts. Rather, it is to show the complications of analysis necessary to gain compassionate insight. And we are suggesting some ways of making the analysis, so as to encourage these people into their own processes of self-chosen growth.

Loss of Sense of Community

All of us must recognize that we live in an era of community (and national and international) turmoil. An encourager must be aware of the ease with which conflicts within a community can erupt into violence against persons and property. In newly developing nations local violence may be preliminary to overthrow of government. In the United States, it is more often an expression of minority frustration against authority or other factions in the local population.

An encourager's responsibility is to try to understand the causes for such violence, and to help find means for reconciling the conflicts that cause it to erupt. This is an enormously difficult assignment. He cannot even hope to meet it unless he has some awareness of how people have lost (or never achieved) a sense of community. They have therefore concluded that they are personally surplus in the place where they live, unwanted, unappreciated. This widespread loss of belongingness has resulted in a loss of the dignity of selfhood.

There are at least two kinds of social experience that historically have contributed to achievement of selfhood. These have been found in family life and community life. It has been pointed out by numerous social analysts that lack of these two social experiences has contributed much to riotous protest. The analysts seldom point, however, that family life and warmth of community relations are being progressively denied to the privileged as well as the underprivileged in an industrialized and urbanized age.

It is not an encourager's responsibility to reconstitute family life in modern times. But he can work upon the building of a sense community, and if such a constructive process deals with the real problems of real people, it will almost certainly turn some attention to family life.

If it is any comfort to an encourager, we can point out that the experts are as confused about the reality of community experience as are the citizens who have lost it. They do not agree upon a satisfactory definition of what they want a community to be. Some experts talk about rural villages or town meetings as the ideal. Others point to small cities, others to metropolitan areas. And still others insist that neighborhoods or school districts, or political precincts or census tracts are the true communities of modern times. Whatever the size of the local social system chosen, it probably no longer exists as a self-contained unit. It is dependent upon decisions and programs that are organized and controlled by forces far away. We define community in terms of the experiences which encouragers can help people to make a part of their lives.

Those Who Have Lost It

Let us list a number of kinds of people an encourager is likely to encounter, who suffer from some loss of community. We will mention first several victims of underprivilege and discrimination. The privileged will be discussed thereafter. Since Negroes have already been mentioned, this is a good classification of humanity with which to start.

Non-Negroes are prone to think about colored people as though they were all alike. As a result of this lumping of them all together, it is possible to make broad but inaccurate generalizations about all people in this category. Such broad generalizations, that tend to "keep Negroes in their place," have long been made by white Americans who are overly conscious of race. By way of reaction, the latter-day Negro racists have come to adopt counterpart condemnatory generalizations about white people.

Various analysts of the riotous excesses of the Freedom Movement have pointed out that the worst violence was perpetrated by a minority in any effected neighborhood. Prominent in this minority are the inheritors of the slavery tradition, sharecroppers from the Old South, cotton field hands displaced by mechanized agriculture, household servants from the pillared mansions now in decay. These people have lacked education, have had no marketable skill, have often been ill-adapted to city life. Added to those disadvantaged have been unemployed youth, school dropouts, victims of cultural deprivation. Others still have been young people in revolt against adult society.

Contrasted with colored people in the riotous minority are the Negroes of great success, actors, athletes, singers, and recently, scientists, writers, lawyers, and others. Then there are many of solid but unspectacular achievement. An increasing number of these are becoming educated and going into professional and other higher-paid jobs. Others have been faithful to lower-grade employment, have established good families, and have brought up children with cultured background and personal hope for the future. These quieter Negroes are often referred to as Uncle Toms by the agitators and racial activists.

Sometimes the different classifications are distributed geographically in an urban area. For example, in one city the more prosperous Negroes live on the southside. Those in the ghettos are found on the northside. The southsiders do not want their children to associate with the northsiders, even in public schools. Sometimes differences may be based upon amount of pigmentation in the skin, the lighter shades being preferred—that is, until recently. To the black nationalists, the darker hues are preferable. Sometimes differences are based upon religion, such as the Black Muslims against the Christians, or both contrasted with those who profess no religious affiliation.

When an encourager hunts for initiators, he must take all these differences (and others he will discover) into consideration. He should anticipate what the probable behavior of initiators of a particular type and reputation will be, as well as what the probable reaction will be to them. Will a riot-prone revolter accept an Uncle Tom as an initiating leader?

Negroes have received so much attention (favorable and unfavorable) that other disadvantaged folk have been neglected. Among these others are the oldest victims of discrimination, American Indians. Non-Indians again are prone to lump these people together without consideration for the differences that make encouraging of development difficult but fascinating.

First are differences between tribes, a separation often quite sharp in the thinking of the Indians themselves. An Anglo-Saxon would-be encourager was talking with an Indian on one of the larger reservations. He listened while the tribal member recited a long list of grievances blamed upon the federal and state governments, and against white man's society in general. The encourager agreed, for the most part, with the condemnations made. Thus encouraged, the Indian went on, finally working the conversation around to his family. He told of his daughter who had recently graduated from a university, with honors. The encourager congratulated him.

"But," said the Indian, "Now she has gone off and got married."

"Oh, and what kind of a fellow did she marry?"

"Nothing but a Choctaw," said the Indian in disgust. (The Choctaw have no reservation, and were therefore apparently regarded as inferior by this speaker.)

It turned out that the new husband had also graduated from a university, with a distinguished record. And the two were going on into a joint professional career that involved further graduate study. But the choice of a husband was to be regretted because he came from a tribe this Indian thought of as inferior.

There are tribal differences in characteristic occupation, in language (some still speak their native tongues as well as English), in handwork, in characteristic dwelling places, in social customs, and so on.

Then reservation Indians are quite different from those encountered off the reservation, even when from the same tribe. In cities they may be found in ghettos where they can be met as a group. Or they may be lost and unattached individuals who are extremely difficult to reach. Those who attempt to reach such unattached individuals are often frustrated by the fact that these solitary Indians often disappear, leaving no trail behind them.

Indians in cities frequently swell the ranks of the poverty-stricken. If so, they may be included in basic nuclei that serve the disadvantaged. A few others become successful enough to fade into the general population.

On reservations, the differences are enormous. Some reservation Indians are tragically poor and apparently hopeless. Others cope with new-found wealth from mineral, forest and land-value sources—provided they have been successful in keeping the wealth out of the rapacious hands of the "Anglos." In recent decades certain tribes through their own tribal organizations, have utilized this new-found wealth to provide scholarships, improve reservation health and education, and even to employ community developers. If an encourager finds himself on or near a reservation, he would be wise to cooperate with whatever tribal council or other indigenous organization is available.

Another classification of the neglected disadvantaged are the Spanish-speaking people. They too may refer to non-Spanish whites as "Anglos." And in some sections they are so conscious of their Spanish background that they will call Negroes "Anglos" also. "Anglos" are prone to lump all Spanish-speaking folk together, but with a particular designation for certain sections of the country. On the eastern seaboard they may all be looked upon as Puerto Ricans, except for Florida, where they are likely to be known as Cubans. In the Southwest, all may be dubbed Mexicans—some of whom may prefer to call themselves Latin-Americans. In some sections of the Southwest, however, will be found small enclaves of old-line Spanish families whose members vigorously resent being classified with any of the newcomers, but especially with the Mexicans.

Then there are the southern mountaineers, of purest Anglo-Saxon heritage. These people, on their home grounds, have been isolated and suspicious of the outside world. They have clung to their traditional ways while the rest of the country is moving into a modern age. But even this isolation is breaking down as a result of road-building, electricity, and radios. (Television sets are more of a problem in some mountain areas, where antennas must be placed on the tops of mountains.)

A researcher into folklore was hiking around in the southern mountains with a portable tape recorder in hand. He hoped to persuade some of the people to sing the old songs to his tape recorder. He encountered a teen-ager on a trail in the woods, and stopped to chat. Finally, he worked the conversation around to the old folk songs.

"Do you," he asked, "know 'The Four Marys'?" (a lovely and poignant song which has been preserved in the mountains since Elizabethan times.)

The teen-ager looked confused. Finally he inquired brightly, "Is it on the Hit Parade?" [a radio program then popular].

In (mostly northern) cities, the mountaineers tend to gather in ghettos that may allow them to preserve some elements of their unique culture and will provide the comfort of shared troubles. These people suffer from stereotyping by nonmountaineers in a fashion that is celebrated in song and story.

Then there are other identifiable groupings of the disadvantaged, the "Pineys" of New Jersey, the Ozark dwellers of Arkansas and Missouri, the agricultural migrants who wander over several states, to mention a few. The identification of the underprivileged with some one geographic location is disappearing, in an age made peripatetic by private car as well as by air travel.

Apart from geography, many of these disadvantaged may live in a culture of poverty. That is, they accept government and privately financed welfare services as their permanent source of family income. A visitor to a small town church in a Southwestern state was introduced to a newly married couple. After the customary congratulations, he asked the husband, "And what will your work be?"

"Oh, we are going to live on relief," said the young man, with the nodding, cheerful approval of his new wife.

When any people (of any racial or national background) have come to accept unemployment and subsidized poverty as their lot in life, the finding of initiators for development is not easy. But it is not impossible for an encourager who will share life with them and who will be prepared to start with the most humble kinds of self-improvement.

But an encourager dare not concentrate solely on the disadvantaged of a community. He cannot make substantial progress with the underprivileged unless he works also with the privileged. Unfortunately the privileged are not easily classifiable into groupings for purposes of community development. Some, a little above the level of the underprivileged, are most uncooperative because they seem to feel a compulsion to look down upon or condemn people of a lower economic, cultural, and racial status. This is their means of reassuring themselves of their superiority.

Closely related are the privileged who cling to property or a minimum position of power as symbols of their (often meager) success. Such people, when they gain a little power and recognition, may become most resistant to community improvement.

Among the privileged, however, are to be found a surprising number of people of conscience. Many of these can be persuaded to cooperate in helping their disadvantaged brothers. Initiation of the development process can often be found among such people cooperating with underprivileged initiators. And they can make good cooperators, provided they avoid the "lady bountiful" attitude. Many outside encouragers come from this company of the privileged with a conscience.

No one can tell in advance how to seek an interested response from people who are classified by themselves and others into various categories of humanity. No one can tell what kinds of compassionate sensitivity will elicit initiative from different categories of people or from different individuals. There is always a question whether an encourager should seek initiators from one faction and then another separately or should combine several groupings from the outset. There is always a question as to what kinds of problems will be likely to arouse the interest of a nucleus-in-the-making and lead to early decisions for action.

Furthermore, as we have said, any classification of people represents at best a temporary listing. Any encourager will have to develop his own ability to analyze social situations to discover which should govern his understanding. He should test his categorization by trying out the approaches to each grouping in an experimental spirit. Above all, he should respect the categories into which people classify themselves—with the realization that these will shift.

Regaining Community

When we talk about regaining community, we are referring to a rediscovery of something the human race has lost or is losing; it is not a loss for most individuals, since they cannot regain something they have never had. For many people now living the gaining of a sense of community represents a new achievement.

Experiences that build a sense of community are holistic; that is, they point people toward an awareness of social wholeness. The wholeness of community means that it includes everyone on the local scene; no person or grouping or faction can be left out. This is why a sense of community should not be built by a single faction striving to serve its own interest in rivalry with others. And even if an encourager starts with a limited faction, he encourages them to think in all-inclusive terms from the beginning. And he expects them to enlarge the scope of their wholeness as they develop.

Achievement of a sense of community is an educational growth over a period of time. This is especially true for those who have never felt the warmth, the personal acceptance, and the consequent achievement of selfhood that awareness of community can bring. The growth of this awareness cannot be outlined, but some episodes can illustrate its gradual emergence.

Within one population of very poor and largely illiterate rural people, a sense of community had been slow to develop. For years they had been beaten down until they were suspicious of the rich, of the government, of strangers, and of their own neighbors. After some cooperative work together, however, they had reached the point where they wanted to construct a small community center. They had discovered that the government would provide them with lumber, sand and gravel, and a few sacks of cement. But they needed money to purchase tools, windows and doors, frames for these, and some roofing. They figured the total amount they needed was about five hundred dollars.

For some communities-in-the-making, this would be no great amount. But to these poor people, it was huge. They sat in a community meeting and worried audibly about such a sum, wondering how they might find it. Friendly encouragers sat and worried with them.

A student in training finally decided to change the atmosphere of worry. He reached for his wallet. A more experienced encourager saw him do this, caught the student's eye and shook his head. The young man's hand came away from the wallet, and he sat through the rest of the meeting in silence. Citizens went home after adjournment, still perplexed.

The student then addressed his experienced compatriot with heat. "What was the big idea? Why did you stop me? I was going to make a contribution."

"I knew you were, that was why I shook my head."

"Well, I can afford to help them out a little."

"Yes, but could they afford to have you help them? They have to figure this thing out in their own way in order to grow in personal and community confidence. They were not in position to match your contribution.

"I still think you should have let me give something," said the student.

"All right then, will you do this? Will you keep your contribution to yourself until the next meeting of the group, and see what happens?" The student agreed, but reluctantly.

At the next meeting various people came in with ideas for raising money, which they had worked out in conversations with their neighbors. Some women would find enough cloth to make dresses to sell; the men were to take the dresses to town for the sale. They would then take this money, buy more cloth, and make more dresses for sale. This process would go on until they had accumulated something over two hundred dollars.

Some other women were planning to prepare food also to be sold by the men in town. For this, they had figured out how much they might make over a period of time. (Incidentally, they did raise the necessary money and built the community center by their own cooperative labor, which added to the emerging sense of community.)

After the second meeting at which the plans were outlined, the student acknowledged his learning: "O.K., O.K. You win. But now I don't feel so generous, since I discovered they can do it for themselves."

Another student grew in achievement of his sense of community as he observed the growth taking place in a small industrial city. He regarded himself as a radical, a militant pacifist who took part in noisy demonstrations for peace. He even had managed to get into fist fights with another student whom he regarded as a militarist. He was much more committed to the cause of peace than to any community in which he had ever lived or had ever heard about.

He had joined, however, with other encouragers-in-training to meet with a larger nucleus group which was planning and conducting a survey of a city. The group had been recruited to be all-inclusive; management and labor were represented as well as all churches and civic groups. A representative from the American Legion drew this student's special interest because he was, by definition, a "militarist."

The student attended meeting after meeting, becoming more and more interested in the process. He was silent at first, then gradually took more and more part in the discussion. Later he explained to some of his like-minded cronies, who had not been involved in the community-building process, "I didn't want to start any kind of a row. I was afraid I might bust things up."

Eventually he discovered that the legionnaire was as much devoted to bettering the community as he was. He found himself working side by side with the "militarist" in service to a common good. The two were shortly on a first name basis with each other, each respecting and asking for the opinion of the other. The student remained a pacifist and said so to the Legion man. The latter stated his objections to such a position and countered with his own views. But the two joined efforts to work together for their idea of community.

Later the student was overheard explaining to his cronies how "we buttered up the American Legion guy,"—this apparently by way of apology for his lack of militancy toward someone in the opposition camp. The search for all-inclusive community good (in which differences of opinion were accepted with mutual respect) had become a stronger motivation than pursuit of a separatist cause.

One more example of the search for community is found in a sprawling metropolitan area where delinquency, dope addition, bad housing, and other urban pathologies were rampant, where the constant addition of rootless newcomers made the problems more acute. The first encourager was the young minister of a middle-class church, located between sections of urban blight and homes which were comfortable to luxurious. The initiators he recruited came first from his own congregation, then from other churches (both pastors and laymen), then from social welfare agencies (both publicly and privately supported) and finally from residents in a low-income federal housing project.

These initiators, constituting themselves a larger nucleus, attracted representation from all other churches that would cooperate, from civic organizations (such as service clubs), from schools and local government (these representatives became resource advisors, not regularly attending members), from basic-nucleus groups that were formed, and from among individual citizens who became interested. This larger nucleus continued over several years, and still is expanding in activity. It has been responsible for various programs which were accepted by the federal Office of Economic Opportunity, yet it continues as an independent solver of local problems, with rotating membership and officership, and with constant expansion of interest into new-fields of endeavor.

An early problem faced by this larger-nucleus group was determination of the size of the area they would study and serve. The entire metropolitan complex was obviously much too large; it stretched across municipal boundaries and spilled over county lines. There were neighborhood areas with names, but the boundaries of these neighborhoods were ill defined, and the initiators wished to serve more than one of these. A casual observer driving through the metropolitan sprawl would not be aware of leaving one named neighborhood and entering another; they all merged into one another. So any choice of an area of service had to be arbitrary at the beginning, and subject to constant revision as the work proceeded.

The initiators poured over maps of their section of the metropolis as they worked their way toward selection of the area of service they preferred. They finally settled upon three of the named neighborhoods. One included the federal housing project, inhabited largely by poverty-stricken minorities (Negro and Spanish); another was made up of a mixture of middle-class (largely Anglo) and lower-income (largely Spanish) families; the third was a largely upper-middle-class neighborhood. They found it necessary to designate certain streets as the boundaries of their area. But none of these selections remained fixed. The activities, the interest, the participation tended to expand beyond all arbitrarily chosen limits.

This difficulty is part of the problem of search for community in an age of metropolitan living. Some smaller geographic area must be chosen as the place where sense of community will be built. But the chosen area is forever subject to revision, either to expansion or contraction, and it must be related and rerelated to larger improvement programs as part of the never-ending search.

Having made their (arbitrary) selection of their area of service, the initiators studied it and its inhabitants. They obtained all the information they could assemble from the census bureau, city hall, county court house, school records, welfare agencies, church federation, and so on. Then they tried to digest all this information in terms of the human needs of the people who lived in the area. Of necessity, they had to select certain problems for first attention and postpone others for later consideration. For example, they concentrated first on youth problems and housing, and delayed consideration of inadequate health services until later.

At the outset, members of the larger nucleus were vaguely aware of a relationship between delinquency, school dropouts, and the programs of the public schools. But not until they investigated did they discover how extensive and serious a problem they had on their hands. They discovered many more school dropouts than they had realized were present in the selected area. The collecting of information for making decisions, and the carrying on of a program after decisions were made, were not separate operations. Investigation and action were intertwined in on-going service to some of their unfortunate neighbors.

In time the school dropout groups lost this title and became merely boys and girls groups—because their members ceased to be dropouts. These groups were of a different character and served a different constituency from that which was normal to similar age groups in cooperating churches. The lower educational and cultural level of the young people alarmed some of the members, who especially protested against the boys "hanging around" the churches. But finally these doubters agreed that it was better for the young people to "hang around" church than around some other places. Eventually, some of the former dropouts became members of the larger nucleus.

These people interested themselves also in culturally deprived children, especially from the minority populations, where broken homes, non-English-speaking families, or absence of books, magazines, and conversation, contributed to a poor start in life. In cooperation with a nearby university, they set up kindergarten enrichment groups and tutoring experiences. These eventually produced Project Headstart and other programs financed by Office of Economic Opportunity.

They also set up a center where disadvantaged people could feel at ease in an apartment of the federal housing development (donated rent-free by the management). They created a separate board of directors to supervise and handle the finances for this center, because the larger nucleus did not want to become an agency-operating body. The board members insist however, that even they are not operating an agency. That, they say, is left to professional social welfare organizations. Theirs is a responsibility to operate a friendly center where people of the housing project and their neighbors can come for warmth of acceptance, referral to professional agencies, meeting of groups and informal classes, and whatever else local people want.

The listing of a few activities does not do justice to the multitude of interests pursued by this larger nucleus. It does not mention many other basic nuclei that are active and others being contemplated. It does not mention the spreading of the influence and participation to adjacent sections of the metropolis, to serve other disadvantaged people and to gain the support (by money and volunteers) from many churches, civic associations and educational institutions.

As far as can be determined by record-keeping and evaluative interviewing, the disadvantaged and the church members as well as participants in and supporters of the process have been gaining a sense of community. There is a growing awareness of a common goal (even though its geographic limits are ill defined) that unites privileged and underprivileged people of different racial backgrounds and people of different (formerly rival) religious connections.

Some suggestion of the growth of community awareness might be discovered in an event that did *not* happen in this area of service. After some three years of operation by the larger nucleus, another neighborhood in this particular metropolis exploded in racial riots that produced destruction of property, looting, arson, and loss of life. This riotous neighborhood was similar to the largely Negro section which was part of this community development enterprise. When the other section of the city exploded, a Negro minister who had been active with his wife in the larger nucleus organized a committee of about forty pastors and laymen of churches. During the period of the rioting in the other neighborhood (generously reported by newspaper, radio, and television) this unofficial committee patrolled their own home territory every night, all night long. Whenever they encountered groups gathered anywhere, they stopped and counselled with them, using as an appeal, "We don't want our neighborhood to be ruined the way ———— is being destroyed." No rioting took place where this committee operated; there was no looting, no lives were lost, the police were not called in, and the fire department put out one small fire that required about twenty minutes of their attention.

Some Generalizations

In a period of history when sense of community is being lost or has been lost for millions, when experts are confused about definitions, an encourager should help people define community in terms of their experience. It is not something which already exists or can be described. It is a living concept that can be achieved in a process of development.

One way for people to overcome their alienation (the individual aspect of urban anomie) is to take part in real experiences of the all-inclusive general good. Out of this they can gain a feeling of dignified selfhood. The experiences must give them recognition as persons, give them the warmth of belonging somewhere, challenge them to make decisions on matters of significance to them, and carry these decisions into actions which they can criticize. They must have the dignity of being deciders, prime movers and self-critics.

Doing things for people (such good things as feeding them, providing better homes, giving better health services, providing jobs and the education that makes them employable, and so on) can help provide a favorable atmosphere for the achievement of selfhood. But all these are external to the initiative that comes from within the participants. The external gifts must be matched by the decisions people make and carry into action. Individuals must have the initiative to cooperate with the good things done for them.

On the question of whether to start building sense of community by mixing people of contrasting classifications or to start with separated groups, there is no assured final answer. Sometimes the question is answered for an encourager, if he finds himself among an isolated population—on an Indian reservation, in a remote section of Appalachia, among Negroes of the Mississippi Delta, in a racial and cultural ghetto of a large city. Sometimes he has a choice, where presently separated classifications of people live near enough to develop into spiritual as well as geographic neighbors.

We believe (from experience) that it is slightly preferable for the all-inclusive larger nucleus to assemble representatives of contrasting populations from the outset. But this preference is based upon two provisos: (1) that an encourager can find privileged initiators who will allow the underprivileged to speak freely, make their decisions from their own point of view, and will not try to press these disadvantaged folks into becoming replicas of themselves; (2) that the underprivileged are not overawed by meeting with the privileged, and become tongue-tied or hesitant to speak their minds.

When these two provisos cannot be met, an encourager may want to start smaller nuclei among separated groups. Then he does two things. (1) He talks, with each separated group, about the other people who are rightly part of "our community"—even though they be strangers and even though members of the separated groups will make prejudiced remarks about the others. (2) He expects and hopes that the separated groups will eventually come together to seek all-inclusive community interests, when the inarticulate underprivileged have gained the confidence of becoming articulate, and when the privileged have lost their desire to make the poor look like themselves.

If an encourager has urged people into development wisely and without condemning their prejudices, if he has expected these prejudices to soften with experience of community, the separated groups will usually themselves choose to mix with other groups from which they have been separated. Either mixing from the beginning or ultimate mixing are goals of his encouraging.

Community does not already exist for most people. It cannot be created for them. They must create it for themselves by finding common interests that unite neighbors, even though they continue to differ with one another.

ADDENDUM FOR SOCIAL SCIENCE STUDENTS

We prefer to use the terms "the disadvantaged" or "the underprivileged" than the more popular "the poor." We prefer these terms because they carry more of an implication of comparison. To refer to "the poor" sounds so absolute and final.

Economists make it clear that poor and rich should be relative terms. They report statistics on gross national product, average income level per person and per family, and percentage of unemployment, by which nations can be compared. Similar statistics report figures for different sections of the country and different selected groups within the population. The comparative figures on annual income are usually used as criteria for determining whether people are to be classified as rich or poor, or in some status in between. The cutoff point on any statistical scale, below which people are to be regarded as poor, is always a bit arbitrary and subject to revision. Thus, to classify families under $3000 annual income (or $3200 or $3500) is relative to the amount of goods that sum will buy with prevailing prices, with the number of persons in the family, and with such factors as whether the chief income-receiver is the mother who must have additional expenses when she is breadwinner.

An intelligent encourager will study the economists and keep up to date on their changing statistics. But he will realize also that other factors in addition to income level must be part of the fate of the disadvantaged. Further, he should be aware that the cutoff point that determines poverty in one local situation is not the same as it will be in another situation. It varies from nation to nation and from one section of a nation to another.

A listing of the disadvantaged in America, which takes into consideration some of these additional factors, will be found in *The Other America* Michael Harrington.[1] His book represents a bible for numerous antipoverty programs. It tells of the problem but provides no solutions, or even approaches to solutions.

For a discussion of community as one of the two great social institutions whose experiences develop persons, even in the midst of poverty, see Arthur

---
[1] Michael Harrington, *The Other America* (Baltimore: Penguin Books, Inc., 1963).

Morgan, *The Small Community,* and *The Community of the Future.*[2] Morgan's basic thinking about community is helpful, but he is not much concerned with the disadvantaged in metropolitan areas. He is inclined to put his hopes upon a return to the rural simplicity of the past.

A more widely applicable concept of community is to be found in Irwin T. Sanders, *The Community, An Introduction to a Social System.*[3] Sanders is a sociologist who ventures beyond a number of traditional sociological limitations. See especially his Part III, "Community Action," which also contains his commentary upon different concepts of community development. He concludes that community developments has four different though interrelated uses; as a process of change, as a method of working with people, as a program of activities, and as a movement to be admired. Any encourager of community development needs to have such differentiations in mind as he uses the term.

---

[2] Arthur Morgan, *The Small Community* (New York: Harper & Row, Publishers, 1942), and *The Community of the Future and the Future of the Community* (Yellow Springs, Ohio: Community Services, Inc., 1957).

[3] Irwin T. Sanders, *The Community, An Introduction to a Social System* (New York: The Ronald Press Company, 1958).

Chapter 9

Some Typical Beginning Activities

If an encourager is true to his responsibility, he will not choose activities for people. They will decide for themselves what they shall do. But can ordinary people be trusted to make wise choices?

The citizens who work with an encourager in service to an emerging community will tend to make wise choices (1) when they have discussed some common problems thoroughly (2) when they have examined a wide array of alternative solutions (3) when they have anticipated (as best they can) the probable consequences of each alternative and (4) when they have been free to dream up new alternatives or to modify old ones. They are more likely also to make prosocial choices if he believes they will.

It is his responsibility to speak and act as though he expects them to choose community-serving activities. He will act this way if he has faith in their ability to discover some generous impulses in the midst of apathy or unenlightened selfishness. His job is to encourage them into discussion and to keep it going. He urges the discussion to be relevant and recommends they reach a good decision. Then his job is to help them put their decision into action.

There is this warning, however: though the decisions a nucleus group make may ultimately be prosocial and wise, these are not likely to be the decisions the encourager would make. He must learn to distinguish between a bad choice and one he dislikes because it is not his. The key questions for him are: Is it a good choice from their point of view? Does it represent a next step in favorable development for them?

From the citizens' point of view, an activity is bad when it violates their ethical code. He can help them make this code articulate and improve it. From his point of view it is bad when it threatens to frustrate the process of development. But since he may be working side by side with them, he must consult his own ethical standards as well. His ethical code should be tolerant enough to allow room for the activity that will help them grow in ethical responsibility.

Some Details of Encouragement

Since an encourager should not attempt to choose activities for people, it would be well to detail some of the things he can do to encourage their wise choice. He can do much to urge them toward careful and thoughtful choosing.

He can give them confidence in their own ability to make decisions and carry these into effective action. Sometimes he builds up this self-assurance merely by being present in meetings, and by being attentive. Sometimes he says a little, but preferably only in response to their requests for reassurance. They will say something like, "Do you think we can solve this problem?" A good answer for him is, "Sure," or "I don't see why not."

He is most convincing in reassurance when brief and matter-of-fact. He should avoid eloquence; any lengthy discourse on how he believes in their competence is likely to sound like he is talking to convince himself. If he feels he must say more, let it be some such comment as, "These people in ————— neighborhood did a good job on this. I'm sure you can do as well or even better."

When he trusts people, he need not talk overmuch about this. He is more convincing when he acts as though he trusted them, in the spirit of "why yes, of course."

It may be desirable for him to be more eloquent in convincing them that solutions to problems can be found, even though none are available early in the discussion. It is often necessary to shift their philosophy of life from "There is nothing anyone can do. It is hopeless," to "There are always some things we can do, if we can only figure them out." This more positive point of view may also take the form of, "Let us get in touch with some expert or organization that handles such problems." He can afford to be eloquent in describing ways out of their dilemma which have been found by other citizens or by experts.

He can keep their discussions from bogging down in attack on or defense of just one of several solutions to a problem. This pro versus con discussion, which tends to divide people into opposite camps, is usually the first one offered as *the* solution, or the one offered by the loudest advocate. Such a head-on clash easily degenerates into personal attacks and paralyzes action.

He can help them avoid the paralysis by calling for or even offering alternative solutions. These he offers, not for adoption, but in the hope of inspiring members of the group to find their unique alternatives. He can later challenge them to bring their discussion to a conclusion in finding a decision for action.

In one smaller city, the churches of every denomination had agreed to conduct a cooperative survey of the religious affiliations (or no affiliation) of all residents. They formed a committee (larger nucleus) to plan the survey, work out the questions to be used in interviewing, recruit the interviewers, and assemble and make the information available to all. They worked together reasonably well until they encountered a question having to do with baptism. Then they split into bitterly opposed doctrinal camps. One faction wanted to inquire about baptism by total immersion, another by sprinkling. Still another did not want any mention made of baptism, but wanted to ask whether people had been confirmed, dedicated, or had ever made a commitment to a church. And there was a further split over whether to accept any such ritual as valid when the decision for it had been made by parents speaking for a young child.

An encourager, not being wise about doctrinal matters, did not know what to do. He allowed the dispute to go on for several meetings. Then, when the wrangling became quieter out of sheer weariness, he asked for the attention of all. He asked, "Do you want to complete this survey or not?"

There were cries of "Yes, yes. That's why we came together."

"Then," said he, "you will have to find some way to get beyond these doctrinal disputes. If you keep on this way, you never will agree on questions, you cannot conduct a survey."

The disputants were sobered by this challenge. They abandoned their wrangling (which many admitted they had been enjoying) and directed attention to the practical matter of how the question should be phrased. They looked at all the alternatives that had been proposed so far, and discarded all of them. Then they worked out their own unique solution, a question that included all points of view. "Have you ever been baptised, confirmed, dedicated, or made a commitment to any church? How was it done? Who was the church official presiding? At what age did this occur?" Interviewers were given a check sheet on which they could briefly and simply check off the replies. The procedure was brief and obtained the desired information.

The solution to the problem was discovered by the group members. The encourager did not propose it. He merely challenged them to find a workable solution that would give them the information they all wanted.

Out of this experience in creating a solution grew a new sense of community and a mutual trust. One of the remarks overheard numerous times later was, "You know, I have never sat down in the same room with a person from the ———— denomination. Now I know Mr. ————, and really he is an awfully nice fellow."

If enthusiasm dies down for a time, an encourager can help people pull themselves out of a slump. In another town, a community council had great success in rehabilitating several public parks that had been allowed to fall into decay. They had organized a number of weekends of cooperative labor on the parks, involving large numbers of citizens who chopped down weeds, mowed neglected lawns, planted new shrubs, fixed paths, built picnic tables, and constructed open-air fireplaces. Then they arranged to make such care a permanent responsibility. After all this, they were tired.

As a result, no new problems were discussed, no solutions proposed in discussion. And, in fact, the council did not meet for four or five months. The encourager did not berate them for lack of zeal. He let them rest for a while, then began coming to their city to be friendly with various council members just to inquire whether they had begun to think about other problems. He avoided making them feel guilty for unfaithfulness to community welfare and improvement.

After several such social calls, an important reason for their reluctance emerged in conversation. For their next action they wanted to undertake a really important and seemingly impossible task, the construction of a new high school (to serve the entire school district—the town and much surrounding countryside). But they saw no way to accomplish such an expensive hope in a poverty-stricken school district. It seemed so hopeless that they hesitated even to mention it.

When this ambitious hope finally became clear in conversations, the encourager took it upon himself to convince them that they could obtain the high school, even though he did not then know how, and did not have access to any money with which to help them. All he could do was offer to meet with them and join in the search for ways to finance and construct the school. With the encourager's help they did find the way. A few details of the solution are found in the next chapter.

An encourager can also warn a group away from selecting a too difficult, poorly thought-out or unwise activity. His decision to warn or not to warn them is a matter of judgment about their level of competence. In one community group, there was an outspoken delegation of war veterans. They demanded that the group decide to build a veteran's hall, to be used as a community center for everyone. The encourager concluded that the group was not yet ready for such a difficult undertaking. This conclusion proved correct when the group voted to purchase cement blocks and other materials without having employed an architect or builder, or even worse, without obtaining clear legal title to the lot upon which their building was to be constructed. He did his best to warn them away from a poorly thought-out decision. But he spoke to deaf ears. The vociferous proponents of the idea insisted they must move ahead just "to show these opponents of ours that they can't push us around." They purchased the building materials and piled them on the property in time to be greeted by a court injunction against the construction, obtained by a man (one of their opponents?) who claimed ownership of the property. The veterans hall was never built. And the community group shortly died.

He can warn them also about the probable setbacks that will almost always follow successes. If their elation is too great, then the discouragements become devastating. If they have been told that every process of development moves through ups and downs, the downs can be accepted with more equanimity, as disturbing events which are likely to be followed by new achievements, provided members continue the process.

He can advise them on numerous details whose neglect could result in crippling disaster. One neighborhood group put on a horse show as a money-raising event. An encourager advised them to take out a one-day insurance policy to cover possible liability for injury when a large crowd was present. During the horse show, an elderly man claimed that he had been knocked over and injured by a horse that came too close to where he was sitting. The insurance company met the claim and the community council was not ruined financially. Similarly, whenever a playground, or a building, or swimming pool, or a public activity is manged by a citizens' group, the operation should be protected by liability insurance.

If any construction is contemplated, the group should be advised early to call in an architect and/or builder. If there are legal aspects to a problem under discussion, a friendly lawyer can be brought in. When some community work period is being planned, the group should be encouraged to investigate the matter of labor union rules about amateurs doing the work. To be aware of all such practical details and draw these to the attention of the group is part of an encourager's responsibility. The point is to warn them of possible disaster from unanticipated difficulties.

As a participant in discussion, he can also introduce basic values as guides for decision-making and for later self-evaluation. Values are best introduced by simple and direct questions. "In choosing between these alternatives before us, how do we decide which is best? What are the short-run, and then the long-run purposes we have in mind? If we decide to do this, what will happen to the people involved? To ourselves? To the dis-advantaged people we are trying to help? To our opponents, even those who (we believe) are oppressing us or our disadvantaged friends?" In the discussion which follows such innocent-sounding questions, there often occurs a wrestling with the most fundamental philosophic and even religious issues, phrased, however, in the language which is meaningful to people, not in the polysyllabic obscurity of philosophers or theologians.

By introducing values into the discussion, an encourager prepares them for the self-evaluation they can be encouraged to undertake later. He can advise them that any activity is incomplete until it has been subjected to critical self-evaluation.

Then an encourager can sometimes help the group by serving as scape-goat. When group members have been frustrated (by other people or by circumstances) they sometimes need someone upon whom to heap blame, in order to obtain some relief of emotion. In one community project, one leader of the group, having reached this point, subjected an encourager to a thorough and eloquent attack in the presence of two less experienced learn-ers. He accepted the uncomplimentary comments and even murmured a few times about correcting some of them.

Afterward, the learners wanted to know, "Why did you let that guy get away with all that? Why didn't you put him in his place?" The reply was simple. "In the first place, some of the things he said about me were correct, at least in part. I learned something from what he said. But, more impor-tant, he obviously needed a scapegoat to blame for what has gone wrong. That is a function I can serve.

"But," he went on, "don't think this man has lost confidence in us. He will be back again for further advice and help, in his own good time." This guess proved correct. The man in question sought out the encourager in about a week. And with an apologetic manner (not with words of apology) sought advice on how to take the next steps with his group.

Finally, an encourager can act as conciliator between conflicting fac-tions, when such a role is necessary. In another project, the encouragers made the (later discovered) mistake of allowing a woman to be chosen chairman of a community group. She was obviously able, energetic, and full of ideas. But she assumed leadership within a population where women were supposed to confine themselves to the home, and men resented their leadership—even though the woman had been elected chairman with their supporting vote. The group came to the point of disintegration when the men grew more and more resentful of her energy. They insisted she tried to push them around.

At length, one encourager pointed out to her a fact that she already had suspected—that she would jeopardize the continuation of the group if she remained on as chairman. Her husband, however, made the final move. He ordered her to attend no more meetings (a masculine order accepted as proper by her and by the neighbors, in this social setting).

The encourager was able to talk things over with the husband, with the woman chairman, and with the men critical of her. He could introduce some ideas of a change of standards to the husband and could assuage the hurt for the wife by enlisting her help in choosing and breaking in her male successor to the chairmanship. He was able also to help men and women remaining in the group to rediscover their enthusiasm for the jobs to be done and for their growing ideas of community.

These are some details of the encouraging job. These are some of the roles an encourager will find himself taking in meetings and in conversations with individuals. He will find himself taking many such roles in both basic and larger nuclei.

But whatever his role, the people must make the choices of activity and assume the main responsibility for carrying the decisions into action. An encourager can take part in the discussion, and should join them also in some of the work to be done. But they must know the idea they are following is theirs, no matter what its original source. The encourager does not dominate. He approves an idea but not enough to force it upon people. He may disapprove but not strongly enough to force his withdrawal from the group. He does not get insulted when people reject him or his ideas.

In working with one group, an experienced encourager had concluded that people's maturity had reached a point that called upon him to remain largely silent during most discussions. But, in one meeting, when encouragers-in-training were present, citizens finally demanded that he speak up to give his best solution to a problem. Thus urged, he offered his ideas. The group listened to his suggestions, discussed them, and finally rejected them in favor of another solution they created. Their new solution was superior to the one he had offered.

After the meeting, one of the learners twitted the experienced encourager about his lack of influence in the group. "They sure put you in your place that time."

"Now look," he said, on the defensive, "they did adopt one other suggestion of mine. So they took one and rejected one. If they followed everything I said, they would be merely endorsing my ideas."

That citizens learn from their decisions is more important than that they always make the right one. They learn from both successes and failures. They often learn more from the mistakes, provided these do not stop the process or destroy the group. An encourager tries to advise them away from such unfortunate decisions.

Self-Help Activities

A major outcome for the process is that people shall develop initiative. They become independent by accepting responsibility to serve an expanding sense of community. The responsibility arises out of participation in the activities of self-help. Such activities were easier to find in the simpler communities of the past. Now when communities merge into each other, when problems become so complex that few can be solved just locally, such activities are harder to find. They require help from some source external to the community.

Even when external help is obtained, however, it is important to emphasize self-help. This is done by calling upon a responsible group to choose the activity and the kind of external help they need.

The following typical activities are suggested on a scale from maximum self-help to much cooperation with external help:

1. Organizing a group that can speak for an emerging sense of community.
2. Conducting such a group in a manner that gives satisfaction to the diverse people and interests included in it.
3. Learning how to discuss controversial issues intelligently.
4. Providing refreshments and other social activities for the group.
5. Collecting and organizing information about people in the area to be served. This includes the obtaining of data from all reliable sources, but may include also a self-survey (a door-to-door or by-mail answering of questionnaires). This has value but is not as objectively reliable as a survey by professionals. Its value lies in the understanding gained by participants.
6. Simple beautification of a small area that can be financed and carried to completion largely by residents, such as installation of window boxes, cleanup of front and back yards, paint-up and fix-up campaigns, cooperative planting of gardens in yards and recreation areas.
7. Organizing "tot lots" on vacant property (with the written permission of owners). Rehabilitation of small neighborhood parks.

8. Organizing larger meetings for recruitment of participants and obtaining of publicity for activities.

When any of the above activities become more complicated or overwhelming, they will require an increase of external help. Various help to needy neighbors falls into this same category. The simple neighborliness of yesteryear that cared for the sick or rebuilt a burned out barn has to be replaced with help that utilizes the skill of experts. For example:

1. A single hungry neighbor can be fed a few meals. But when it comes to distributing Thanksgiving or Christmas baskets, the job had best be done in cooperation with a wise social welfare agency. Services to migrants or responses to appeals for aid received in the mail should be checked through charitable organizations that can keep good-hearted citizens from being victimized.
2. One community nucleus developed a program of reading books (to a tape recorder) for the blind. But they did this with the guidance of an agency that served the blind.
3. Others have taken an interest in child or adult health, but not to prescribe their own remedies. The task is to refer or actually to take sufferers to clinics, or doctors or hospitals, or to seek to make these services available, when lacking. Some nuclei have induced a doctor to settle in a community. Others have provided a building in which a clinic of the professionally trained could operate.
4. Then there are simpler construction jobs that can be done by citizens (being careful to avoid violation of labor union rules and zoning ordinances) such as repair of stairways and broken windows in homes (private houses or apartments), beginnings of road and bridge construction, and even erection of small flood-control installations. But when any of these activities become large scale or costly, they should involve professionals. The nucleus of citizens can build up the interest and even make a few beginnings, but the main construction jobs call for the specially trained.

A nuclear group of citizens can bring about the organization of agencies that will employ professionally trained workers. But it can also keep in constant touch with the professionals, helping or planning and offering work activities to supplement and humanize the services of the experts. Road builders, pavers of streets, installers of street lights need reminders to get the job done. Recreation leaders and teachers do a better job when citizens have authorized their work and continue support for the service. It is possible, however, to persuade professionals to leave some portion of their work to be completed by amateurs. Here are some examples:

1. One nucleus turned over construction of a swimming pool to a builder, but left beautification of the area surrounding it to citizens.
2. Another employed an architect and a builder to construct a school building, but themselves laid tile floors, installed desks, and painted some of the rooms.
3. In one large city, citizens began rehabilitation of a hospital by painting discolored walls.

Perhaps the most important function of all is the uniting of many interests, agencies, and persons to meet discovered need. This uniting is a responsibility most difficult to meet in an age of specialization. As one minister of a church told an encourager, "I am too busy working for the church to have any time to give to the community." To overcome this specialized loyalty that ignores the common good is a great challenge for a larger nucleus.

Obtaining Help
from External Resources

There are resources of help for development everywhere. Most of these, in or available to any community, must be sought out by nucleus groups aided by an encourager.

Most obvious and already mentioned are social welfare agencies. These are both privately financed and tax-supported. They include services to almost every kind of human handicap, but frequently are surrounded by limiting rules as to how they are to be used, and by whom.

Then there are civic associations that can become interested. These are more flexible than the agencies, but require more skill to approach. There are service clubs (both male and female), chambers of commerce, labor unions, veteran's organizations, women's clubs and even industries (national and local). Often it will be found that these civic-minded associations are grateful for the opportunity to cooperate, at least financially. A local nucleus can often help them find a place to put their money.

Educational institutions are important for local development. Public elementary and high schools will often provide teachers or administrators to join in discussion of problems, especially when school-type education is involved. They will often add recreation to their curriculum, and will modify their work or introduce new programs when a need is made clear. Universities will often respond to calls for help through extension services (agricultural and more recently urban studies) or through academic departments (sociology, anthropology, geography, school of business, and so on) or through the interest of individual professors.

Churches represent a largely unutilized reservoir of people of good will. Sometimes church members will take the initiative in nucleus formation. Or they may be recruited for many kinds of cooperation for specific public service enterprises. This cooperation is especially welcome when church people from formerly rival denominations can work together for the common good. Community-serving activities provide an opportunity for churches to become practically ecumenical.

Charitable foundations are also a source of financial help, but applicants need to understand the particular emphases which each foundation regards as its own. The best known of these are national. But many local (usually city) foundations can be interested in community-service activities.

Local governments are almost always sources of help for nucleus groups, and officials, either elected or appointed, will usually respond when they are convinced that a nucleus represents grass-roots voters. There are mayors and city councilmen, but even more, there are various committees, offices, agencies, and special responsibility groups, such as Human Relations Committees, Boards of Education, Planning Commissions, and so on. The planning offices may have city-wide, county, or regional responsibilities. These are discussed more fully in the next chapter.

Various state offices and bureaus can be reached. Each is set up to serve some special function such as fair employment practices, road building and maintenance, public education, recruitment of industries for cities, and so on. The latter are sometimes referred to as development bureaus or even as agencies for community development.

The federal government has been increasing the number of its agencies that provide help to local initiative. In addition to agricultural extension are various urban programs, federal participation in welfare and relief services (unemployment compensation, payments to widows and orphans, vocational rehabilitation for the handicapped, distribution of surplus foods, to mention a few), and newer national programs with clearer community reference (area redevelopment and various local projects under the Office of Economic Opportunity). It is difficult to predict what further possibilities will be opened up by the Department of Housing and Urban Development when it becomes more active.

Who is to make the actual approach to any of the many sources of help we have mentioned? Preferably, nucleus members should take the responsibility so they may learn from the experience. In the early stages of their growth in responsibility, an encourager may decide to accompany them in the expectation that they will eventually take over without depending upon his presence. He may clear the way for them by speaking to the resource person in advance, or by giving people the name and office location of the agency to be reached. But he should avoid depriving them of the experience of contact by offering the help without their seeking it.

The town nucleus group that wanted to build a school expressed all kinds of wild and impracticable ideas about the kind of building they wanted. Many of these were so structurally unsound that an encourager knew the building would collapse in the first high wind that blew through. But he refrained from criticizing their naive ideas. Instead he pointed out that they must meet the standards set by the state Department of Public Instruction. Most of the members did not know such a department existed and had no idea of how to obtain help from it.

The encourager told them the department was located in the state capital, many miles away. "Oh," said the people in the nucleus meeting, "we couldn't possibly go there for help."

"Why not?"

"Well, that office is run by a bunch of bureaucrats. And everyone knows how hard it is to get anything out of bureaucrats."

"How do you know these bureaucrats are so bad? Have any of you ever met any of them?"

"Oh no. But then everybody knows ——"

"The things everybody knows are frequently untrue," said the encourager. "Why not give these people a chance to be helpful? That is their business, you know."

Reluctantly they agreed to drive a carload of local people to the state capital to ask for help in building their school. The encourager did no more than supply them with information as to which building they should enter when they arrived and which office they should seek out in that building.

Several days later, when the delegation returned to the group after their trip, they were ecstatic. They had been treated with the utmost courtesy, had been given sample blueprints, instruction pamphlets, and advice on how to go about their difficult task. Furthermore, representatives of the office had agreed to come periodically and meet with the nucleus to guide them further. In fact, the feared bureaucrats had proved themselves almost pathetically grateful that a delegation of inquiring citizens would come all that distance to seek their help!

In another state, a nucleus group had concluded that their county had been neglected on road building. They looked up the relative size of contribution to state taxes from their county to the state budget and the relative amount spent on road construction. They concluded their county had been neglected. They decided, with encouragement, to get up a petition asking for more roads, black-topping of some in existence, replacing of bridges, and so on. They circulated this to obtain several hundred signatures.

When the petition had been circulated and signed, they debated whether to mail it to the state capital or to take it by hand. The encourager recommended the personal contact for better results, again arguing against the fear of bureaucrats. Finally a carload of local citizens drove to present the petition to the state bureau of roads. They were received with a certain amount of reserve, but the "bureaucrats" promised to study their request.

Within three weeks a bulldozer and black-topping equipment appeared to work on roads in the county. The work crews and machinery kept working until cold winter weather shut operations down. With the better spring weather, another delegation visited the bureau of roads again, and once more the road building operation began. The request had to be repeated each spring. But it always brought results. And the nucleus gained in strength with this evidence of its influence.

A nucleus group in a large metropolitan area made contacts with the police for information about delinquency and drug addiction, social welfare agencies for health, family and recreation needs, the schools for changes in classroom procedures, the churches for more volunteers and financial support and help on racial conflict problems, the service clubs for further financial support, the university for trained personnel, research help, and student volunteers.

There was one difficulty with this extremely active larger nucleus, however. The clergyman encourager carried too much of the burden of activity himself. He became widely known locally for his service to the common good. But his reputation overshadowed public appreciation for the group.

The test of whether or not an encourager has asked participants to take an adequate amount of responsibility is to be found in the way in which they develop, in whether they become good selectors of wise activities, and in whether their group becomes accepted as spokesmen for the community good.

Encouragement for Choosing

Although an encourager expects citizen members of a nucleus to choose activities and learn from this choosing, he cannot divest himself of his responsibility. He has a role to play—in the discussion that leads up to choosing, in the actual decision, in the work that carries decision into action, in the obtaining of help to carry the activity forward, in the self-evaluating analysis that makes learning articulate.

He encourages people to choose some relatively easy self-help activity early in the development process—one which is simple, yet significant in their thinking, and likely to produce visible results. He hopes for this kind of choice because the active experiences it brings about will (1) give them confidence in their own ability to solve problems (2) help them build up habits of cooperation, which can be applied to more difficult tasks (3) begin to establish the group's reputation for devotion to the common good.

He should warn them away from unwise choices. But he should also cheer them when they have been discouraged by bad results. He may deflate overconfidence when elation has become overheated. He tries to help them maintain an attitude that allows them to adjust flexibly to whatever happens.

He also attempts to balance conflicting interests and points of view, so that wise choosing is more likely to occur. He conciliates between contending factions.

Above all, he is a patient friend who allows people to work things out in their own way and to learn from the experience. He tries to help them avoid the choices and experiences and attitudes that might impede or terminate the on-going process.

ADDENDUM FOR SOCIAL SCIENCE STUDENTS

There is a considerable literature accumulating which describes the beginning stages of community development as an applied social science. The publications listed here are selected from the writings of several authors who are important contributors.

A pioneer book is Baker Brownell's *The Human Community*.[1] The writing is based upon the author's work in Montana. It stresses the virtues of small town rural life.

Jean and Jess Ogden have two important books, *Small Communities in Action* and *These Things We Tried*.[2] These are additional pioneer works

---

[1] Baker Brownell, *The Human Community* (New York: Harper & Row, Publishers, 1950).

[2] Jean and Jess Ogden, *Small Communities in Action* (New York: Harper & Row, Publishers, 1946) and *These Things We Tried* (New York: Harper & Row, Publishers, 1947).

that have become classics of the rural emphasis. They give more descriptions of what actually happened than the Brownell book.

Richard W. Poston's early *Democracy Is You* is a "how to" book that presents a formular-like outline. His later book, *Democracy Speaks Many Tongues*,[3] changes his formula somewhat, especially in relation to overseas operation.

An early book by William W. Biddle has already been mentioned, *The Cultivation of Community Leaders*.[4] This practical approach represents a point of view derived from experience with smaller populations. This writer too has modified his position in later books that deal with city problems.

Saul D. Alinsky's point of view is important, but it is difficult to list publications that give an objective description of his work. His writings are largely polemics and descriptions of his work tend to be either breathless in admiration or equally exaggerated in condemnation. The clearest contributions to social scientific thinking are a paper, "Citizen Participation and Community Organization in Planning and Urban Renewal," [5] and a statement before a Senate subcommittee on juvenile delinquency.[6]

In *A Neighborhood Finds Itself*,[7] Julia Abrahamson presents a detailed account of a city community development enterprise that contrasts sharply with the Alinsky methods, and in the same city, Chicago.

In *The Death and Life of Great American Cities*,[8] Jane Jacobs gives a critique of urban planning and renewal. But in addition her book contains some analytical wisdom about neighborhood community development in cities.

Community Organization for Citizen Participation in Urban Renewal [9]

---

[3] Richard W. Poston, *Democracy Is You* (New York: Harper & Row, Publishers, 1953) and *Democracy Speaks Many Tongues* (New York: Harper & Row, Publishers, 1962).

[4] William W. Biddle, *The Cultivation of Community Leaders* (New York: Harper & Row, Publishers, 1953).

[5] Saul D. Alinsky, a paper presented before the Chicago Chapter of the National Association of Housing and Redevelopment Officials, Chicago, 1962. Published by the Industrial Areas Foundation (8 South Michigan Ave., Chicago 3, Ill.).

[6] In Eugene L. Hartley and Gerhart D. Wiebe, (editors), *Casebook in Social Processes* (New York: Thomas Y. Crowell Company, 1960), pp. 346–376.

[7] Julia Abrahamson, *A Neighborhood Finds Itself* (New York: Harper & Row Publishers, 1959).

[8] Jane Jacobs, *The Death and Life of Great American Cities* (New York: Random House, Inc., 1961).

[9] William C. Loring, Jr., Frank L. Sweetser, and Charles F. Ernst, *Community Organization for Citizen Participation in Urban Renewal* (Boston: Housing Association of Metropolitan Boston, 1957).

by Loring, Sweetser, and Ernst gives a detailed description of a successful program in one American city that has sought citizen participation.

T. R. Batten has two important books that develop a point of view from overseas operation, *Training for Community Development,* and *The Human Factor in Community Work.*[10] These give case studies of work with newly developing peoples.

Peter du Sautoy also has distilled much wisdom from work with newly developing peoples in *The Organization of a Community Development Programme.*[11] He is also editor of the *Community Development Journal,*[12] a quarterly publication with international circulation that keeps abreast of current programs in the field.

The books given represent a selection of several contrasting points of view, each based upon the writer's unique experience. A serious social science student might start his critical review of the literature by reading all for both contrasts and underlying agreements.

---

[10] T. R. Batten, *Training for Community Development* (London: Oxford University Press, 1962) and with the collaboration of Madge Batten, *The Human Factor in Community Work* (London· Oxford University Press, 1965).

[11] Peter du Sautoy, *The Organization of a Community Development Programme* (London: Oxford University Press, 1962).

[12] *Community Development Journal* (22 Kingston Road, Didsbury, Manchester 20, England).

Chapter 10

Some More Complicated Activities

A vital community development process has leading-on qualities. It moves from one interest to another, through the selection of activity after activity. It is this leading-on characteristic that an encourager has in mind when he joins in discussion for selection of action projects. He raises questions but he does not choose the problem or the action. The people make the choices. He should be guided by the conviction that the process will, sooner or later, bring the people around to consider those problems he might choose as important.

When an encourager first came into contact with the town that moved from rehabilitation of deteriorated parks to construction of a high school, he thought the problem citizens should select was in the field of health. The town lacked a sewage-disposal facility, depended upon private, inadequate septic tanks and old-fashioned privies, and had suffered disease epidemics from bad sanitation. Children had died in one such epidemic within the year before the first contact. But when the encourager tried to direct attention to health problems, there was no interest. Citizens were ready to talk about cleaning up a graveyard, setting up a fire department, obtaining telephone service—anything but health. When they finally settled upon the park project, the encourager believed this was unimportant compared with the problems he thought they should consider.

When they came around to the problem of building the high school, two years later, the nucleus planning committee discovered the school district was obligated to install running water for a gymnasium and toilets and a sewage-disposal system. Some citizens then began saying, "If we have to

132

construct a sewage-disposal plant in order to have a new high school, why
don't we build a larger one to accommodate all homes as well? After all,
we have had too much sickness from bad sanitation." (Had the earlier
words of the encourager been heard? And were they finally giving heed to
his advice?)

Nucleus members carried the matter to the governing town council and
obtained action to build the sanitary facilities for the entire town. As a
result of such action, other public health improvements followed. People
had eventually brought themselves around to some of the problems considered important by the encourager.

As the problems discussed become increasingly complex, they tend to be
the kind that can be handled most efficiently by a larger nucleus. Such a
group will probably have a greater array of experienced members. The
determining factor in deciding to undertake the more difficult activities is
the level of sophistication available among participants. But even when
sophistication is lacking, people will often prove to have greater wisdom
in choosing and be more efficient workers than an encourager would have
predicted. Even a basic nucleus may sometimes be encouraged to undertake
very difficult activities when able people are members.

Another factor that favors the organization of a larger nucleus to handle
difficult problems is that such an association, which represents many
organizations and factions in a larger community, is more likely to have
contacts with agencies, government offices, and various other sources of
help, either for expert advice or financial support.

Doing the Impossible

When the nucleus group just mentioned began to talk about
building a new high school, the encourager was very dubious about the
people ever succeeding in bringing their overambitious dream to reality.
There simply was not enough tax money in the school district to pay for
the kind of school they wanted. And these were not worldly-wise people
nor were they sophisticated in financial or legal matters. Besides, the
encourager himself was ignorant about how to proceed in the face of such
major difficulties.

Nevertheless, because he was convinced that devoted people who use
their intelligence can find answers to problems, he encouraged them to go
ahead. He urged them to expand their group by taking in wider representation and more experienced members. He urged them also to make contact

with various authorities who could help them, such as lawyers, experienced money-raisers, architects, builders, and state authorities. He gave them the confidence to proceed and advised them on expanded membership and on which authorities were appropriate and competent. As a result of his advice and of counselling with these various authorities, they created their own action pattern for obtaining a high school, which the school district apparently could not afford.

It might be pointed out that they followed the encourager's advice part of the time. At other times they depended more upon the experts they consulted. But most of all they were using their own critical judgment.

They discovered that under state law, a school district could rent classroom space and other facilities using state-supplied funds. But this legislation presupposed that some properly constructed and safe buildings were available for rental, and no such facilities were to be found in this town. Then, might a separate nonprofit corporation construct a school building with the necessary landscaping, playgrounds, and other appurtenances that could be rented? Yes, this was possible under the law.

So the larger nucleus created a separate legal entity, a nonprofit foundation. Its purposes were to raise money for a new school, purchase property, construct buildings that met state requirements, and then rent these facilities to the school district. Funds from local school tax revenues supplemented by state contributions were to provide enough income to amortize the debt incurred by the sale of school bonds issued by the foundation. The school district would increase its collection from taxes up to the legally allowable limit. As part of the decision to adopt this procedure, members of the community group calculated the probable amount of money they might raise from voluntary gifts for operating expenses and purchase of property, the amount of bonded indebtedness they would probably incur, and the income they might expect to receive from rentals to the school district.

We have recounted some (not all) of the complicated and interlocking details which constituted the pattern of action these people worked out and adopted. It was all legally proper, approved by necessary authorities, and realistic in terms of the people's abilities of the future probabilities. After its adoption, the complex plan was put into effect; the money was raised (more than had been anticipated, because outsiders heard of the enterprise and contributed), the bonds were sold, the school was built, the school officials took over, and the rental payments are now retiring the bonds as planned. An unanticipated source of revenue for the school has appeared: the school is a showpiece in that part of the state, attracting pupils from other school districts who pay tuition.

Incidental to the total achievement were many efforts and episodes that had to be planned and carried out. Among these were carefully thought-out publicity stories for newspapers and radio, parades at different stages of progress, money-raising events (county fairs and fish fries, as well as parties to collect pledges), and several dedications and family-type suppers (after the school was in use). All these events required careful timing and the cooperative effort of many committees that involved the responsible officers of the nucleus group, of the foundation, and of numerous nonofficial citizens, such as housewives and young people from the school. The whole enterprise required an amount of organizational detail that awed the encourager. These people, with little previous organizational experience, worked out and put into action an answer to their problem which no one had even dreamed of at the beginning.

A further example of doing the impossible is found in a large city, where a larger-nucleus group has been working for some years to provide a humane balance for some of the excesses of overenthusiastic urban renewal. In the neighborhood in question, a large university together with city government has used federal and other funds to rip out many blocks of deteriorated buildings, replacing these with attractive (but higher-priced) apartments, as well as park spaces. This kind of urban renewal, though it brings about physical improvement of a neighborhood, ousts poor families who most probably leave to swell other slums elsewhere. (This is a guess. Who knows for certain where they go?) And much of the sense of community is lost. Unless the planning is guided by humane values, this kind of urban renewal constitutes social planning by a bulldozer.

The neighborhood larger nucleus has drawn attention to humane values in the midst of the expenditure of millions of dollars for reconstruction of buildings. At many points, the group has thrown its financially feeble influence on the side of the planning that serves human need. Sometimes it is successful, sometimes less so.

Concluding that there had been a loss to this neighborhood and to the entire city in the departure of artists as a result of urban renewal, the group sought some way to bring these creative persons back to the rebuilt neighborhood. They constructed a center for artists where these nonconformist and usually penurious persons could feel at home, at rentals which they could afford. The center is financed largely by money raised as subsidy for creative activities. Property had to be acquired and the proper buildings had to be planned and constructed so that studios, exhibit and sales rooms, little theatre, and so on, were made available. All this the larger nucleus accomplished and continues to maintain.

The Art of Planning

Such difficult and complex activities obviously require careful planning. But many people, from ordinary citizens to prominent political figures, resist planning. It impresses them as unexciting and laborious, or even as undemocratic.

In undertaking some "impossible" tasks, members of community nuclei have the opportunity to modify their habits of thinking. And an encourager, has the opportunity to help the people achieve the self-discipline for study and thoughtful decision-making.

In the early stages of the process, citizens will exhibit the very human tendency to give attention to the most obvious problems, and to adopt the most immediate actions as solutions. This tendency toward immediacy is good for the beginning, but it normally leads to planning if in the process citizens are persuaded to undertake more and more difficult tasks. It is an encourager's responsibility to give people the confidence to plan as he draws their attention to the progressively more difficult problems.

A contrast between citizens who have not enjoyed the benefit of the development process and those who have will become apparent to an encourager at this stage. A frustrated citizen of a metropolitan neighborhood came to consult a community expert about the threat to his own home. Urban renewal authorities were putting pressure on him by raising tax rates, according to him. He suspected that they were planning to oust residents from the beach neighborhood where his family enjoyed the sea breeze in order to put in public parks. He demanded that the expert provide him with an immediate solution to his (personal) community problem.

The expert then acted like an encourager. He recommended that the citizen and his neighbors form an association in order to search for their own solution. The citizen immediately lost interest. He wanted a prepackaged "correct" answer that would save his home, but spare him the discomfort of study, attending meetings, discussion, and using his own intelligence.

Members of a developing larger nucleus are more likely to welcome the challenge of searching for solutions. When they have gone through the experience of coping with simpler immediate problems, they can be persuaded to accept the self-discipline required for planning. This is an encourager's opportunity. He can introduce seemingly impossible problems in such a way as to invite the search for planned solutions.

The learning of the art of planning means several changes in habits of thought. People must first agree to postpone the immediate triumph in favor of the long run hope. Then they must have willingness to wait for accomplishment through many disappointments. And since longer periods of time are involved, they must be flexible enough to modify their procedures and next-step goals in order to serve the distant hope. They learn to remain faithfully committed to the distant goal while free to modify the means for getting there.

Finally, they learn to increase the scope of their cooperation. They work first with their friends within the nucleus group to plan and to execute plans. Then they carry this same ability to work with others to friends outside the group, to the experts and agencies that will help them work out ways of proceeding, but most of all, to whatever professional planners are available.

Increasingly there are planning bureaus or commissions to be found in American cities, counties, and states. Sometimes these bodies have the word "planning" in their titles; sometimes they have other names. (One state planning commission is called an economic commission, because state legislators wished to avoid any accusation of "socialism.") These planning offices, together with specialized functions that have planning implications, are controlled by human beings. The bureaus are not just impersonal assemblages of computerized thinking. Administrators who are bound by legal requirements, and who punch the keys on the computers, are still human.

One city neighborhood larger nucleus has regularly invited representatives of the county planning commission to address their meetings and to help them in determining how their area of service could be preserved as a good interracial residential section. Another, in a city not too far away, offered to collect data for a master plan which was being drawn up by a firm of professional planners employed by the city council. Members of the larger nucleus themselves surveyed the buildings of the city, using also the services of volunteer college students. It was then no surprise when they were invited to join in the decisions which were embodied in the city's master plan.

Citizens who try to cooperate with planners should realize that these professional people also suffer from confused motivations and ambivalences. They want to evolve plans that are a credit to their profession and are workable. Yet they want to have democratic participation in the evolving and adoption of their plans, lest their blueprints remain forever in dusty files. Stated in another way, they want people to be a part of the planning process, but do not want to be bothered with the troubles of seeking people's participation.

Because of the discomfort of this ambivalence, most planners will welcome the opportunity to work with a community nucleus whose members are learning the self-discipline necessary for planning. If citizens need to learn the difficult art of planning, planners need to learn how to gain democratic participation. An encourager can contribute to both by finding ways for nucleus members to sit in with planners and for the planners to come to help at nucleus meetings.

Relating to Larger Social Systems

The ambivalence found in planners is not unique to them. It is found also in the behavior of administrators of great programs of social improvement, in city, state, or nation, or in combinations of all three. These administrators are planners, although they are seldom thus designated. They also exhibit human frailty in carrying into action programs which were meant to improve the human lot, yet are experimental and difficult to administer democratically. They are not to be regarded as enemies when programs fail to meet their purpose fully or when democratic implementing proves difficult.

They also are struggling to find ways to carry democratic hopes into planning. An encourager can help nucleus members to get in touch with these administrators. Some of them will welcome the cooperation as a means to help their programs serve the people they are meant to serve.

The question will continue to be asked: To what extent do large-scale programs of improvement (for rural betterment, urban renewal and re-habilitation, area redevelopment, elimination of poverty, and so on) accomplish their avowed purposes? Do they serve the people they are supposed to benefit?

A tentative answer is available from experience to date: These programs serve their purpose to the extent that they are based locally upon some bona fide citizen initiative in the planning and in the executing of the plans. The program serves its democratic intent to the extent that citizen initiative comes from local citizens. Basic nuclei, building up to larger nuclei that can and will cooperate in planning, provide the means for democratic implementing of the great programs. To help members of these nuclei become articulate and achieve the self-discipline to plan with administrators, are among an encourager's opportunities.

After three years of independent work, a community council in the southern mountains was invited to become a part of a state-wide planning commission set up by the governor. In another section of the country, a citizens committee that had worked on road and agricultural improvement draw up a plan for county improvement that was adopted quickly by administrators of area redevelopment programs. (A very eloquent chairman with a flair for flowery literary expression helped in getting the attention of the planners and program executives.)

A city committee that had worked on enriching the background of culturally deprived preschool children was among the first to receive funds from the Office of Economic Opportunity. A neighborhood nucleus in another city, that worked on interracial harmony, was able to gain the cooperation of the mayor, of his committee on human relations, of the police, of the city planning commission, and was able to lobby in the state legislature for new laws. Another city human relations council (an un-official body which was a larger nucleus) worked on obtaining better housing for minority groups, then on getting more jobs for them. Later it guided the President's Committee on Fair Employment when it began to work with local factory employers. It also was able to put on pressure for enactment of state and national civil rights laws.

Whenever citizens' groups gear into programs of larger social systems, they should not be absorbed into the city, or state, or federal planning agency or office. The nucleus must have its own existence, must give voice to ordinary local people and even be free to criticize the larger-scale effort. It is possible to criticize in such a way as to make further cooperation possible—always remembering that the administrators are human too. They are probably as eager to serve needy people as are their critics. But they need help to learn how. So do most of their critics.

Part of the separate identity for citizen groups is established and maintained by building up a favorable public picture of the nucleus group. Members need to acquire a judicious skill to use the available instruments of publicity. One trouble is that citizens new to cooperative activity for the public good are often fearful of newspapers, reporters, and television people. Actually, these purveyors of publicity are also human and will often respond to a human approach. One publisher and his editor expressed indignation to the writers because a nucleus group in their area of a metropolis had failed to give them stories about citizen meetings and work. Most newspapermen want stories, and will interpret negatively only when they feel citizen groups are trying to be secretive.

In one city an encourager, starting work with a neighborhood nucleus, decided to seek the backing of the editor of the one newspaper in that city. He tried to persuade other initiators of the process to go with him to talk to the editor. Everyone refused. The editor was a remote sort of person whose employees blindly accepted his orders, a tyrannical figure both feared and placated by most people in the city—and one often ill-informed in his editorial policy. The encourager, finding no one willing to go with him to interview the editor, finally said he would go alone. (Should he have insisted that some of the group go with him? Yes, it would have been better.)

When he reached the inner presence of the editor's office, after making his way past numerous receptionists, secretaries, and other underlings, he told of his plans to form a nucleus to work on better human relations. "Huh," replied the editor, "I suppose you are going to try to upgrade the Negroes."

"Yes, that is part of the idea."

"Well, you are dumb to try this. If you do-gooders would just leave these sorts of problems alone, they would take care of themselves, in time. You are always stirring things up when Negroes should be left alone to make progress without a lot of uproar."

"You may be willing to let time take care of injustice," said the encourager, "but I am not willing. I think we should do everything we can to make our ideas of democracy work for everybody, and as soon as possible."

"You're playing with dynamite. Do you realize?"

"Yes, I know. But I have played with dynamite before, and will again, in search of fairness for all people. I suppose sooner or later I will get my silly head blown off. But until I do, would you be willing to hold off publicity until we think it would be wise to have it? And then we will give your reporters first chance at every story. We would like your help."

Surprisingly (or was it surprising?) the editor agreed to give every publicity support to the endeavor, though he still insisted the course of action was unwise. He proved as good as his word. He held off when his reporters were asked to delay a story, and then gave good coverage when the time came. Later, when the nucleus group and the encourager were attacked by a newspaper from another city, he came to the defense of the enterprise— and won much public support. Furthermore, he became a personal friend of the encourager even though they continued to differ in mutual respect.

Revolutionary Confusion

There are advocates of social change who contend that the troubles of our time are so great that only revolutionary solutions to problems will suffice. And they add that community activities should fit into some such revolution. It is not clear to other community workers what they mean by such language.

Many proposers of community change convince themselves of their own importance by talking about revolution. They insist that they are contributors to "the revolution of our time," or even that they personally are conducting a revolution. Such talk tells more of a desire for sensationalism than of their determination to solve great problems in a fundamental way.

If certain people find satisfaction in using the word "revolution," others fear it. To them it carries an implication of conspiracy and subversion. Many who fear are citizens whose cooperation a nucleus will need for community enterprises.

Because of this fear, an encourager will be wise to avoid use of the word as description of his work. In fact, he should not be and should never become a destroyer of the social order. By using or endorsing the idea of revolution, he can find himself disqualified to act as a mediator between factions in controversy. A revolutionary seeks the triumph of certain social classes over others. An encourager seeks the development that benefits all.

An encourager is an expediter of change, but of the changes people shall think out under the discipline of search for a common good. He can expect to see the citizens he encourages propose many changes. He can expect them to do so in concert with many persons who might have been thought of initially as enemies. He can expect them to encounter some die-hard opposition to important changes, even to those that have majority support. He should be in position to encourage them to win over as much of this opposition as possible. But he should expect also to help them learn how to carry their proposals into action with as little injury as possible to both friends and enemies.

All this means that he seeks the most fundamental changes of all, those which can occur in people's way of thinking and in their consciously chosen schemes of value. People will be changing themselves while they redesign their communities. The encourager will encourage them to achieve a self-chosen discipline to adjust to fundamental changes, even to "the revolutions of our time."

Incidental to this process, there may be times when an active nucleus will decide to take part in events that some activists describe as revolution. Sometimes this will be an extraneous episode. In one city an interracial citizens' council had made more progress in four years than had been made in the previous fifty (according to important Negro leaders). But the news services shortly became filled with headlines and stories about "The Negro Revolution" spreading over the nation. Members of the council (larger nucleus) felt they must get "in the swim." So they set up a parade down the main artery of the city, a demonstration with banners and slogans, generously photographed and reported by the press. But the real job of solving racial problems had been going on for several years, and continued in spite of (?) or on account of (?) the headline-producing parade.

Sometimes the episode fits into the central process of thoughtful prob-lem-solving. It is therefore not perceived as revolutionary. In another city, a neighborhood council also working on interracial problems, faced a situation of the defacement of two houses that had been sold to Negro families in a hitherto all-white city block. During the night unknown vandals painted swastikas and vituperative slogans on windows, doors, and stone walls of the buildings. The council seized upon the unhappy event as an opportunity. Members of the group persuaded a professor in a nearby uni-versity to excuse students who would volunteer to clean up the unsightly mess. The job proved difficult because the paint had sunk into pores in the stone. It had to be sandblasted off, an operation that required many hours of labor.

Again the work was generously photographed and headlined by the city's newspapers. The mayor was persuaded to issue a vigorous public condemna-tion of such practices and to endorse the idea of good homes for all races. The police started on a search for the culprits, who proved to be "invaders" from another part of the city. The total outcome of the defacement and the much-publicized response to it was a considerable growth in public accept-ance of the idea that families might live anywhere they could afford to pay for a home, irrespective of race.

In both episodes, the important thing to note is that the process of self-chosen growth by citizen problem-solving is central. The pressure on public opinion through publicity is secondary. Since an encourager is not a revolu-tionary, he is in a position to help nucleus members choose the episodes of pressure that will contribute to the central process. He is in a position to help them learn self-discipline from episodes of pressure. Even when these have been described as revolutionary, a skillful nucleus can reinterpret them to serve a positive purpose.

A great challenge for citizen nuclei is to discover how pressure for justice can be applied in such a way as to lead to ultimate reconciliation. The cooperation that builds better communities does not come about be-cause anyone proclaims it. It is achieved through learning that is often pain-ful in conflict. But a nucleus should not stop with the conflicts. After the demonstrations, the tumult, and the headlines, comes the quieter, reconciling search for ways in which conflicting persons and factions can live together in mutual benefit. Unfortunately, there is no formula to guide citizens in choosing the kind of pressure that leads to ultimate reconciliation. Nucleus members, with guidance from an encourager, will have to search for the episodes of pressure and publicity which will make for progress yet will allow for the healing of the wounds of revolutionary action.

Giving Up before Starting

Are there problems, in a community and beyond, so complex that peaceful solution is impossible and revolution is the only recourse? We do not know until we, as humans, have achieved much more disciplined thinking to replace the emotional sloganizing that still is accepted as thinking. An encourager has the privilege of helping some citizens begin to achieve this disciplined thinking. Who knows how far people will be able to go with such encouragement?

A warning is pertinent at this point. An encourager should not succumb to the fallacy of giving up before he starts. It is easy to conclude that problems are so difficult as to be beyond whatever human capacity is available. Here is a religious worker who has lived for years among disadvantaged people in an area of "hopeless" poverty. He has concluded that the persons he serves will not respond to his hopes for them. He says so in conversations, speeches, and in writings. Out of his experience he can "prove" that these people cannot grow into the competence to solve their very complex problems.

But this same man, several years before, refused to start a community development process among these people. He was disheartened and sure that the process would not work. So he never tried it. He gave up before he started.

ADDENDUM FOR SOCIAL SCIENCE STUDENTS

At the end of Chapter 6, we followed psychological emphases into the development of individuals. At the end of this chapter, we will follow sociological interests to deal with social structures and the change of such structures. The emphasis upon structures has led sociologists to study communities as social systems. An excellent example of this approach is found in *Community Structure and Analysis,*[1] an anthology of many contributions edited by Marvin B. Sussman. The various writers discuss community typologies (classifying the types), structure, problems, methods of analysis, action, development, and change.

---

[1] Marvin B. Sussman, (editor), *Community Structure and Analysis* (New York: Thomas Y. Crowell Company, 1959).

The action emphasis for change has long been in the forefront of some sociological thinking. An early evidence of this is found in Arthur Hillman's *Community Organization and Planning.*[2] A more recent example is Clarence King's *Working with People in Community Action.*[3] This is an international case book very useful for the newer programs of the Peace Corps and for antipoverty work in the United States.

The whole profession of planning reflects the structural emphasis of sociology as well as the statistical emphasis of economics and the construction emphasis of the builders. Until recently it has not been deeply concerned with the human side, either in outcome or in participation to evolve plans. The bulk of the writings have been directed toward architects, engineers, economists, public officials who lay out streets and plot properties, statisticians who collect data for location of shopping centers, schools, churches, and so on. We shall not offer references to this nonhuman concept of planning.

Instead, we will draw attention to the newly growing sensitivity among planners to human factors. A good beginning is to be found in two magazines. One is in a special issue of the *Journal of the American Institute of Planners,* "Planning and Politics: Citizen Participation in Urban Renewal." [4] The other article is "Individuals: Neglected Elements in Planning," by William J. Platt.[5]

Another reference gives a summary of enphasis in planning, up to the date of publication. This is "The Study and Practice of Planning." [6] One other, of more recent date, gives the application of science and technology for planning in less developed areas. It is "The Political Implications of Urbanization and the Development Process," by Lucien W. Pye,[7] in the volume *Social Porblems of Development and Urbanization.*

On the matter of social change and conflict, there is a very extensive

---

[2] Arthur Hillman, *Community Organization and Planning* (New York: Crowell-Collier and Macmillan, Inc., 1950).

[3] Clarence King, *Working with People in Community Action* (New York: Association Press, 1965).

[4] "Planning and Politics: Citizen Participation in Urban Renewal," *Journal of the American Institute of Planners,* November 1963.

[5] William J. Platt, "Individuals: Neglected Elements in Planning," *International Development Review,* Vol. V, No. 3, September 1963.

[6] "The Study and Practice of Planning," *International Social Science Journal,* Vol. XI, No. 3, 1959.

[7] Lucien W. Pye, "The Political Implications of Urbanization and the Development Process," *Social Problems of Development and Urbanization,* Vol. VII of *Science, Technology and Development* (U.S. Government Printing Office, Washington, D.C., 1963).

literature, most of it hortatory and polemic. We will not summarize these writings, but will draw attention to two publications that put the questions in a more objective social scientific context. The first is an address by Nevitt Sanford at an annual meeting of the American Psychological Association, "Social Science and Reform." [8] The other is a more recent sociological treatment, "Types of Purposive Social Change at Community Level," by Roland L. Warren.[9] The additional readings recommended in this second reference, a brochure, are suggestive but incomplete in dealing with the creative possibilities in the community development process.

---

[8] Nevitt Sanford, "Social Science and Reform," American Psychological Association Annual Meeting, August 28, 1958.

[9] Roland L. Warren, *Types of Purposive Social Change at Community Level* (Waltham, Mass.: Florence Heller Graduate School of Advanced Studies in Social Welfare, Brandeis University, 1965).

Chapter 11

An Encourager in Action

An encourager will find that the kind of friendship he establishes with people contributes more to their self-chosen growth than any specific activity he recommends. That relationship is a highly personal thing, for him, for them.

Should he operate from an office or from his home? Should he live somewhere else and come to people for limited time periods? Answers to these questions depend upon some other questions. Does the encourager have an institutional connection or is he an unattached individual? If he is employed by an institution, to have an office is acceptable. But he should avoid the professional manner that puts him behind a desk and causes citizens to act like applicants for help. If he is tempted to play the role of an executive granting favors, he had better minimize this tendency by operating from his home in the neighborhood.

Should he be a resident in the area of his responsibility or should he live elsewhere and commute in? There are advantages in both arrangements. An indigenous encourager will usually prove more convincing if he lives in the neighborhood. An outside encourager may live elsewhere but should be within easy driving and phoning distance. The question is not basically whether he has an office or where he lives. It is, more importantly, which decisions on these and other questions will bring him into the best relationship of trusting and reciprocal friendship.

Should he attempt to encourage more than one process of citizen development at any one time? Again the answer is not easy to state with finality. If he is an outside encourager with a car, he may simultaneously handle several separate processes with separated groups of people. If he is an indigenous encourager a single major process seems most advisable, although he may meet with half a dozen or more basic nuclei in various parts of his area of service.

His decision as to numbers of meetings, many of which will occur at night or on Saturdays and Sundays, will follow from the schedule he sets for himself. An encourager works most often on the off-hours for citizens. He will have to schedule his time to meet people's availability, but will have to take into consideration also his own convenience and strength.

Relationship to Citizens

His relationships to people must be as profoundly ethical as he can make them. By profoundly ethical we mean that he goes beyond mere truth-telling to concern for people. He should maintain his own personal interests and judgment about people and their activities. He keeps himself free to have his own purposes, apart from their purposes. He communicates his judgments at times and in such a manner as to encourage them into self-correction of their failings.

To members of the nucleus groups he tries to communicate his motives as accurately as possible, but casually. He does not hesitate to mention his motives which differ from theirs, but he works his motives into the conversation so that these are stated without making an issue for dispute. The outcome to be sought is not controversy but the attitude that "of course, intelligent and independent friends have differences. We respect each other's differences."

He should be as open as he can, realizing that this is difficult in an era when all of us tend to shield ourselves behind false fronts. So much is this true that most of us do not even know which is our true self. The encourager should realize that people will have difficulty accepting him as he is, partly because they too are uncertain about their real selves. Still he should remain as open as he can, even though he thereby makes himself vulnerable to misinterpretation.

He should be as honest about himself as he can. This is difficult in an age when most people speak for effect rather than for communication. Again, he may not know which statements are most accurate, in view of the competing motivations with which he must contend. He probably is a complex person with desires that contradict each other, and he may not know which desires will predominate at any one time. Nucleus members may be confused by his inconsistencies, partly because they will be unwilling to grant him the freedom to vacillate as they do.

He should have as great a devotion as he can to people's total growth. They should become convinced of his commitment to serve the overall good, even when they may misinterpret some of his desires. They should conclude that he is to be trusted, even if they misunderstand him.

To nonnucleus citizens he should also try to be open. But if he is realistic he will expect much more misinterpretation from those who know him less intimately. These relative strangers may conclude that no one could have such motives as he claims. They may decide that there are hidden motives, that there is a catch somewhere. This suspicion will reflect their own antisocial motives which they will ascribe to him.

Ethical Behavior Is Complex

To be ethical is not a simple matter. An encourager's intensions to be open, honest and in favor of the common good must be disciplined by other ethical impulses. Openness and honesty must be restrained by compassion. Such a statement is not a justification for dishonesty. Instead it provides a basis for considering how things should be said and how they will be heard. The satisfaction in having spoken the truth or done the right thing is not enough. The encourager must ever be concerned whether his display of virtue will expedite or hurt the growth of nucleus members, and of other citizens in the community.

Ethical behavior must be self-controlled. An encourager should not become or seem to become self-righteous. His ethical conduct needs always to be controlled by a sense of humor. This sense of humor is certainly an awareness of the ludicrous in life. It is also a willingness to accept disappointments as part of a process, and even more, to be amused at the events that put him into an embarrassing position. The attitude we have in mind is an acievement of a perspective, an ability to see people and events in meaningful relationship to long-time trends and objectives.

With this perspective, many annoyances, discouragements, failures, and personal miseries can be seen as amusing in the long run. The most important long-run factor that puts present unhappiness into perspective is compassion for the struggles of an erring humanity. It is this amused compassion that keeps an encourager from becoming unpleasantly self-righteous or so devoted to a noble cause that he cannot laugh at himself.

A contrast is important at this point between his role and that of the dead-in-earnest advocates of needed social change. These necessary people (who are often willing to become martyrs in the cause of voter registration of the underprivileged, or in opposition to war, or in elimination of racial discrimination) are to be admired. Theirs is, however, a determinedly devoted and humorless role. The encourager should understand them. He should appreciate them. He should be thankful that they draw attention to ingrained injustices which he hopes to see corrected. But he has a different role.

Because of their determination to correct some specific injustice, these advocates seldom achieve the long historic and balanced interpretation of events and of themselves. They are more likely to find their satisfaction in suffering for the righteous cause they serve. An encourager should plan to make use of the situations these dead-in-earnest people create. His role is to make the progress that is possible after they have stirred things up. More details on how this is to be done will be found in the next chapter.

Some years ago one of the dead-in-earnest organizations serving Negro rights had organized a single-day campaign to force every restaurant in a city to open its doors. A campaign headquarters had been set up and teams of interracial activists had been recruited to blanket the entire city. The activist teams had been trained as to how they were to act and what they were to say or do in the event they were refused service or even thrown out or beaten up. Each team was to report back to headquarters at the end of the day.

As each team came in, the coordinator of the city-wide effort asked its members how they had fared. One team captain made the reply, "Aw, the whole thing was a flop."

"It was a flop?" asked the coordinator hopefully. "You mean you were refused service? Or you had a rough time?"

"No, nothing like that," was the disgusted reply. "We were served every place we went and nobody objected. It was a complete flop."

In another city, when the interracial council had obtained agreement from all movie-house managers to allow anyone to sit any place in the house, the council spread the word quietly among Negroes. A Negro student who had sworn to boycott all theatres decided to attend a theatre. He confessed later that he had been unconvinced that he would be welcome in an orchestra seat, but had finally decided he would give the theatre one more try.

"And what happened?" inquired a council member.

"I sat through the main feature three times around."

"Why? Was it a good movie?"

"No. It was lousy. I just sat there in the orchestra hoping an usher or the manager would tell me to go to the balcony or get out. I had a wonderful speech all made up to blast him with. But no one interfered with me. I had to sit through a boring movie waiting for something to happen. And I still have that wonderful speech bottled up inside me." It might be added that there is no pain quite like an undelivered speech.

A year and a half later, when eating places were being opened up in the same city, a simliar announcement told Negroes they would be served at every drugstore luncheon counter. A few days after the announcement, another colored young man encountered a council member. The young man was looking bedraggled and unhappy.

"What's the matter with you?" asked the member. "Are you sick?"

"Yeah, I feel sick."

"Why don't you go home, call a doctor, and go to bed?"

"Oh, it isn't that. No doctor can help me."

"Why not?"

"I'm so full of cokes I slop."

"You are? How come? Are you so fond of cokes as all that?"

"No, I'm not. But you see, I didn't half believe drugstore counters would serve me. So I started out and hit every store I could find. And do you know, everyone served me. And I had to drink all of it. I was trying out a scientific experiment, and the experiment backfired on me."

It should be added that the young man recovered and became one of the best of encouragers.

In a southern state an encourager was employed by a state university. The state had a rule that any public employee who worked for racial equality could be dismissed from his job without hearing or without recourse. This particular man regularly violated the rule, being friendly with Negroes, attending their meetings, encouraging them to demand their rights, and even putting on some interracial social-educational events. His prestige was such that state authorities neglected to apply the rule against him, as long as he did not receive too much publicity for his activities. And he often joked about his working for social acceptance of Negroes so much that he might be fired any minute.

At one time a traveling delegation of racially mixed visitors from a northern state, was due to visit some of his citizen groups. The visitors hoped to stay for a day or two. Where could the Negroes in the party be put up for two nights? No hotel would accept them. The encourager scouted around quietly to find some way of getting his colored guests beds and some meals. Finally he found a most unlikely solution to his problem. The women's auxiliary of a war veteran's organization volunteered to take them all in. They were led to volunteer by one woman whose husband had been rescued under fire in the Korean war by a Negro fellow soldier. Said she, "If a Negro is good enough to bring back my husband alive to me, I guess a Negro is good enough to sleep in our house and eat at our table."

After the Negroes, with their white friends, had been entertained in homes, the encourager said cheerfully, "Well, I guess I'll get fired for this one." He never was.

Building Optimism

Part of the ethical attitude toward citizens is an optimism about their potential for becoming better. An encourager will not urge people into processes of self-chosen improvement unless he is convinced that they are capable of such development, and unless he can convince them. How is such optimism established and maintained in the face of contrary apparent facts and discouraging experiences?

We start an answer to this question by pointing out that an encourager is probably already prone to optimism. His decision to become a volunteer to help people proves this. In fact, his cheerfulness about people may be so great as to be unrealistic and naive. It probably needs some disciplining to be useful in helping people. He should expect to have his hopeful expectations destroyed by events again and again. But he should persevere after each setback.

The next point to make in answer is to recommend searching for the long-time perspective. Immediate results are often disheartening because people change slowly. So do social customs and laws. But they do change, and sometimes for the better, if people keep working hopefully.

One of the satisfactions an encourager of community development looks for is the evidence that his influence has had a long-time favorable effect. Months or even years later people will recall gratefully the things said and done which the encourager may have thought at the time were failures. An encourager has to believe that his efforts, if thoughtfully and ethically planned, will have good outcomes—though not always the ones he expected. The experience of a community developer supports this expectation of favorable results, as long as he has an open mind to appreciate the accomplishment that is more meaningful to the developing people than to any formula preselected by the encourager or by the institution that employs him.

An encourager's optimism tends to be contagious; it helps to create hopeful attitudes in citizens, over a period of time. But hope is potent medicine, to be used with care. It is dangerous when people are led to believe that improvement will come easily, or that they can gain wealth or privilege by seizure from others. It is realistic and useful when it refers to those accomplishments which are within the range of people's own capabilities.

An encourager's responsibility is to keep his hopes realistic in terms of what people can accomplish. But he needs to realize that they will often surprise him—later in the development process—by accomplishing things he had not thought they could do.

Record Keeping

We have delayed mention of record-keeping until this essential activity of ethical relation of an encourager to nucleus members could be discussed. Record-keeping is necessary for the proving out of experiments that search for answers to problems. But it is important also for the unique development of the process through which a group moves. The experiments that participants try out will prove little unless records are kept of the process. This means that a research purpose runs through the work done, and an encourager should acknowledge this fact to citizen participants. The research is not set up to produce social science monographs but to help citizens solve their problems and understand the process.

As he gives attention to keeping records, he does so in the light of his ethical relationships. He avoids any recording of discussion and events which is done behind participants' backs. He avoids any research which reduces them to the status of subjects under investigation. He gives attention to the matter of who sets up the experiment and who is to experiment upon whom. If someone external to the process seeks to use people for research purposes, an encourager tries to protect them against any assault upon their dignity of self-direction.

The research that uses people without their participation can do injury to the achievement of personal dignity. In an area of the southern Appalachians, some encouragers had established a relationship of trust with local inhabitants. A graduate student collecting data for a Ph.D. thesis asked for introductions to give these people tests. He wanted to make a study of the personality types of mountain dwellers. The information he wanted was legitimate from his point of view but the process of obtaining it would have reduced them in self-perceived importance. The encouragers refused to allow him to exploit their ethical relationship.

In the same area, two or three years earlier, some other investigators had made a survey to discover the extent of poverty. Interviewers went around from mountain shack to shack, asking what pieces of furniture, dishes, and other "artifacts" (material possessions) each family owned.

Early in the research, the word had been passed around that some strangers were coming around to ask about the things they had in their homes. Who were these inquisitive people probing into other people's business? For want of a more accurate answer, the rumor was passed around that these were representatives of the tax collector's office, and that if they admitted to owning much property, the taxes would go up.

Under the circumstances, is it any wonder that the "scientific" findings about poverty in the area were less than accurate? The relationship between social scientist and people had not been given consideration. But, in addition people had been investigated to obtain static facts about them, rather than encouraged into a process that would open up their potential for favorable change.

Fortunately, there is a type of social science research which is dynamic and which increases people's dignity of self-direction to discover their favorable potential. This is known as action research. In this method, people become researchers upon themselves. This dynamic method gathers information about a process while it is going on, information which is then fed back into the process to expedite or correct it. Thus feedback is part of the process.

Because it deals with dynamic processes of becoming, action research does not work well unless participants are involved. They authorize each experiment, keep some of the records themselves, and use the information accumulated to evaluate, criticize, and correct the process. That is, citizens achieve the dignity of becoming experimenters. They experiment on themselves in collaboration with encouragers and with whatever social scientists can be persuaded to join the cooperative effort. Some scientists will want to write case studies and monographs to publicize the findings of such research. If they are ethically responsible, they will ask citizen participants to be aware of their preparation of conclusions. One of an encourager's responsibilities is to help any cooperating scientists to achieve greater sensitivity to people's developmental needs.

It is always to be realized that the extent and kind of research citizens can indulge in varies enormously from one nucleus group to another. The educational background and previous experience of participants will be determining factors. But even the most unsophisticated people are capable of understanding that they are part of and can help to direct a social experiment. Even illiterates can talk with those who are keeping written records, can recommend changes in the form of recording, and draw attention to events to be recorded. All can join in the self-criticism when records are used for evaluation.

Those with better educational background and wider experience can help on actual record-keeping. The extent they can or will do this is to be discovered by an encourager in each nucleus. Citizen participants become a part of the research to whatever extent their capability will allow—and that capability can always be increased. Even if they do not want to give the time required, it is important that they know and approve of an encourager's keeping records. It is important too that these records be available to them.

What kind of records can be kept? There is no final answer, for citizens must be in on choice of method and forms to be used, as well as on authorization. First, we give an example of an authorization which was not adequate and resulted in insufficient participation. Then we give an example of the same technique of recording, set up and utilized by participants, and used by them as feedback.

In one neighborhood nucleus in a city, the encourager asked if he might make a tape recording of discussion in meetings. There was no openly-expressed objection, so he set the machine up in the midst of the group. At first there were many glances at it, and some evidence that discussion was restrained. Then, participants seemed to forget its presence until one man, expressing opinions freely about other citizens not present suddenly demanded, "Say, is that damned thing still running?" From the general demeanor of other members, as well as this outburst, the encourager concluded that he would be unwise to continue such record-keeping.

In another city neighborhood nucleus, the citizens themselves chose to use a tape recorder. They used it first on a community development expert called in for training sessions. Then they used it on themselves, at regular meetings. They played back the training sessions for new members to be oriented into the work of the group. Then they listened to their own voices replayed at evaluation meetings. They criticized their own contributions to discussion. "Say, did I sound like that?" "Boy, I sounded awfully uncompromising, didn't I?" "I see now how this big row got started, way back in that meeting two months ago." Finally they edited tapes, cutting out irrelevancies and repetitions, in order to make the process clearer to themselves.

This same group also kept running records of conversations, meetings, training sessions, activities, and contacts with resource helpers. (Many nucleus groups have done this. We regard this running account the most basic type of record to be kept.) As a result, participant members were able to gain some idea of the flow of the process through which they were moving. It was also possible for a social scientist to write up and publish (with the interested approval of nucleus members) a case study of the process. The study was then used for training of community development workers.

What is a useful form to be used for such a running account? An encourager is urged to create his own forms, in cooperation with nucleus members. The form created should be easy to fill out after each event, should contain basic needed information, and be such that it can be placed in an accumulating chronological file. The following basic items of information are needed: 1. What was the occasion being recorded? 2. Who was present? 3. The date. 4. The time of day, and time of beginning and ending. 5. What was said, agreed upon, disagreed upon, done? 6. Any sidelights of conversation, conflict, changes of opinion or attitude that would make the process more apparent.

Some record-keepers include also: 1. A statement of the purpose of the recorded event. 2. A judgment (by the record-keeper) of how successful the episode was in serving the purpose. 3. A further judgment as to the emotional reactions exhibited by participants—hostile, friendly, disturbed, calm, apathetic, enthusiastic—and were some people trying to "put something over," or resistant to such salesmanship. But if these judgmental items are included, they should be separated from the factual items. They are useful if several people (the encourager and two or three members) all record the same event. Then it is possible to contrast the judgments of each writer.

Finally, there should be some means of summarizing these accumulating and (hopefully) brief reports. The summary is also something an encourager can work out in cooperation with citizen participants. For greatest value both to participants and to social scientist collaborators, this summary should reduce a large file of separate events to a flow of process that can be used as data for evaluational meetings. When a summary is informative for citizens, it is at the same time valuable for social scientists who want to make action research studies of the process of problem-solving.

Some Generalizations

The keeping of records is not just an exercise in paper work, to be sent to supervisors in some distant office. It is an activity which is integral to the process through which citizens are growing. It helps them understand that process, and correct and guide it. Such records are essential to self-evaluation and redirection of the process. They provide material for the conscious change of personal lives that can occur in the process.

Such record-keeping and record-using makes a fundamental contribution to people's achievement of a tolerant sense of humor, about themselves, about other people, about their shared enterprises. The sense of perspective thus gained rests upon an awareness of the process through which they are moving, of the history they are living. If that perspective is nonexistent in the beginning, it grows gradually as a result of using record summaries to evaluate the process and their work. In the appreciation of that process, people can afford to be a little amused at human frailty, including their own.

If they lose some of their dead-serious, rigid righteousness, they gain the confidence to use the process that will more surely solve their problems.

It is an encourager's ethical relationship with people, and their trust in his good will toward them, that makes record-keeping possible. He can encourage them into a realization that they can contribute to important research. But his relationship of trust can contribute also to their further ethical growth—and to his own.

In his relationship to citizen participants he provides an ideal for the kind of relationship they shall develop toward fellow citizens. He does not teach ethics. He provides an ethical sensitivity attractive enough to make them want to imitate. This is a tremendous and even fearful responsibility.

If presenting himself as a model for citizen self-development seems too great a responsibility for an encourager, he had best overcome his fears. Once he became a volunteer to work with people in communities, he (perhaps inadvertantly) accepted such a role. He can comfort himself with the assurance that there are other persons in any community who also act as models, who may not exhibit as much ethical responsibility as he should.

ADDENDUM FOR SOCIAL SCIENCE STUDENTS

In a time of rapid social change, it is important for people to have a sense of history, to realize that they are a part of history-in-the-making. History is not usually regarded as one of the social sciences, but it should be related to them, and social scientists should have an understanding of the flow of the history of their time.

Such a utilization of historical thinking becomes possible as historians emphasize more the history that is lived. The discipline becomes something more than a record of a bygone past; it is also a continuing record of events that are happening now. These are events which might give some direction to the future. The decisions that individuals and groups make, and their activities that follow decisions, all contribute to the ongoing flow of history.

At least two consequences emerge from utilization of a sense of history to guide development processes. First is the realization that the history that is lived is not concerned only with the great and powerful; it has to do also with the actions of small numbers of people in groups that live in local communities. Even relatively unknown people may contribute to the totality of historical trends.

Second is the realization that those who make the decisions for action have an ethical obligation to consider the consequences of their actions.

If they are helping to guide the future for themselves and their children, they must take responsibility for their contributions to the history that is to be.[1]

The problem of the ethical relationships and responsibilities of social scientists is one which has increasingly disturbed the consciences of such scientists in recent years. The behavioral group in the social sciences [2] has been especially troubled. In fact, they have developed almost as much worry about the impact of their activities as have the physical scientists who released atomic energy in the bombs of mass destruction. Gone is the day when scientists could remain objectively aloof from the human consequences of their research.

Various social, but especially behavioral, scientists point out that though their work may not have the devastating consequences of an atomic war, their skills may be misused to produce all kinds of antisocial results. Among the numerous writings on this ethical question, a recent issue of the *Journal of Social Issues* presents a good introduction, "The Social Responsibilities of the Behavioral Scientist." [3]

On the matter of citizen and social scientist responsibility for guiding the future, M. M. Coady's *Masters of Their Own Destiny* [4] is valuable. This book gives an account of how depressed people of Nova Scotia developed themselves with encouragement from St. Francis Xavier University. Coady was aware of the beginnings of social scientific significance that was found in this religiously inspired experience.

A more recent case study of a developmental program is found in Jack D. Mezirow's *Dynamics of Community Development*.[5] The writer is concerned with a community development process in Pakistan. Mezirow is optimistic about results in the development of people. He concludes that the

---

[1] For a further consideration of the interrelationship of sociology and history, see C. Wright Mills, *The Sociological Imagination* (London: Oxford University Press, 1959).

For an examination of historical concern for social change, see *The Social Sciences in Historical Study* (New York: Social Science Research Council, Bulletin 64, 1954).

[2] The behavioral sciences are usually listed as social and clinical psychology, sociology, cultural and action anthropology, the human aspects of economics, political science, and sometimes, social psychiatry.

[3] "The Social Responsibilities of the Behavior Scientist," *Journal of Social Issues,* April 1965.

[4] M. M. Coady, *Masters of Their Own Destiny* (New York: Harper & Row, Publishers, 1939).

[5] Jack O. Mezirow, *Dynamics of Community Development* (New York: Scarecrow Press, Inc., 1963).

failures of the program were due to institutional rigidities of government bureaucracies. He found it easier to be optimistic about people than about the superstructure of leadership that would control them.

A few years earlier, the National Society for the Study of Education brought together a number of social scientific contributors in its annual yearbook, entitled *Community Education.*[6] This book tells of a number of typical programs as well as of training efforts and some philosophical and social scientific backgrounds. Especially noteworthy is the contribution of the anthropologist Margaret Mead. In Chapter III, she tells of the rapidity with which human beings can change in three case studies, and draws optimistic conclusions about human capacity for guiding change when people are wisely encouraged. The whole book is worthy of careful study, however, because many of the other contributors give further evidence in support of Mead's optimism.

Certain other writings of Margaret Mead should also be read for details in support of an optimism about man's developmental potential. See her *New Lives for Old,*[7] *Cultural Patterns and Technical Change,*[8] and *Continuities in Cultural Evolution.*[9] Mead's writings, like those of other author's who tell of specific instances of human improvement, must be read with discerning attention to catch the implications for an historical process in the midst of the details of change.

Many more records need to be kept, however, both by citizen participants and by cooperating scholars, to build up a theory of the history that is lived and can be somewhat guided by those who live it.

---

[6] *Community Education* (Chicago: The National Society for the Study of Education Annual Yearbook, 1959).

[7] Margaret Mead, *New Lives for Old* (New York: William Morrow & Company, Inc., 1956).

[8] Margaret Mead, *Cultural Patterns and Technical Change* (New York: UNESCO, 1953).

[9] Margaret Mead, *Continuities in Cultural Evolution* (New Haven: Yale University Press, 1964).

Chapter *12*

A Citizen Group in Action

If an encourager is competent, he will give attention to two kinds of social relationships in citizen groups. They are relationships within and outside the group. The two are separate but interrelated. His concern for one will probably predominate over the other at different stages. Normally he will give major attention to the internal functioning of the nucleus group early in the process. He will give more attention to external relationships and responsibilities later.

The internal activity will likely seem more important in the basic nucleus group. The external responsibilities will loom more important in the larger nucleus. There is no clear dividing line between the internal and external social relations. The greater concern for development of individual members found in a face-to-face group cannot be satisfied finally except as experience with great social forces comes through a larger nucleus.

It is easy to become so preoccupied with the personal adjustments and maladjustments of group members as to forget social obligations. And some community developers do just this. They offer training to learners in the field that increases sensitivity to their own motives and their ability to get along with other group members. This inward-turning emphasis represents a group form of the self-interest condemned by psychiatrists.

It is easy to become so preoccupied with the social obligations of the group as to be indifferent to individuals. And some community developers do just this, especially those who talk overmuch about the necessity of organizing a community. They become so interested in coordinating agencies, organizations, or social protest factions, that they ride roughshod over citizens in or out of the groups they are coordinating.

159

We shall try to keep the internal and external dynamics of nucleus groups in balance, so that persons are served while social forces are coordinated to solve those problems that must affect people's lives.

Bringing People Out of Isolation

Many professionally trained helpers of people express surprise when they learn that encouragers are expected to search people out not to sit and wait for people to come to them. The surprise turns to dismay when they are asked to become encouragers who move about. Any educator wants learners to come to his classes. A recreation worker asks people to come to his community center. A minister feels himself a failure if people fail to attend his church. Some social welfare workers prefer to have clients wait upon them in their offices. These professionals, and others, frequently resent the time required to find people wherever they are.

It is elementary in community development that an encourager casts off his professional manner (if he has one) and searches for people in their isolation. This is one reason why a nonprofessional volunteer is so important to the process.

An encourager sets out to reach people who are so apathetic, or suspicious, or resistant that they will not spontaneously come to any center for services. He goes to their homes, if he can get in without their feeling that he is intruding. He goes to their places of recreation. Sometimes these are not very pleasant. The people he seeks may be found in saloons, or in places where gangs gather, or in camps for migrant workers that lack the decencies of life. Sometimes these places are difficult to enter, such as slum dwellings or the apartments of inhospitable residents in high-rise urban renewal buildings. Sometimes people will be found in supermarkets, or in parking lots, or talking over the back fence. An encourager will have to study the people he hopes to reach, to discover what the places are in which they can be met on a basis of simple human exchange. The place should be one where they are at ease, not the encourager. Part of his training is to learn to feel at ease in places strange to his background but where people can be at ease to accept him.

In approaching people he had best assume that they will be unsure of themselves and possibly unwilling to reveal their inner thoughts. He had best assume that the group he encourages them to form will be initially small in size. It is wise for him to make these assumptions about reluctance of response among disadvantaged people, but also among many who are privileged. A few of the people he approaches will respond more readily than others. Some of these can be initiators of a nucleus group. But the ultimate targets of his most conscientious efforts should be those who do not respond easily, those who must be sought out with much patience.

Sometimes he will be able to see a nucleus take form from a population that seems quite homogeneous—all teenagers, all of one race, all poor, all apartment dwellers, and so on. But such seeming homogeneity is likely to be an illusion. The encourager would be wise to assume that there are great individual differences among people who look alike. And if the process is moving toward larger nucleus interest, new and strange persons can be expected shortly to join the nucleus.

When people do come together, beginning even in the exploratory stage, they will need help to come out of personal isolation. Their awareness of their own individual differences will tend to inhibit their ease of communication. The normal process of meeting together and worrying about problems of common interest will tend to bring people out of such isolation. But when certain group members are slow to come out of their shells of timidity, an encourager may want to intervene to increase the social skills of communication, for both the timid and the overbold. He may have to urge the tongue-tied to speak up and the talkative to listen. And he may wish to advise all to be patient with each other's peculiarities, including his own. He may find himself explaining one person to another. His purpose should not be to become an amateur psychiatrist but to build up the atmosphere of tolerant understanding that will encourage group members to come out of their shells.

But this intervening in a process which people work out for themselves is a very delicate operation. An encourager should not attempt it unless he knows the people well and they trust him. In one city project, an inexperienced encourager turned a misunderstanding into a nucleus-destroying conflict when he intervened without the knowledge of the rest of his team. The citizen group was interracial, and the misunderstanding was superficially racial. But there were additional personality frictions that went beyond the Negro-versus-white difficulty. The inexperienced encourager failed to take the complexities of personality relations into consideration. He also failed to give heed to members' desires to protect their own dignities.

The citizen group, still in the basic nucleus phase, was on its way to becoming a larger nucleus, related to a neighborhood and to the whole city. The misunderstanding arose in a meeting when individuals who differed in a dispute lost their tempers. They openly accused each other of foul motives, called each other liars and cheats and stamped out of the meeting by way of adjournment. The unwise encourager then called upon several of the partisans in the conflict, in their homes. He reported to each person just what his opponents had been saying about that person in private conversation.

He said later that he had done this because he was sure no reconciliation was possible until all had faced up to the unhappy "facts" of the situation. The actual result was that all persons in conflict concluded he was a nosey busybody who had revealed thoughts spoken in confidence. They would have nothing more to do with him.

The misunderstanding became so bad that other encouragers on the team felt it wise to do nothing for two or three months, in the hope that tempers would cool off. Then one of them had to go through the process of listening to protagonists—by that time somewhat less angry—describe the unhappy meeting; he kept accusations to himself and passed on only the desires of each person to reconstitute the nucleus. He was able to persuade the antagonists to meet again in the attempt to make progress on the problems that still lay before them. The group members came together, warily at first but with gradually increasing confidence. They ultimately went on to make their group into a most successful larger nucleus—with much encouragement to forget the harsh accusations once made and to seek reconciliation in attention to common purposes. But the unwise encourager had made himself persona non grata. He was never welcome in the group again. And some members of the group dropped out permanently.

Normal misunderstandings had been exaggerated by an unskilled encourager who had failed to be sensitive to people's reactions. He had blundered ahead to tell the painful truth without watching faces or waiting to discover how his intervention was being interpreted. Any encourager who attempts such interference in citizen-directed processes, should do so warily. He should watch for people's reactions and be prepared to desist, and to back off and apologize if he goes too far.

The internal dynamics of the group should be a matter of constant concern for an encourager. He can do much to smooth people's interrelations. But no one is skillful in every situation, and people have a right to resent interference. The encourager should intervene gently. Most of all, he should expect the actual experiences of the process to do most of the job of bringing people out of isolation into sensitive communication with each other.

Making Internal Conflict Creative

He will be wise to anticipate that every nucleus will develop internal stresses and conflicts. Such an expectation is certainly realistic when the group includes human beings of diverse backgrounds and interests. The encourager should not fear conflict within a nucleus. Instead he should prepare to use the conflict creatively. He should cultivate the skills that can use conflict to speed the maturation of group members and increase the group's ability to cope with contending points of view.

Sometimes the antagonisms are personal frictions that require no more than an increase of patience and tolerance of other members. Other members of the group will often spontaneously caution those expressing hostility. If they fail to intervene, a quiet request from an encourager will often induce them to do so. They may need only the encouragement of discovering that someone else feels as they do.

But other antagonisms within the group are deep-seated, reflecting basic differences in ways of thinking and in schemes of value. In the town that built the high school, there were verbally violent wrangles over the decision to undertake such an expensive venture. There was a faction that loudly feared an increase of property taxes. These tightfisted economizers argued against the school in meeting after meeting. Then when they finally discovered they were outvoted, they dramatically stalked out of the meeting, all but banging the door after them. They did not return to the nucleus for several years.

When the school had been built and was being paid for, when other sources of financial help had been tapped, when taxes had not risen as much as the economizers had feared, they were mollified. They returned to the group. But they never proved to be energetic workers for the community good.

Are there citizens who always remain complainers and objectors, motivated mainly by self-seeking impulses? It should be an encourager's hope to win such people over to more generous motivations. He will succeed with some; no one knows how many.

An account of citizen growth, that comes from the southern mountains, more definitely fulfills the hope of favorable change. Sometime prior to development of a nucleus, several landowners had held up progress of road building in a county, by overpricing the value of a right of way across their property. Construction of the road that would benefit everyone had been delayed for over two years; it took that long for their demands to work through the courts. Eventually they did receive a little more money than had been offered initially, but they still complained that they had not been granted as much as they deserved.

Then a community-serving nucleus was formed and many of these people became members. In the area, no awareness of community had existed prior to this nucleus. The loyalty to a local common good had to be built by citizens out of their experience of working together. Shortly these same tightfisted complainers found themselves giving their time for a variety of cooperative work efforts. Finally they contributed money, along with others, to purchase tools and equipment for roadside parks. They became generous enough to provide facilities for visiting tourists that would use the road whose construction they had once delayed.

Some greater complications of citizen change are to be found in a city development project. A larger nucleus split apart on the issue of how to make progress toward preserving and creating a good interracial neighborhood. The split occurred over deep differences on objectives. The differences had never been openly discussed in meetings. They came to group attention in the heat that was generated over the use of the term "block organization." Certain white members of the group spoke strongly in favor of the creation of a block-by-block organization to educate newcomers into the niceties of city living. But every time the term was used, most Negroes stiffened in opposition and demanded, as an alternative, the setting up of a city-wide publicity campaign for open occupancy of houses.

The encourager was at a loss to know why the split occurred or what to do about it. He could not account for the heat engendered by the dispute. It took him weeks of patient inquiry to discover the reason. He found that some years before a white citizens council (now defunct) had tried to set up a block organization to keep Negroes out of the neighborhood. The memory and the term lingered on in Negro emotions.

But the contemporary whites, who held no discriminatory purpose, insisted they knew nothing of this history. Many of them, however, were associated with a university whose administration feared the neighborhood campus would be engulfed by hordes of low-income Negroes. The colored people in the group distrusted the whites from the university, identifying the personal motives of these group members with the administration of the institution that hired them. But these complications of attitude toward other nucleus members had never been admitted in the meeting. In fact, the emotional heat that was produced left the impression that the motivations were largely unconscious.

Additional difficulties lay in the fact that each antagonist spoke not just for himself, but for people and interests he thought he represented. Each seemed to feel that he should uphold a partisan position. If the whites spoke for the university, threatened by a human wave of slum dwellers and slum makers, the Negroes spoke for house-hungry people. Some of these latter were so eager for decent places of residence that they condemned any cooperation with whites as yielding to an enemy that wished to shut them out.

The split was further exaggerated by an arrangement which had been adopted early in the life of the nucleus. Two chairmen had been chosen, one white, one Negro. These two alternated in conducting meetings. This was bad, because it drew attention to racial differences and even antagonisms. An encourager had protested this cochairmanship, at the time it was set up —but not loudly enough.

A solution to the conflict was eventually found, after many stormy meetings. But before adoption of the solution there had been numerous angry exchanges between members. The solution was a simple and obvious one: They would put on a publicity campaign for city-wide open occupancy *and* carry on the educational work with newcomers. The city-wide publicity was obtained through the newspapers which were persuaded to write up events sympathetically. The educational efforts went forward first in the hands of committees; then it was turned over to sections of the neighborhood, each of which had a captain appointed by the nucleus. Negro members never did overcome their antipathy to the term "block organization," so a substitute structure was developed. And the whites were satisfied with the substitute.

That is, a creative solution grew out of the process. The problem for the encourager was not to propose a solution but to keep the process going. To keep people attending meetings was difficult enough in the midst of episodes of open, but unexplained anger, and of verbal attack. But then the process in a vigorous nucleus gave members an opportunity to find their own solution.

Using Expert Resources
without Surrendering to Them

Assume that an encourager has helped a citizen group to grow to a point of consciousness of their own collective identity. They have come out of isolation and apathy within the group. Now, how do they relate, as a group or as separate members, to outside resources of help? They need help from organizations that employ experts, have connections, and can give financial help. The encourager has a responsibility to help them adapt their group skill to their dealings with outsiders.

In making contact with an organization, the approach to its representative should be kept as friendly as possible. Although nucleus members who approach organizations are spokesmen for an important citizen group, they are more convincing if they do not speak as the representatives of power. They are well advised to avoid threats. They should not talk as though they had votes to frighten elected officials or the influence to make life miserable for employed bureaucrats. They should be reluctant to gain cooperation by insisting that they have the backing of powerful people. The proposed plan of cooperative work should speak for itself. The enthusiasm of nucleus members is often contagious. Representatives of organizations and experts can be invited to meet with the group, so that they have a chance to discover that enthusiasm.

Some organization representatives, especially from sources of financial help, will refuse to meet with a nucleus. With them, it is important to demonstrate the competence of the group, that it has studied the problem, knows what it is talking about, and has a worthwhile solution to propose. Competence is added to the enthusiasm of spokesmen for the group.

The organization representatives who can be regarded as experts are more likely to come to group meetings. Before they meet with the group, an encourager can advise them to be human. They may be asked to avoid demanding the honor they may think is due them and the professional manner that invites the honor.

It is possible to assure experts that they will gain recognition out of the merit of their work when it is pertinent to the people's level of understanding. The problem is to help them discover how they may adapt their expertness to the needs that people can articulate. The problem of helping experts to adapt their great skills and knowledges to people's needs is not easy to solve. An encourager will have to be patient with them after assuring them that recognition for their worth will come.

An encourager works with both nucleus members and organization representatives to improve the equality of communication between them. One rural development process reached a point where agricultural extension workers were called in as consultants. These experts misunderstood the invitation, assuming they had been called to take control. But the people proved most uninterested in the mimeographed outlines the experts produced. It took some time for an encourager to persuade them to be more interested in the people than in their outlines. He finally helped them learn how to work out cooperative activities with the people.

Another agricultural extension man had received instructions from his state office to offer free vaccinations for all dairy cattle. He dutifully sent letters to all farmers, but was deeply disappointed by lack of response. When he learned of a community development process, he made contact with an encourager. "What am I doing wrong?" he asked. The encourager pointed out that these farmers insisted upon their right to throw their mail into the wastebasket. "But then," the extension man said, "how do I reach them?"

"Let me draw your dilemma to the attention of the citizen group. Perhaps they will extend an invitation to you."

When the citizens were approached they said they would be happy to invite the agricultural expert to a meeting. They listened attentively. Then all dairymen agreed to set dates for vaccination and to persuade their neighbors to avail themselves of the service. The expert began to learn the difference between a "know-it-all" manner and a "let's-work-this-out-to-gether" procedure.

It is important to maintain the independence of the group that asks for help. This is true especially in the era of federal funding. A nucleus group should not be formed just to receive outside help. It must have a life of its own, so it can survive a refusal of help. It should also be able to survive the granting of funds.

Another citizen nucleus which had sunk a community well and installed water pipes to homes, discovered that its town and surrounding farm area were suffering from a plague of grasshoppers. The group took the initiative to send a delegation to the state capital to ask for help in spraying crops. There they encountered uncooperative officials and returned empty-handed.

When the delegation reported to the group, great was the general indignation. They decided to move ahead to obtain their own equipment and supplies. They assessed each member a small amount and obtained other contributions from neighbors who then joined the group. They assembled enough money to purchase a spray rig and the necessary chemicals. Then they obtained information on operation of such equipment from the state university. They trained some of their members as operators. They then controlled the grasshoppers so successfully that their services were requested by other farmers. Shortly they rented out their equipment and their operators. From this rental income they obtained enough money to repay their expenses.

The cleanup of the grasshoppers was important. So was the raising of money to pay for their venture. But more important than either outcome was the experience that built the independent strength of the group.

A larger nucleus in a city slum neighborhood concluded that poor use of English was one of the major causes for poverty. It took the initiative through an encourager to obtain help from a literacy-teaching organization which had local offices. Experts were sent in who trained people to act as literacy teachers. The experts were good, not only in their field of specialty, but also in the ability to pass their skill on to other people.

A Nucleus in Action Has Influence

Not only can a nucleus serve its community by utilizing help from outside resources, it can have influence upon outside organizations and individuals of power. A larger nucleus is especially influential. Such a group works most convincingly when it is active in the spirit of cooperative community development.

In a small city, a human relations council discovered it could make substantial progress in the racial integration of publicly used places of business. It quietly persuaded all motion picture theatres to do away with segregated Jim Crow balconies for Negroes. Then it set out to open the restaurants to all customers of every race. The theatres were not too difficult, though several months of persuasion by nucleus members were needed. But the restaurants presented more of a problem.

Some years before attempts had been made to force integration upon the city's eating places by sit-ins and picketing that made the newspaper headlines. As a consequence, restaurant managers had formed a mutual protective association to refuse service to Negroes, in spite of the fact that such action was contrary to state law. The protective association had successfully resisted all pressure toward racial integration for five years. Its strength began to weaken only as the human relations council grew in influence and persuaded one restaurant after another to open its doors to Negroes. Members of the human relations council were successful in persuasion because they were friends of the managers and carried the spirit of their group to them and to the community as a whole.

One restaurant resisted, however. Its manager had been the original organizer of the anti-Negro protective association. He knew of the human relations group, but was stubborn against its influence—until another demonstration erupted in his establishment, the largest restaurant in the city. Then he changed his strategy; he called a member of the council (a friend of his) to complain about damage done to his business. The nucleus member agreed to come down and talk this matter over with him, bringing an encourager of the group to join the conversation. But he pointed out to the manager that no one connected with the human relations group had known of the demonstration until the phone call from him.

After listening to the manager's side of the story, the two visitors did two things. They sympathized with the owner-manager, assuring him that they wanted him to succeed in his business. Then they recommended that the restaurant serve Negroes on an experimental basis for one month to see if such change of policy would increase or decrease the volume of business. They assured the manager they were convinced no injury would come to his business. The manager thought this over and finally agreed to a tryout period, "because I don't want those wild characters coming back again and disturbing my customers." But then he asked for the help of the council. Would they select some nice Negroes and introduce them gradually, one in a group the first time, two the next time and so on. The council members agreed and set a date for the first racially mixed party.

The first service to a Negro in this experiment occurred after the theatre one evening. The one Negro present was a member of the human relations group. He was treated with the utmost courtesy (the manager had instructed his waitresses well). After that memorable evening meal he said, "Gosh, all my life I have wanted to eat there. Now, I don't think so much of the place. And as for the food, it wasn't so hot either. But then they were awfully polite, too much so, in fact."

Thereafter, the number of Negroes increased in parties at the restaurant, including women as well as men, and older people as well as students. There were no unhappy incidents of any kind. No one complained, and there was no newspaper publicity. At the end of the month, the encourager and council member checked with the owner-manager of the restaurant. Had his business suffered any? "No, not at all." Had it improved? "Oh yes, a little, but that might be seasonal, I don't know."

"Well, do you think you might serve Negroes from here on out?"

"Oh yes, I think so. They seem to be nice people." Then after a little thought, "But I reserve the right to put anybody out who creates a disturbance and annoys my other customers."

The community council quietly passed the word that all Negroes would be welcome thereafter. The encourager and several members told the manager that he did not need their services to introduce Negroes any more. He agreed and finally remarked, "Say, tell those Negro guys I will be glad to serve them now, if they will behave themselves."

Why did the stubbornly resistant manager finally agree to grant Negroes the dignity of service in his restaurant? Perhaps because the prevailing spirit of the times was changing in that direction, aided by the work of the human relations council. But even more, because a group of his fellow citizens (for whom he had gained a grudging respect) granted him the opportunity to discover for himself that a community-serving ideal would work.

Might other resistant persons and the institutions they control respond similarly if given the opportunity?

Some Conclusions about Citizens' Groups

The procedure for making group life satisfying and productive is something an encourager will have to search out in each unique nucleus with which he works. There is a spirit he should seek to develop in the group; there is no predictably proper methodology. He should build up an atmosphere which helps members to cope with their group conflicts so that they may acquire skill to be transferred to other conflicts and pressures external to the group.

There are some suggestions for building that atmosphere. In order to make these clear, a distinction should be made between his presence as an encourager who takes part in discussion as contrasted with his activity in interrupting or redirecting the nucleus process.

He should constantly contribute to the group atmosphere by being present, by staying awake and attentive, by smiling, by making remarks or raising questions in discussion. He intervenes, however, when he concludes that something has gone wrong and he is called upon to take the initiative. The initiative he shows could result in disaster and expose him to condemnation. But if intervention is wise and skillful, it will tend to increase the amount of citizen control of the process.

1. When meeting with people, he should watch faces and listen to tones of voice as well as to spoken words. He should try to understand the frictions and misunderstandings between members, than cultivate a manner which shows he has confidence in their ability ultimately to work their way through to creative compromises. He should interrupt the process when he believes he can expedite growth of ability to create their solutions to problems.

2. Often antagonisms between people are unconscious or are only dimly conscious to them. These unstated conflicts are usually more devastating than those given open airing. When the unconscious conflicts erupt, they often surprise the person who explodes as much as they do his friends.

   He should not necessarily intervene at the time of emotional explosion but should try to understand what is going on. This understanding tends to guide his manner and tone of voice. If he speaks up at a time of emotional tension, he should do so cautiously, watching for subtle reactions from members.

3. He should time his interventions carefully. When people are excited in the heat of anger, for instance, they do not welcome any conciliator, even one who understands and believes in their ultimate growth. It is better to wait until they cool off or otherwise reach a more receptive mood.

4. Conflicts within the group express both antagonisms between persons and their awareness of pressures upon them from outside. These pressures can come from families or friends, or more characteristically, from factions or organizations group members believe they must represent. Usually a member will be more inflexible and stubborn when he believes he is spokesman for a faction in the community than when he is spokesman for himself alone.

An encourager should be patient to allow for these (often self-appointed) spokesmen of community conflict to have their say. He can try to persuade other members of the group to be equally patient—up to a point. When the airing of grievances from community factions interferes with the on-going work of the group, he will have to intervene to help the process continue.

5. He should do all he can to build up the self-assurance of group members so they can meet representatives of outside help on a man-to-man basis. That self-assurance can be built by keeping awareness of the nucleus group central. When members approach external sources of help, they do so in the name of the group. They bring whatever help they are able to recruit back to the group and they invite outsiders into group meetings.

6. He should try to humanize the experts and others who come to the group. This is a point at which he has much to contribute. Most experts and persons in positions of prominence prefer to protect themselves behind fronts of professionalism or status. But some, perhaps many, long to find ways by which their expertness and prominence can be adapted to the understanding and needs of ordinary people. He can help those who have this longing to search for ways of effective adaptation. He may find that many more experts want to cooperate with citizen groups than he would have predicted before starting to search for them.

7. He should realize that the isolation and apathy of individuals can be replaced by the self-respect that is achieved when people discover they have influence in the community in which they live. He will be able to help many people find the dignity that comes when important people listen to them.

8. Some items of wisdom he can offer to citizens in groups that seek influence are these:

   a. Seek for prosocial motives even in opponents. They may surprise by being generous, in their own way.

   b. They should be wise enough to interpret the other fellow's generosity as part of the total interest of all citizens.

   c. They should not be pious about good impulses. They should assume the person they want to influence has the selfish motives they have. But they should assume that the other person has good motives also, motives at least as good as theirs, or maybe even better.

   d. In influencing persons to change, they should always leave them some opportunity to make a decision by their own choosing.

They should not force them into the position of merely doing as they say, especially if the change asked is a generous one. They should let them take the credit for doing a community-serving act in their own way.

ADDENDUM FOR SOCIAL SCIENCE STUDENTS

For a summary of research on the internal dynamics of groups, see *The Human Group* by George C. Homans.[1] This book also presents some case studies of groups in a number of activities of modern life. The author starts with the internal life of the group and goes on to consider external pressures upon members. The book was published in 1950. In a later book, published in 1961, *Social Behavior, Its Elementary Forms,*[2] Homans brings the summary up to date. The author is, however, overly concerned with controls exercised by a leader. This emphasis is understandable, since he is writing about many of the existing forms of group behavior found in gangs, industrial organizations, and community associations, set up to control citizens. In community development, the emphasis is upon another type of group, that which is controlled increasingly by members.

For a research examination of this latter concept of group life, see *Group Centered Leadership* [3] by Thomas Gordon. The author's subtitle is quite significant, "A Way of Releasing the Creative Power of Groups." The book gives a case study of an experimental workshop group that found its own leadership in a highly permissive atmosphere. It gives an account of what happened when several people were assembled together for the experiment. Their motivations grew out of their interest in the experiment. This contrasts with motivations of participants in community development processes, which grow out of a desire to serve community need. The findings of this experiment are not, therefore, directly applicable to community-serving citizen groups. But they are suggestive for experiments in the community context.

A research account that carries the analysis of internal group function-

---

[1] George C. Homans, *The Human Group* (New York: Harcourt, Brace & World, Inc., 1950).

[2] George C. Homans, *Social Behavior, Its Elementary Forms* (New York: Harcourt, Brace & World, Inc., 1961).

[3] Thomas Gordon, *Group Centered Leadership* (Boston: Houghton Mifflin Company, 1955).

ing into community living is found in an issue of *Human Organization*.[4] Three articles are collectively entitled, "Community and Regional Development: The Joint Cornell-Peru Experiment." The first two articles tell of a community development experiment in the Peruvian Indian community of Vicos. The accounts are valuable in that they tell of a process that encouraged villagers to work out their own goals while bringing themselves more into the world of modern life. The first is "The Processes of Accelerating Community Change," by Allan R. Holmberg and Henry F. Dobyns. The second is "Summary of Progress and Reactions," by Henry F. Dobyns, Carlos M. Monge and Mario C. Vazquez.

It is, however, the third article which is of greatest interest to this chapter, "Integrating Communities into More Inclusive Systems," by Harold D. Lasswell. The author is keenly aware of the personality factors, conscious and unconscious, that effect the behavior of members of the controlling council of citizens. He relates their personal interactions to the pressures and social forces of the surrounding community.

---

[4] "Community and Regional Development," *Human Organization*, Vol. 21, No. 2, Summer 1962.

Chapter 13

Reconciling
Community Conflict

A community-serving nucleus which an encourager helps local people to create has an obligation to mediate the conflicts that surround it. It cannot avoid dealing with many organizations, movements, social forces, and individuals in controversy. But it should go further. It should act as a conciliator of conflict since it seeks the kind of community that makes room for variety. It can become that voice of responsible local welfare which has been sought by separate social agencies, clashing factions, and administrators of federal improvement programs.

A neighborhood larger nucleus should be a social instrument for conciliation of clashing interests and for cooperative planning. But often program administrators are reluctant to turn over money or responsibility to such a group (even though they may call loudly for citizen participation in federal planning). How can they be persuaded to use such an independent group? The answer lies first with the citizens and with the encourager who might stir their initiative. They must bring such a group into being and establish its independence by having it carry on some active projects without outside help. Out of such activity will grow the members' awareness of the group's importance as a coordinator of community interests.

Then members of the larger nucleus and the encourager should let the executives of government, of private agencies, of competing factions, and of service programs know that an authentic voice of community-seeking interest is available. In time these executives should learn that there is a coordinating function for the larger nucleus that will never be taken over by welfare professionals. Part of the responsibility for an encourager is to make this function clear both to nucleus members and to program administrators of local and federal government. The function will be made clear by talking about it, but even more by carrying various activities to successful completion.

The Nature of Community Conflict

It is possible to describe and classify community conflicts as irritant worries. It is more useful to classify them according to hopes for reconciliation. The nucleus which citizens have created with an encourager's help should be set up in such a way as to make this reconciling function possible.

The key to resolution of community conflict is to be found in the establishment of personal relationships between the disputant organizations and factions. The pattern for personal understanding and tolerance found within the nucleus is extended to organizations and factions external to that group of friends who can differ with each other. Nucleus members do the extending, out of the richness of their satisfaction with these internal relationships.

Note that the ideal these members seek is not agreement, in either nucleus or in surrounding community. It is rather understanding, which searches for ways of living together in the midst of differences. The clash of points of view and of competing interests will always exist. Nucleus members are encouraged to cultivate the skills to help people live positively in the midst of mutual antagonisms. These skills are cultivated by working together to solve specific problems.

The most manageable conflicts are those of indigenous local origin. These may vary from simple personal dislikes between individual neighbors to factional rivalries and organizational competitions. An encourager's temptation will be to oversimplify by reducing complex misunderstandings to a single sloganized rivalry. Thus what appears to be a conflict between the underdogs and the privileged may have all kinds of complications of individual likes and dislikes, of varying amounts and kinds of personal inadequacy. Thus it is very easy to believe a conflict is one between Negroes and whites, without taking into consideration the factional differences among Negroes and the differences of attitude among whites.

In addition to these personal or factional disputes are competitions between agencies and organizations that work on the local scene. Sometimes these take the form of rivalry for no more than attention or funds. Or they may be more deep-seated in competition for members, or between churches.

Or these may emerge in open and publicized disputes that verge on violence, as in strikes or boycotts or in protest demonstrations.

More complex, and more difficult to mediate, is the local conflict which is an aspect of a national or international dispute. Local labor-versus-management trouble may reflect a more extensive dispute. It is difficult for a neighborhood or even city-wide nucleus to help resolve a strike that involves their neighbors when the real decisions on settlement must be made in a distant city. Church rivalries may also reflect national or even international denominational policy. Finally there are national organizations for combat that may have local chapters, or may send in representatives, to stir local people into protest.

A neighborhood-based nucleus can offer mediation for the local aspect of the large-scale problems. There always is a unique local solution to be found, even though it be part of a national trend. In order to help citizens find this solution, nucleus members need to inform themselves about policies adopted and decisions made elsewhere. Then they must pass this information on to citizens outside the nucleus, so that more people realize that the local conciliation is important to the national solution of the problem. Nucleus members coordinate their local mediation with problem-solving in other localities on the national scene.

Even more complex is the dispute which local protagonists believe is part of a great movement or historic cause. Mediation is difficult enough when the cause is part of the program of a distant national organization. But it is even more difficult when a cause is interpreted as an often ill-defined righteousness. The protagonists may be either local citizens or outside "invaders."

It should be noted, however, that the defensive reaction against outsiders is almost always an alibi for doing nothing. The cry that "We have had good relationships with our own people until these foreign agitators came in and stirred them up," is one heard in every section of the nation. It usually means, "We do not want to face the problem. We want everything to remain as it is." The blaming of outsiders is to be regarded as a doubtful explanation, not because the accusation may be untrue. It may be true. It is to be doubted because the alleged good relationship is usually one of master to servant. The harmony that has supposedly existed in the past is not one of equals who respect each other's differences as a basis for negotiation of change.

The presence of agitators, indigenous or foreign to the local scene, should be welcomed by nucleus members who seek reconciliation. The agitators will not succeed over a period of time unless they draw attention to some genuine grievance. To bring the grievance to public attention is good, even though nucleus members must be careful to avoid becoming partisans themselves. If conflicts are to be resolved, grievances must be faced. If there is to be genuine reconciliation, eloquent spokesmen must be found for all conflicting interests. The difficulty in community after community of the past has been that too often most of the eloquence and access to news media was found on the privileged side of each argument. The agitators tend to establish a balance in conflict, which can then be conciliated.

When something near a balance of eloquence and publicity exists, a dispute can be mediated creatively by nucleus members. It becomes possible for them to set up the occasions for negotiation between mutually respecting equals, and to press for change that meets the interests of all factions in the controversy.

How can a neighborhood nucleus mediate the many controversies that will come to its attention? We do not yet have enough experience to have sure answers. We do not have too many episodes to cite. An encourager must struggle with this uncertainty. We can suggest some approaches for his beginning. Then he must experiment further for better answers.

Bringing Conflict into the Nucleus

One method for resolving community conflict by personal contact is to bring the antagonists right into the nucleus. This occurs best when representatives of clashing interests become members. But an encourager must often take steps to be sure that the frequently excluded interests and factions are invited in.

In one community project, the initiators of a larger nucleus in a small city came from the chamber of commerce. The encourager was convinced the initiators' motives were generous, that they meant to serve all citizens. But he had to recommend strongly that nucleus membership not stop with the chamber of commerce. Specifically, he called for representation of women's groups, organized labor, and churches. (There were no ethnic minorities in this city at that time). The initiators were surprised at his demand, but willing to follow it once the matter had been drawn to their attention. Prior to the encourager's insistence, they had just never thought of inviting other interests into a community improvement program. They had not realized that in failing to invite these others they might be creating a future opposition. Inspired by the idea of all-inclusiveness, they then made a survey of all organized factions and groups in the city, to make sure they had not excluded any that might be significant enough to turn into a future opposition.

It is wise to include the normally excluded factions from the beginning. It is possible, of course, to invite them into membership at the time of an open conflict, but then explanations and even apologies are necessary to account for their having been overlooked earlier. But it is better for an invitation to come at a time of crisis than not at all.

In including representatives of clashing factions, it is wise to inquire whether all important subfactions have been invited. For example, all labor interests will not be represented by including a person from just one union, usually the noisiest. Churches of all denominations should be welcomed, not just those the initiators belong to. Not all those invited will respond, but the door of welcome is left open for them to come in later. And, in the meantime, nucleus members should keep in touch with the self-excluded factions by keeping them up to date on problems discussed and progress made.

The wisdom of including rival interests is illustrated by a larger nucleus in a small city that had representation of both management and labor from the beginning. There was one huge factory which dominated the local scene. There were several labor unions in this and other business enterprises, but the largest union was a local of a national federation. The citizen group also included churches, civic and veterans groups, service clubs, and womens associations. The group had been meeting in the cafeteria of the factory until a strike, called by the national union, set up a picket line in front of all entrances. Then the meeting was shifted to the basement Sunday school room of a nearby church. Union members would not cross the picket lines, and no one, not even those in management, wanted to force labor representatives to violate their union loyalty.

At a meeting held during the strike, citizens came together to discuss not the strike, but garbage collection and disposal. At first, the management and labor representatives sat and glared at each other. Perhaps their antagonism was increased by the discomfort of the chairs; they had to squeeze adult bodies into chairs designed for children. But after a time, their interest in the proper handling of garbage was so great that they forgot their discomfort and antagonism. They joined together to seek solution of a problem important to both factions. They agreed upon a solution to the garbage problem. Then a week later the strike was settled.

Within a nucleus group, a step toward resolution of conflict can be taken by working together, not necessarily on the dispute that separates members, but often upon some other mutually worrying problem. The experience of common concern and common endeavor tends to produce mutual trust which eases attitudes toward other problems in dispute. Cooperation on lesser problems makes solution easier for more difficult controversies.

Members of a nucleus tend to learn from the process of dealing openly with a dispute. They can learn to look upon conflict as an opportunity for increasing their social skills. They can develop abilities to differ in mutual respect and to listen to each other. They can be led to acquire the habit of collecting facts before making judgments. They can learn to experiment with a proposal that all or most have agreed upon. To expedite such learnings is part of an encourager's obligation. Out of such experience comes the further willingness to try again and again even though any one suggestion is found faulty when tried out. All this is possible within a larger nucleus, assuming that antagonists can be brought to discuss and work together. A period of time is necessary, during which members use the continued association of dissimilar people to establish new habits, new attitudes, and new expectations.

There is another way of bringing antagonists into a larger nucleus. This is to use such a citizen group as a sounding board for the statement of clashing points of view. The process of personal change that rests upon continued association cannot then be counted upon, so the main benefit gained is an airing of grievances. Some better ways of using a nucleus to resolve community-wide conflicts need to be found. It is possible to use the existence and spirit of a nucleus to pervade the community as a whole, if members will experiment with methods of mediation.

Using a Nucleus Experimentally

Beginning suggestions for community-wide reconciling activities of nuclei can be found in some stories of religious conflict. In one project, when the encouragers first came into a rural area, even before a larger nucleus was formed, they heard tales of the bitterness between a Roman Catholic priest and an Episcopalian rector. One never knows how much to credit such tales. But any encourager will encounter them. And they will cast a pall of gloom over the work, whether true or not.

In this case, the encouragers heard how one man had called his religious rival all kinds of hard names. He said he would punch the other on the nose if they ever met. The opponent had replied in kind, according to eager informants.

The encouragers managed to start a community development process with an active nucleus or more accurately, several nuclei in succession. One had to be started, and another, until a permanent one was finally developed. Both of the religious rivals and their churches became interested in the process. The Episcopalian rector became active first, helping in the earliest stages. The Catholic priest came in later, and worked even harder than his rival to speed the process. For a time, both men came to visit the nucleus meetings and to bring various kinds of support—but on different days.

About this time, the encouragers wondered if the two rivals would eventually come to cooperate on some work project. The two men were finally brought together on a hot afternoon, when half the countryside had turned out to work together. They greeted each other warily at first, then in a more and more friendly fashion as they indulged in physical labor together. They became friends though they remained denominational rivals.

In this case, a process of reconciliation began to occur outside the nucleus, but was spurred on by the nucleus. Its members extended their skills and concern for the common good to include clashing factions beyond the group.

In a state where Catholic priests are allowed to join the local (and usually Protestant) councils of churches, the reconciling authorization was preceded by a number of episodes of community cooperation across denominational lines. Several years earlier there had been a history of bad blood between the two religious groups. There were tales of fist fights and spitting back and forth, of church windows broken by vandals, and so on. Whether these tales were true or not, some community development encouragers were informed that "you just can't cooperate with people in *that* church."

Despite the tales of conflict, several community development nuclei began working together for the good of people in all churches—and even those in no churches. Out of these many local experiences came friendships among laymen, then between ministers and priests. Whether these episodes led to the official approval of Catholic membership on councils of churches is quite uncertain. But we may say that an accumulation of many local experiences can produce changes of attitude that eventually effect distant administrators.

In many local nuclei all over the country, it becomes important for encouragers to take this initiative as reconcilers in a time when major disputes tear communities apart—and when activist protesters have disturbed so many consciences. The issues in dispute are often national or international, but these can erupt in disturbances on the local scene.

In cities all over the land, the race issue, the poverty problem, the clash between factions on war and defense policies, and labor-management disputes by the dozen, have been so publicly protested that consciences have been rubbed raw. What follows from the soreness? Continued rubbing? Resistance against the discomfort? Callousness toward further disturbance?

Or can some positive steps be taken to right whatever wrong has been agitated?

Larger nuclei are peculiarly qualified to meet this challenge, beginning on a neighborhood basis. They are set up in such a way as to utilize the work of the activists. They can mediate local conflicts in a manner that serves the good of all citizens, not just the interests of the agitators. Dramatic protests seem likely to become a permanent feature of the life of American cities. Community development nuclei can become the local social instruments for reconciling the impulses that grow out of the resultant disturbed consciences.

There are at least two developments of our time that promise to make publicly dramatic expressions of dissent a permanent part of American life. One is the emergence of a new breed of agitator, one who appeals to an uneasy democratic and Judeo-Christian conscience, one who cannot be dismissed as a foreigner with an alien ideology. The other is a greater disposition to tolerate such public protests, rather than cut them off with the ruthlessness of the past.

The prototype for the new breed of agitator is found among the members of the New Left. These disturbers of complacency are characterized by freedom from doctrinal loyalties, such as adherence to the various brands of communism, socialism, or Marxism. Instead, they advertize themselves as people who will put on a dramatic demonstration of dissent whenever their consciences are outraged—and on any issue.

They do not appeal to any ideology which can be convincingly described as anti-American. And the conscience to which they respond is shared by many less demonstrative Americans. There are many who entertain at least minor doubts about the rightness of things as they are. These citizens, disturbed by appeals to conscience, call for a tolerance of the New Left. But community development nuclei are in a position to go beyond mere toleration of these nonideological disturbances. They can use the uncomfortable consciences to provide motive power for positive improvement. The clash between complacency and awakening consciences is the starting point for reconciliation.

Another but related opportunity for neighborhood nuclei is found in the clash between Negroes who demand first-class citizenship and whatever "establishment" denies them recognition. In states of the old confederacy, this clash is likely to take the form of Negroes versus "the southern way of life." In northern states it is more likely to take the form of the black man against various welfare services, the police, and white property owners.

In either south or north will be found demands that Negroes be granted special privileges to compensate for the generations of slavery and bad treatment. A community development encourager, will not be in position either to grant or refuse this demand. That decision will be made by other people in authority. Instead his task will be to stir these victims of discrimination into initiative to help themselves. It will be his job further to bring these newly energized victims into cooperation with those privileged people whose consciences have been stirred.

His job, in other words, is to stir Negroes, and all other victims of injustice, out of the expectation that their salvation lies in gaining power to force concessions. Whatever is granted to these unfortunates is less important than what is done *by* them *with* the help of sympathetic friends. Any permanent progress for them must be made within the context of a better community for all citizens.

A nucleus, which should contain Negro as well as white members, will seek to find total-community-serving answers to conflicts produced by either the New Left or by Negro demands.

A first step for a nucleus that proposes to utilize either of these demands upon conscience is to improve attitudes of its own members. Members need to be convinced that a legitimate grievance lies in back of dissent or demands, no matter how much they may disapprove of the excesses of protesters. Then their obligation is to study the situation that produced the protest, to talk with the demonstrators, and even more with the victims in whose behalf the protesters claim to speak. The grievance, the injustice, the contending points of view, should be made as clear as possible to nucleus members, and then to all citizens. A nucleus which has developed a reputation as a seeker for the common good will usually find that some newspapers will publicize their interpretation of the grievances, even though editors and reporters may not agree with the demands.

A next step is for nucleus members to realize that there is almost always need for victims of injustice to find authentic and responsible voices. Permanent voices are needed which can make grievances articulate and can keep drawing attention to injustice until solutions are found. These voices should be permanent, to negotiate solutions and renegotiate them, and try these out, again and again, over the years. Members of the nucleus then should encourage the victims of discrimination to perfect their own organizations, choose their own spokesmen, and give these voices of grievance an opportunity to be heard. They can invite them to address the nucleus first, for improvement of their presentation, then to address other community meetings and organizations.

The training of spokesmen for victims of discrimination is necessary for the years to come, because the ingrained injustices of the generations will not be quickly or easily corrected. Neither the complacent who want no change nor the protesters have the answer. There are too many hidden and long-unrecognized grievances to be corrected. There is too much indifference among the privileged and too much inarticulateness among the victims. The problems are too complex to be solved by emotional sloganizing. Nucleus members can thank the protesters for making an issue of hidden injustice. But they will not expect the protesters to settle down to the long, patient pull of discovering workable solutions.

A responsibility for nucleus members, therefore, is to make sure that people with a grievance have adequate spokesmen. These spokesmen need to be informed and persistent, even stubborn, in continuing to state their case. They need also to be encouraged into negotiation with the representatives of privilege. If a nucleus is to bring about reconciliation, there must be a clash of contending points of view. The spokesmen for privilege usually are already eloquent; the spokesmen for the victims of injustice need to become so. Then workable programs of improvement are sought in the midst of the clash of sharply stated opposing interests.

The essence of conciliation is not found in an early harmony of consensus. It is achieved out of the travail of open dispute. But disputants need to achieve the faith that a community of good for everyone is discoverable. Nucleus members are the sharpeners of clashing differences, but they are also the builders of the faith that a creative compromise can be found that will benefit all factions.

Nucleus members take the initiative to bring the disputants into the same room, so that people who have been attacking and threatening each other in absentia meet each other face to face. Often a nucleus can bring about such a confrontation for the first time. Nucleus members then urge each contender to state his case—but then to keep on meeting together again and again, until some consensus can arise out of discussion.

An encourager or nucleus members can seldom propose the consensus which will finally be adopted. He and they can offer sample solutions by way of priming the pump of discussion, and by way of strengthening the hope that solutions can be found. But that which is finally adopted is usually something which grows uniquely out of discussion. His job, and that of the nucleus is to keep people meeting until some commonality of interest emerges. He can draw attention to the points of essential agreement by way of encouragement to wrestle more optimistically with the disagreements. If nucleus members can persuade representatives of contending factions to keep talking hopefully, then such problems as those that stir the New Left and agitators for Negro rights can be expected to find resolution.

An encouraging nucleus needs to discover and perfect skills that speed the process of finding creative consensus. When the disputants come together, it is possible to get them to agree to certain ground rules. Each point of view should be given the floor, but for an agreed-upon limited time period so that all may be heard. The selection of a neutral chairman or discussion leader (sometimes from among nucleus members) will facilitate adoption and enforcement of ground rules. Then it is possible for nonpartisan nucleus people to press diplomatically for the achievement of some proposal to be acted upon. The purpose of discussion is to arrive at some conclusion acceptable to most or all present. Finally, nucleus members can quietly build the expectation that any agreed-upon solution is to be tried out experimentally and then modified as it is evaluated. But in trying it out, each faction will expect to contribute to the action, each in its own way. These expectations are built into discussion from the outset by quiet words of comment and even reassurance.

If the discussion reaches a stalemate, other initiatives by nucleus members are possible. It is often possible to recommend the finding of some problem (even a relatively unimportant one) which most of the parties in contention will agree to concentrate on for a time. The experience of agreeing to discuss, or even better, to do something about the shared concern will often make easier the reexamination of the stalemated important issue. This method for speeding consensus is carried over from the experience of a closely knit nucleus.

Many cities, wounded by episodes of dramatic dissent, or fearful of such demonstrations, have influential citizens who wish to move toward solutions of important problems. Their eagerness to move presents an opportunity for a nucleus of nonpartisan but community-seeking citizens to bring together assemblages of contending factions. Such committees for conciliation can be set up by a nucleus on a neighborhood basis. Then several nuclei can be combined to represent a city as a whole. It is often desirable to obtain the blessing of city authorities, but the actual assembling can be done unofficially.

A neighborhood nucleus can bring into being an assemblage of social forces, organizations, and agencies to evolve programs for federal support. In city after city, federal funds for antipoverty programs has been delayed or even spent for questionable activities because there was no genuine focus of total citizen interest. The factional community fragments have never had the opportunity to seek a consensus. A nucleus that encourages a process can call them together in an assemblage that will meet continuously until they come up with creative ideas. A nucleus takes the initiative to call the assemblage together and to keep it meeting. It does not become an operator of a program. It remains free to be the interrelater of conflicting factions and the expediter of the process that produces the consensus for a program.

This is the way an encourager can pass on his function and skills to the larger nucleus he helps citizens to create. He urges the nucleus to pull together noncooperating factions for community decision and action. These fragments of community are organized not for conflict, not for acquiescence to welfare planning, but for good will that serves everyone.

When Reconciliation Fails

What does an encourager do when a nucleus fails to mediate conflict in spite of his best encouraging? There are many reasons for such failure. The laws that govern local behavior may be antiquated or contradictory and difficult to change. Social custom may grant advantages to the privileged which they will not even discuss, let alone surrender. Certain people will enjoy disrupting whatever process of reconciliation is undertaken. They may do so because of their own inner maladjustments or because of loyalty to some ideology that seeks to prove democratic cooperation cannot work.

In the face of failure he may have to admit that the conflict is beyond his competence to handle. This is especially true when he is probably on the local scene for a limited period of time, for the abuses of the generations require time-consuming change in people, customs, and laws. It is even more true when he admits he is a nonprofessional (and even the most competent authorities are not in agreement upon how to resolve conflict wisely or to bring about social change constructively).

His admission of inadequate competence does not mean that he gives up, however. He keeps pressing for reconciliation for as long as he is active as an encourager. And he hopes that some encourager who follows him will do the same. Since he proceeds experimentally (the record-keeping described earlier is part of this), he keeps hoping that some reconciliation will ultimately succeed when he or those who follow him are encouraging the process.

Some Generalizations about Resolution of Community Conflict

The whole process by which a nucleus becomes the instrument of conciliation pays respect to the belief that problems can have a rational solution. The problems which we face, as a human race, are to be resolved not by pressure or emotional sloganizing, but by obtaining the best contributions of all the intelligences that can be assembled. The intelligence is released when sufficient mutual good will and understanding have been built up.

Conflicts are resolved by the gaining of cooperation among factions that have distrusted and misunderstood each other. Considerable disturbance may have to occur, built up by dramatic dissent that causes both the complacent and the discouraged to move. They are more likely to move after the stirring up when some social instrument of known good will, such as a larger nucleus, takes the initiative to call them together.

The habits of cooperation and the desire to cooperate grow by doing things together. The shared activities cover a wide range—coming together face to face, discussing both differences and agreements, concentrating upon some problem of common concern (often one unrelated to the main issue in conflict), then searching for a solution together, and finally working to carry the solution into action and evaluation. Thus the process within the nucleus is extended to the surrounding community.

There is, however, danger for the mediator of conflict. The danger threatens both the individual encourager and the active nucleus that mediates controversy. People or factions in conflict may say, "You're no friend of mine if you do not hate my enemies as I do." In this case, the encourager and the nucleus he urges into the encouraging role insist that it is possible for persons of good will to have friendly relationships with factions on both sides of any controversy. Detractors will not believe him when he first makes this assertion. But he should persist in saying it and act as though he believes it. Sooner or later he will convince some or perhaps most of his critics.

He can draw certain skills of conciliation to the attention of nucleus members. These they can acquire by a conscious effort as they mediate conflicts in community confrontations of factions.

1. He should develop a group atmosphere in which differing with others is expected and regarded as honorable. People can be urged to differ not in anger or recrimination but in respect for the point of view that is strange. Opponents are always to be treated with consideration, even while their points of view are regarded as incorrect. Quiet words of guidance will build this atmosphere of friendly dispute over a period of years.
2. He should develop some devices for calling time on the overzealous or the overeloquent. This stopping of a flow of words can be accomplished with politeness, even with a sense of humor. The responsibilities for this delicate halting of eloquence rests upon nucleus members, not upon partisans.

3. He should build up the concept that any proposed solution to a problem is not an adoption of change that will last forever. It is rather an idea to try out and is always subject to later reexamination and modification.

4. He should exhibit a calm assurance that some solution of good will is discoverable, no matter how stalemated and discouraging the discussion seems to be at any given time. Several nucleus members in a strong nucleus who will exhibit this calm can do wonders to make the atmosphere hopeful.

5. Above all, he should press for continued meeting, continued discussion. Even though there be postponements, he should bring the group back together again. One strong persuasive point for bringing disputants back into meetings is the conviction demonstrated by nucleus members that some positive action will eventually come out of meetings. Part of the atmosphere of the meetings is built by the manner in which people are urged to keep on attending.

6. He should make it clear also that whatever solutions to problems are finally adopted must be of benefit to all disputants. No faction is going to be forced into capitulation to another. All are going to live and work together, even though this means evolving new patterns of local living, even though everyone will eventually make changes in himself.

7. He should realize that much depends upon the atmosphere that prevails in meetings. By being neutral toward factional or personal hostility, yet committed to the common good, nucleus members can create an atmosphere for community meetings that makes problem-solving likely.

ADDENDUM FOR SOCIAL SCIENCE STUDENTS

The literature on social conflict, in community, in nation, in the world, is voluminous. The literature on reconciliation of conflict is much scarcer. We will not attempt to list the many books, articles, and instructional manuals on controversy and how to defeat opponents. We will draw attention to a few of the social scientific treatments of the methods of conciliation.

The most basic work is that of Kurt Lewin, especially in his book, *Resolving Social Conflict*.[1] This book has become a classic among social

---

[1] Kurt Lewin, *Resolving Social Conflict* (New York: Harper & Row, Publishers, 1948).

scientists but not among social activists. See especially Chapter XIII, "Action Research and Minority Problems."

Another book is more popular with practical people close to the scene of action. This is *Roads to Agreement* by Stuart Chase.[2] This book describes and classifies a number of methods of conciliation that have worked.

For an even more specific case study of community conflict and resolution, see the issue of *The Journal of Social Issues* entitled "Trigger to Community Conflict."[3] This is a symposium that centers a number of contributions upon the problem of fluoridation of a community's water supply. Some procedures for dealing with conflict can be identified in this issue of the journal, but their usefulness is somewhat limited by consideration of just one controversial issue, and not one of the most emotionally disturbing of our times.

---

[2] Stuart Chase, *Roads to Agreement* (New York: Harper & Row, Publishers, 1951).

[3] "Trigger to Community Conflict," *The Journal of Social Issues,* Vol. XXIII, No. 4, 1961.

Chapter *14*

The Ethics
of Influence

We have already pointed out that an encourager's relationship to people must be profoundly ethical. We wish to restate this point and examine, in deeper analysis, the responsibilities that an influencer of other people must accept.

We wish to look also at an encourager's responsibility for persuading citizen groups to influence their fellow citizens. Even though he is an encourager of citizen-initiated change, he cannot free himself of responsibility for nucleus decisions and actions, and for the process of development through which people move. Citizens are responsible also, or they become so as a result of his efforts. But he must realize, again and again, that they would not have started on their road of development if he had not intervened to stir them out of whatever handicaps and negative attitudes have paralyzed their initiative.

He cannot avoid responsibility for the results of his intervention. The nucleus group he influences cannot avoid responsibility for its interventions in the life of its neighborhood or city. The citizens outside the nucleus will hopefully be brought to greater ethical responsibility as a result of his efforts as his ethical spirit has an impact through nucleus actions.

Inevitable Influence and More

By what right does an encourager of development impose his presence, his ideas, his ethical standards upon residents of an area where he serves? The nobility of his intentions, or of the institution that recruited him as a volunteer, will not compensate for the unfortunate things he may do. And he may do some very irritating things that will cause people to become negative.

Will his influence prove beneficial to the people he hopes to help? And who decides whether the changes that occur in people's lives are beneficial? May citizens conclude that he is a nosey busybody, messing into their affairs? May they not reject his ethical idealism as impractical and other-worldly? Or, on the contrary, may they not conclude that he is a clever confidence man trying to manipulate them to accept his ideas, rather than to seek their own concept of the good?

The first answer is easy. It is impossible for anyone living to avoid influencing other people—and, in some instances, to keep on affecting people even after departure or death. To live is to have impact upon other people's lives. Everyone influences his associates openly or subtly. Then the ethical question is to what extent does that influence make life more interesting, more complete, more rewarding for people whose lives are touched? To what extent does a person help other people fulfill themselves in their own unique ways?

But there is a related question that requires more complex answers. By what right does an encourager go beyond the minimal influence of being alive? An outside encourager goes out of his accustomed environment and into the environment of other people who may not have invited him, or have given a nominal invitation only, without anticipating the disruptive effect his presence may have.

An indigenous encourager does not escape this difficulty. He may be working in the social environment to which he was born, but he will disrupt some of the accustomed routines of living. He will find himself pressing for new ideas that will confuse or redirect the processes of change that go on spontaneously, or follow some other influencer's efforts.

Means for meeting this ethical dilemma can be found when an encourager realizes that influence is not the same thing as control. He can influence in such a way as to decrease his domination and increase people's control of their own future. He will find a self-congratulatory satisfaction when people do the things he wishes to have them do. But he should find the deeper satisfaction that arises when he sees them create their own patterns of conduct and develop their own schemes of value, which are not a copy of his. He offers recommendations in discussion, but he expects them to create proposals of their own.

If an encourager expects members of a nucleus to come to resemble him, in point of view, behavior, or objectives, he will utilize the methods of conscious or unconscious control—and the unconscious are the most difficult to hold in check. But if he expects nucleus members to develop according to their own ethically seeking experience, he will participate in a process of citizen-motivated growth into which he can feed his ideas, along with the ideas of all other members.

In the first case he consciously or unconsciously seeks power over people. In the second, he chooses to avoid this power, in the expectation that the ethical standards of citizens will be refined out of experience with the process and also out of contact with him. He sets out to be an influential member of the group, along with other friends, but never its director.

The choosing to avoid control is not just negative, not just a renunciation. He should make a positive choice to believe in people and in the process they can conduct with his help. Unless he chooses to avoid control in favor of this faith in people and in the process of their experience, he is constantly in danger of yielding to the delights of power. Unless this faith is active and vigorous, he will never explore the methods of community development which strengthen people to choose their growth wisely.

In other words, the probability that he will search experimentally for better methods of encouraging development, such as we have recommended throughout this book, is dependent upon his making an ethical renunciation of control over people. And by this choosing to avoid domination, he increases the probability of ethical growth in the nucleus and among its members.

One final note of realism before we pass on to the ethics of a nucleus: an encourager's renunciation of power to control applies initially to a small number who become active in any neighborhood, about four percent at any given time. This is in the intimate ethical relationship he can have with nucleus members. But he extends this ethical avoidance of power also to the larger crowds who may become involved later. He may see as many as thirty percent of local residents turn out for mass activities. He extends his renunciation also to members of subcommittees that plan details. These may involve as many as ten or twenty percent of a neighborhood population during intense periods of activity.

But his willingness to avoid power extends also to the entire neighborhood and city. His reliance upon processes of ethical seeking forces him back upon the activity of a nucleus or of several nuclei. He counts on these active participants in the process to be creators of ethical values whose influence will eventually come to pervade an entire area of community-seeking activity. He surrenders the expectation of power over people in favor of ethical growth that will be most observed in the development of nucleus members. These persons who give most time and devotion to the creation of a community gain the greatest benefit of favorable change.

The fact that an encourager has chosen to be a volunteer to help people means. that he already has generous impulses. His ethical problem is, therefore, not to discover good will in his motivation, but to discipline this good will, lest it do more harm than good. He disciplines his generous impulses by giving greater heed to the effect of his actions upon other people than to his own conviction of being right. But even more, he disciplines his well-meaning influence by helping the nucleus members to develop their own ethical sensitivity.

Ethical Responsibility in the Citizen Group

Every active citizen nucleus has influence upon the surrounding community. It cannot escape ethical responsibility for the way it exercises that influence. An encourager has an obligation to help members accept that responsibility. He begins by encouraging them to organize their group to serve their concept of a community good.

Beyond this beginning, he will find two ways he can influence their ethical decisions without dominating them. The first is negative, the second positive. He can avoid asking them to indulge in antisocial behavior, such as violent attacks upon enemies or demonstrations that tend to increase antisocial impulses in opponents. Then he can raise questions that encourage group members to create and revise an ethical code of their own choosing.

In this process he can point out that the group has an obligation of restraint toward the community it seeks and serves. There is a self-discipline which group members need to learn, if their influence is to prove effective and long-lasting.

They can learn this group discipline; it cannot be taught as a copybook lesson. They will learn it through experiences which he can encourage and help them to understand. The self-discipline achieved always represents a delicately balanced choice that comes from group discussion and critical self-evaluation. Gradually he can help them build up a code of acceptable group conduct. This code refers to relationships within the group, but even more to obligations to outsiders.

As members of a nucleus rise from hopelessness, in the process, they tend to be overly impressed by their new-found power. They gain self-respect and the dignity of their own importance as they discover that their wishes can have some effect upon public decisions and events, that other people will pay attention to them.

But having gained this influence, they are subject to the well-known corrupting effects of power. They suffer from this corrupting effect, as do all human beings; the corruption occurs even though the amount of power gained or even hoped for is not great. The very experience that has given them self-respect tends to cause them to take advantage of others who may also suffer from hopelessness. Until they have learned the lessons of self-restraint that rest upon an expanding experience of community, they may become quite as self-centered and oppressive of other powerless people as their former oppressors.

Certain community developers are so sympathetic to the victims of poverty and discrimination that they choose the bringing of power to the powerless as their chief aim in life. Their well-meaning enthusiasm can easily outrun their wisdom if they are unaware of the corrupting influence that pursuit of power can have, upon themselves, upon the citizens they encourage. Some increase of influence is necessary for development. But achievement of power is not the sole objective of the process. Growth of ethical obligation to all one's neighbors is more important.

It is this ethical sensitivity which provides the means for citizen self-restraint upon the unbridled pursuit of power. Sense of community and growing awareness of obligation to all the people in it provide the ethical imperative for citizen self-discipline. An encourager has an opportunity to encourage people into the ethical awareness that grows out of emerging sense of community.

He does not become an instructor in ethics, nor does he rely mainly upon the hope that citizens in a nucleus will adopt his standards. Instead, his chief reliance is upon building up an awareness that they are part of a common good called community. And he draws constant attention to the need and opportunity to serve all of their neighbors. This encouraging of nucleus members into ethical obligation is a quiet urging of attention that occurs many times a day in dozens of small contacts, as well as in the affairs of great consequence.

In fact, it is in the small discussions and decisions, day by day, that the chief loyalty to community is built. It is difficult to recount illustrative episodes because the growth of ethical sensitivity is usually so undramatic and unremarkable at the time. It is only later that citizens come to look back at the changes which have occurred in themselves, by gradual shifts in attitude, to which an encourager may have contributed.

He should not expect a citizen nucleus to be as wise as he should be, however, especially in avoiding involvement with community controversy. He should not be surprised if they take sides on disputes they would be more wise to conciliate. They may oppose points of view or factions in the neighborhood or city, before they reach the more inclusive level of sharing hopes for the future with opponents. Their learning of an all-inclusive idea of community will come gradually, after they have learned numerous sad lessons from unwise controversy. He can be a key to that growth despite misadventures. He can try to build up in them an admiration for conciliation knowing they will adopt such a function after they have had unproductive experiences of striving for partisan advantages. For some time they may prefer to serve a fraction of the population, before they achieve the more inclusive concept of total community. Part of the encourager's ethical responsibility is to help them gradually to achieve this broader concept of community good.

The kind of influence toward which he encourages a nucleus to move is that of creative resolution of community conflict. But the road to this ideal is long. He can help nucleus members move along it with greater speed through his tactful influence.

The Slow Growth
of Ethical Responsibility

Although the slow development of ethical sensitivity provides few dramatic episodes, one or two illustrative highlights can be mentioned. The first of these stories has to do with the growth of ethical sensitivity among some students who were learning to become encouragers. The second tells of ethical sensitivity developing in a nucleus that served a city neighborhood.

A group of students was living and working to speed development in a population foreign to their comfortable, middle-class background. In addition to the many daily activities planned and worked upon with a citizen nucleus, the young people tried to become friendly with many citizens not necessarily active in the nucleus. They encountered many problems that grew out of poverty as a way of life. How should they, who had never known want, relate themselves to people who had known nothing else?

They tried every way they could to raise standards of living, by improving health, providing education that was requested, and helping people to qualify for jobs. But the climax of their learning of ethical sensitivity came on the day when the students were breaking camp to return home. In their visiting, they had discovered a mother with twin babies whose husband had been killed in an accident just after the twins were born. She had struggled to find enough food to keep her babies and one older boy alive. The students had helped her for some weeks, giving up some of their own food to share with this tragic remnant of a family. They had provided her especially with the powdered milk which was one of the staples of their own diet. Then on breaking up the camp to leave, they found they had half of a five pound can of powdered milk left over. They conveyed this to the mother as a parting gift. She expressed tearful gratitude.

When all the students' gear was packed, they piled their goods and themselves on trucks to leave. But before they started out, they noticed the older son of the widow trudging up the trail to the campsite. When he came up to the trucks, he opened his fists to reveal two eggs which his mother had sent as her parting gifts.

The students, in agitation, asked the boy to wait while they conferred, out of his hearing. What should they do? Should they accept the eggs these hungry people obviously needed? Should they accept when they had no stoves or dishes unpacked to cook the eggs? Or should they insult the widow's generosity by refusing the gift?

One of the older encouragers said, "This is a real ethical dilemma. The gift of the two eggs represents the true widow's mite. Dare we refuse the gift which is more precious than much gold? Perhaps her gesture of generosity is more important to her than the food value of the eggs."

The students wrestled with this dilemma while the boy waited. Finally they reached a conclusion of ethical sensitivity; they would accept the eggs with gratitude and send their appreciation to the widow, through the boy. Then they would take the eggs and give them to someone else in need.

A simple story with unimportant details? Perhaps, but it illustrates the many small and undramatic episodes that in the aggregate build ethical sensitivity that may then apply to the great issues. The next story has to do with some of the great issues of our time, which tear at the fabric of metropolitan life.

The larger nucleus of an interracial neighborhood had been trying to preserve a residential area to serve both Negro and white families. They had contended for months with the tactics of real estate brokers who were engaged in blockbusting. To open up homes for Negroes, but also to enrich themselves, the dealers deliberately created a panic among white owners so that these householders would sell their homes for cheap prices. Then the operators would sell to Negroes at high prices, making an often fabulous profit. The blockbusting real estate men, who sent out scare letters and put in frightening phone calls to create panic selling, were both white and Negro.

Members of the larger nucleus brought into meetings samples of the letters used to create panic. They told again and again of phone calls and rumors spread to increase the fright that assured the profits. As a consequence, nucleus members had concluded that the whole breed of real estate brokers were bad; they were looked upon as the enemies of good community life.

In meeting after meeting, an encourager heard real estate brokers berated. He heard the allegation made that these "bad characters" would independently decide that a certain area of the metropolis was to be opened for blockbusting activities while other neighborhoods remained lily-white. It was further rumored that no government office had any control over these real estate operators, so they constituted the real power in deciding whether and how various parts of the city were to be desegregated.

The encourager listened to these accusations against real estate dealers for several meetings. Finally he decided the time had come to seek for a more ethical point of view. He began raising questions about real estate dealers. At several meetings he pointed out that he did not know any of the dealers personally, but he wondered if all of them were as bad as described. He mentioned the fact that he knew real estate operators elsewhere who were kindly and community-minded individuals. They were loyal to their professional field to be sure; but they were individuals, not all to be classified as villains, and some were devoted to their idea of the common good.

Such questions and remarks seemingly fell on deaf ears. For a time there was no response. So the encourager began wondering out loud if any members of the nucleus knew real estate dealers personally. And if so, were any of these friends nice people? And did any of them know such a dealer well enough to invite him or her to attend a meeting of the citizen group?

Members of the nucleus heard the encourager but did not offer arguments against him. Their condemnations diminished in frequency and vigor, however. Finally, one member confessed to friendship with a real estate dealer. When no one berated him, he proposed that he invite his friend to one meeting, to hear what these citizens thought of those who desegregate a city by blockbusting. After a little discussion, the group extended an invitation.

The dealer came, and paid attention to accusations against his profession. The accusations were less condemnatory than they had been several weeks earlier. Citizen members decided they liked their visitor; he was a nice fellow. They invited him to come again. He countered by suggesting that he bring two of his colleagues. The meeting agreed and invited them also.

This began a series of meetings of the nucleus with various real estate dealers present. Some defended the practices of their profession; others admitted there were unethical practices and specifically condemned both blockbusting and the refusal to show homes to Negro buyers or renters. In the exchange of points of view that followed, it was apparent that the real estate brokers had many points of view, and that citizens of the nucleus also differed among themselves. But out of the exchange of points of view, there began to emerge new ethical standards for both dealers and citizens.

Eventually some of the dealers carried their concern for a better city back to the real estate brokers' association. They proposed a resolution condemning the practice of creating panic and calling for a policy of allowing nonwhites to live wherever they could afford to throughout the city. They argued this resolution with sufficient persuasiveness to have it adopted by the association. There were negative votes against it, and all dealers did not make their practices more ethical as a consequence. But the publicly approved standard of good practice among real estate agents was changed for the better. And this resolution helped to change the whole atmosphere of the city, to welcome nonwhite residents. The newspapers gave approval, and the mayor gave open occupancy his blessing. The problems of good homes for Negroes and city-wide desegregation have not all been solved. But the city-wide ethical atmosphere has been changed in such a way as to make cooperative solutions more likely as factions work together.

Part of this community-wide ethical improvement was found in the greater sensitivity within the citizen group. Members redirected their energy toward the reconciling of antagonisms rather than to the condemning of adversaries. Learning how to win over real estate brokers became a generalized skill applicable to newspapers, to the city government, and to other accumulations of power in the city.

Some Generalizations

It is difficult to discipline one's own goodwill impulses. It is easy for the desire to help people to become the influence that dominates them. A sensitivity to their ways of thinking will help to diminish one's impatience with their refusal to accept the good chosen for them. Once an encourager has controlled his tendency to dominate, he is in a better position to help citizens in a nucleus gain the same self-discipline.

When an encourager is sent to serve a people of another nation, he should anticipate a "culture shock," the discovery that they hold to standards quite alien to his concepts of what is good. When he goes to work with fellow citizens of his own land, but among those with different economic, social, or even religious backgrounds, he had best anticipate a culture shock also, even though it be milder. But even when he works with his own neighbors, he is well advised to expect some shock of discovery that they hold to standards he does not like. The willingness to have other people start the development process with ethical standards strange to one's background is most important. One then anticipates that their standards, and one's own, will improve as a result of development together.

It is difficult to set forth any rules to guide the encourager in helping citizens discipline their desires for influence. It is so easy for them to be corrupted into ambitions for the power to control.

So much depends upon the already existing community atmosphere and how it is perceived by both the powerful and by those who believe themselves to be powerless. Relations between factions in the population may vary from an entrenched social class structure that no one believes ever will change, to a highly fluid society in the flux of shifting class and personal relationships. The best advice is to avoid prejudging any community situation. An encourager should try to make changes through ethical citizen-group initiative. The situation may prove much more fluid than he had first supposed.

So much depends upon how present holders of power react to the discovery that the disinherited or other "lesser" folk ask for or demand influence. Some persons in authority are ethical enough to welcome evidence of initiative among the underprivileged. Sometimes a few of the privileged are willing to join in efforts of change and will attempt to win over a majority of their fellow privileged. But, on the other hand, the holders of wealth or political position may exhibit a pathological fear of change and of those who propose it. It is always difficult to predict how the privileged and powerful will react, especially as individuals. It is difficult to anticipate how many might be approachable for conciliation. The encourager should encourage a citizen nucleus into the ethical approach which gives the holders of power a chance to become more ethical.

So much depends also upon the attitudes and methods of those seeking to gain influence. These may vary from long-standing habits of subservience and lack of faith in themselves, on one side, to belligerent demands that can erupt into violence and senseless challenge of existing authority. The more irrational demands for justice tend to arise in situations with a long history of subservience. Both the extremes of subservience and of fury against oppressors are to be avoided in community development processes. The preferred ethical balance is one sought rationally by citizens who learn to respect themselves and their opponents. The leadership of a community-relating citizens group is most important in establishing this balance as a local standard of good conduct.

An encourager can modify the attitudes of the privileged only slowly and indirectly, usually through the initiative of a citizen group. But he can do much to facilitate the influencing of that group. He should not dominate the group; he should seek to influence it in ways that make members more ethically competent decision-makers. This concern for citizen development will provide principles to guide his influencing. He must advise with compassion, not only for the people who need to gain the experience of increasing influence, but also for those who are reluctant to yield power.

One of the paradoxes of community development he will discover is that cooperation and reconciliation can be proved to work only by encouragers of the process who believe these ethical methods will work. Citizens in nucleus groups will not believe the more ethical methods of influence will work until they try them. And usually they will not try them until they are encouraged to do so by someone who believes the methods will work.

The highest ethical influence he can have is to encourage citizens to develop the better ethical standards they shall choose.

ADDENDUM FOR SOCIAL SCIENCE STUDENTS

The social scientists who have given most adequate attention to the responsibility of agents of development, are the anthropologists. Two names especially can be mentioned, Sol Tax and Ward Hunt Goodenough.

Sol Tax has been the advocate of action anthropology, a method by which development agents seek to bring about changes in which local participants are choosers. A book which he edited, *Horizons of Anthropology,*[1] gives a little introduction to his concept, especially in the chapter he wrote, "The Uses of Anthropology." A more concise presentation is found in an address, "Action Anthropology." [2] Tax and his students have done much action anthropology research among American Indians, which has value for other disadvantaged populations.

Ward Hunt Goodenough has produced the book already mentioned, *Cooperation in Change.*[3] This is a closely reasoned analysis of change among underdeveloped peoples, in which they cooperate with the influence of agents of development. His Part I, "Theory," presents an examination of persons in relationship to social customs and values, but in process of change. His Part II, "Practice," is even more useful for encouragers. He goes into questions of social sensitivity and of the limitations set up by administrative controls. He is especially good in his treatment of the problems of culture shock. His entire presentation leans heavily upon overseas experience with less advanced peoples. But much of his thinking is applicable also to work with people in advanced nations such as the United States. His whole point of view calls for the decision of citizens to participate in the process of change.

---

[1] Sol Tax, *Horizons of Anthropology* (Chicago: Aldine Publishing Company, 1964).
[2] Given at the University of Michigan, March 20, 1958.
[3] Ward Hunt Goodenough, *Cooperation in Change* (New York: Russell Sage Foundation, 1963).

The whole question of influence which groups of citizens can achieve has been clouded over by a concept which has gained currency in both popular and sociological thinking. This is the conviction that every town, city, and metropolis (and even state, and nation) is dominated by a power structure which must be fought or manipulated into proper action.

The best known expression of this point of view is found in a book by Floyd Hunter, *Community Power Structure: A Study of Decision Makers*.[4] This study of an American city (Atlanta) has been interpreted to prove that there is always a monolithic and often impregnable organization of those who run everything.

The monolithic interpretation, following Hunter, has been challenged by a number of other social scientists. Notable among these is Scott Greer in *The Emerging City, Myth and Reality*.[5]

At the end of his book, Hunter calls for formation of citizen groups similar to the nuclei we have described. He does not tell how these are to be formed, however. Many who follow Hunter's thinking about power structures fail to note his recommendation for dealing with them. Nevertheless, the concept of a community power structure persists and has a fascination for many social science researchers. It has become a cliché of work and of thought for many practitioners of community improvement and action. For example, *A Manual of Intergroup Relations* by John P. Dean and Alex Rosen [6] presents a series of methods for coping with the power structures, in an often manipulative fashion.

The community development process calls for experimentation with the cooperative approach stressed by Goodenough, more than with the approach that coerces power structures.

---

[4] Floyd Hunter, *Community Power Structure* (Chapel Hill, N.C.: University of North Carolina Press, 1953).

[5] Scott Greer, *The Emerging City, Myth and Reality* (New York: The Free Press, 1962).

[6] John P. Dean and Alex Rosen, *A Manual of Intergroup Relations* (Chicago: University of Chicago Press, 1955).

Chapter 15

The Process
Continues

The process an encourager helps people to start should have no ending. It can be accepted as nonterminal when people realize that problems are seldom solved once and for all. The important ones require attention over the years to adjust solutions and find new solutions.

Many efforts of community (and other kinds of) improvement rest upon the expectation that the problem under consideration can be disposed of by some great effort for which people's enthusiasm can be whipped up. The assumption that the difficulties which plague humanity can be settled once and for all may or may not be openly stated in the publicity that urges citizen action. But the tacit assumption is present in most community action programs that end in futility. "If only you will make the extra effort called for in this money-raising campaign or push of publicity or demonstration against authority or construction of some buildings, then we will have solved our problem." Such reassurance is naive in an era of rapid and accelerating change.

A more realistic assumption, which should be part of the thinking of nucleus members, is that they will have to keep seeking better solutions to problems and that new problems will arise constantly. Therefore, the community effort to be sought is one of adjustment and readjustment for today and for the years ahead. Community improvement is not something to be sought by a single dramatic campaign or even by several. It requires continuous attention to changing needs and to grievances expressed by one injured group and then another and another.

Some social instrument in communities is necessary to carry on this nonterminal adjustment and readjustment process that presses for improvement. One such instrument is a larger nucleus, relating first to a neighborhood, then relating to a whole city or other large area, together with other neighborhood nuclei. By encouraging and continuing such groups an encourager is introducing a consciously chosen and ethically sensitive influence into the unplanned processes of change which are already occurring and will increase in speed.

Building in the Expectation
of Continuation

It is part of his responsibility to persuade initiators to enter upon the community development process, expecting it to be nonterminal. The citizens they recruit are encouraged to become part of the process, not for a single great effort, but for the long pull of planning a community-serving future. He should ask all to make a commitment to stay with the nucleus, through success and failure, for a period of time. Usually three years is a realistic minimum as a start. Such an early commitment pledges citizens to faithfulness until the process is well started. It does not obligate individuals to nonterminal participation even though the process is set up to last indefinitely. The individual citizen may look upon his participation as limited in time, with obligations passed on to others.

The concept of rotation in nucleus membership should be discussed as part of the original pattern of the group. One should recommend that initiating members seek out new members so that rotation can take place without loss to the on-going process. Especially is change of personnel important in officerships. It is wise to recommend that chairmen, for instance, serve for a limited time period, perhaps a year or two. Then regular elections can be scheduled as part of the pattern for action, with opportunity for passing the responsibilities around.

Citizens will respond differently to recommendations for rotating responsibility in different development processes. In one interracial nucleus, an encourager raised the question as to whether the members of the newly formed group did not want to choose a chairman of one race and a vice-chairman of the other. Then group members could reverse the racial choice at the next election, a year later. He was promptly notified by both Negroes and whites that his idea was ridiculous. They accepted rotation of officers, but wanted to be free to choose the best man for the job irrespective of the color of his skin.

In another interracial larger nucleus, the same encourager found members insisting that a white man should be chairman, year after year, until all were convinced that a Negro holding the office would win wide support in the community at large. Their concept of rotation was tied to the impact of the group upon surrounding citizens who were not yet involved in the process. The encourager concluded he had best accept the rulings of both groups, even though the policies chosen seemed contradictory to each other.

Subcommittees and smaller constituent nuclei are some of the best recruiting grounds for new members to be brought into the central larger nucleus. An encourager keeps this possibility in mind as he works with these smaller groups. And he asks officers and important members of the larger nucleus to use the smaller groups this way also. Smaller nuclei can shift in membership more rapidly than should the central body. This central larger nucleus provides the greater continuity for the continuing years. But even its membership will also change in time.

One other idea he builds into people's thinking, as an aid to continuation, is that any outside encourager is expected to work himself out of a job. He also makes a commitment to stick with the citizens who have committed themselves to staying with it until the process is well started. But his commitment also has a time limit. He expects to stay with the larger nucleus until it is well enough launched to go on without him. In the meantime he is training citizens through experience and interpretation to take over and run the process after his departure.

This phasing out by an outside encourager is anticipated from the beginning, and steps are taken to build up citizen competence to continue. We have seen outside encouragers who agreed to stay with a process until all the people involved (including themselves) were convinced that they could leave without hurting the ongoing development. One unspecified time period of this sort lasted for six years. In other instances we have seen outside encouragers set a limit of three years, at the end of which time they promised to withdraw. The latter arrangement seems to produce better results because all the people involved can work with a phasing-out date in mind. We do recommend less than a three-year commitment for outside encouragers.

Handing Over the Process

When the time comes for an outside encourager to phase out, there are several hands into which he can pass the group. By all means the most satisfactory receiver is an indigenous encourager (or several) who has been trained for the job of encouraging, and can be broken in to responsibilities over a period of several months. Incidentally, the indigenous encourager should not expect to dominate. He or she or they should be just known as members of the group. If a single person, he may accept a minor officership such as secretary or treasurer, but is wise to avoid the chairmanship. He is the person who is going to live with the group for a long period of time and should therefore be less subject to rotation in and out of office. In addition he should be more interested in pushing other members into prominence than himself. All of this role of encouraging others into leadership is part of the training which an outside encourager should offer to the indigenous encouragers who take over.

After having worked with a city human relations council for about eight years (too long for outsiders, not for insiders) some encouragers were forced to consider phasing out. They were about to leave this particular city and were therefore forced into their termination. They searched about for some persons on whom to cast their mantle. After considering and interviewing several nucleus members, they finally settled upon a couple associated with the college located in the city. This husband-wife team had been active in the group, but had not thought of themselves as encouragers. In this situation, with the original encouragers leaving, they agreed to carry on with the same spirit and point of view on method.

The transfer of encouraging responsibility worked well. The indigenous encouragers found they could do many jobs they had not known they could. Among these was the recruitment of new members and officers. Shortly, they proved more successful than the first encouragers in spreading the participation. So the transfer was successful even though it had been forced by circumstances.

In another community development project among underprivileged rural people, the phasing out had been talked about from the beginning. But these were unsophisticated people who needed much help. Among the tasks they asked the outside encouragers to help them on was the raising of money to purchase tools and supplies for their cooperative work. They insisted they had no idea of how to approach government bureaucrats or donors of wealth. Would the encouragers show them how?

The encourager pointed out that he was as ignorant of money-raising skill as they. Then why shouldn't he go with them to visit various sources of help and learn how with them? The nucleus members accepted this proposition somewhat dubiously, but went along on money-raising expeditions, leaning heavily upon the encourager who fumbled his way into obtaining grants of help.

At first the participant citizens thrust the encourager forward as chief spokesman; they were tongue-tied. The encourager was inept, but his lack of smoothness proved to be an asset. Potential donors apparently concluded he must be sincere since he lacked the money-raiser's normal glibness. And they became generous. As a result citizens achieved a bit of courage and began to take over the role of spokesmen.

After two to three years of such cooperative money-raising expeditions, a committee of the nucleus group announced one day that they were about to take off in a couple of cars to ask for help from a distant government office. When the encourager learned of this he asked his citizen friends to wait while he changed out of his work clothes and into a suit to impress the government people. When he appeared ten or fifteen minutes later, the committee looked him over approvingly, then pointed out unanimously that they did not need him any more. He could change back into his work clothes and let them go on their way without his helpful presence.

The first reaction of the encourager was deep disappointment, bordering on anger. Here he had dressed up in splendid raiment only to be informed that he was now unnecessary. But the second reaction was one of jubilation after they had gone and he had changed his clothes again and cooled off. After all, this was the very thing he had been working for all these months. The nucleus members had taken over and were now assuming responsibility for the continuation of the process.

Among members of the money-raising committee were several emerging indigenous encouragers who took over after the original encouragers phased out. The local people still remember the original encouragers, talk about them, and welcome them on visits. But the process is now theirs.

An indigenous encourager has his own way of phasing out. It does not usually take the form of departure from the scene of development. Instead, he avoids becoming the indispensable leader. He seeks out and trains other indigenous encouragers to spread the influence of the process. Above all, he makes it clear that he expects other citizens to take over more and more of the responsibility.

Sometimes it is possible to hand over the process to an agency or institution that operates in the area. In part this was the case with the couple from the college in the city. Even better, however, is to persuade an educational institution, or a social work agency, or a church, to make the encouragement of the development process a regular part of the organization's program. We have seen agricultural extension officials thus take over a process, or a group of church people, or sometimes school officials. The great difficulty for an encourager in almost every such case is that he will doubt that the agency will do as good a job as he has done. There are often grounds for the doubt. The institution, in taking over, may revise objectives and methods because of loyalty to the traditional practices of the organization. This possibility is always present in any phasing out to institutional encouragers.

In the instances we have mentioned, however, local citizens had become strong enough and experienced enough with the process to be able to keep going despite institutional interference. The original encouragers had been successful in starting a process that had its own momentum in the lives of the citizens. As a result these encouragers and citizens were able also to influence the agencies and institutions to modify their purposes and methods somewhat. This will be part of an encourager's job in phasing out. He should try to persuade any institution that takes over from him to understand the philosophy and purposes which he has built into the process.

One encourager stumbled upon a workable pattern for phasing out, almost by accident. He had a grant from a research foundation for conducting two community development processes within a three-year period. One was to be in an urban neighborhood, the other in a low-income rural section. The time for departure was, therefore, established from the beginning. And the encourager carried on both experimental projects with the date for termination agreed upon, throughout the three years.

Because of this arbitrarily set date, the encourager carried on his work in such a way as to assure continuation. He was on the alert to find citizen leaders who could be trained to become indigenous encouragers. He tried to interest local institutions to make the process a part of their program responsibility. But, above all, he sought an early growth of responsibility among larger nucleus members.

In the city project, several university professors were trained to become indigenous encouragers—in spite of the fact that the institution which employed them would never give any official endorsement. (The administrators of the university were happy to accept credit for the larger nucleus, however, when the newspapers gave favorable stories of the achievement of the citizen group). Public school and social welfare individuals later became indigenous encouragers without specific approval from their employing organizations.

In the rural project, a religiously supported mission school became the institutional inheritor of the process by assigning one of its teachers. This man also benefitted by on-the-job training through experience. The school assigned this teacher to give most of his time to the continuation of the original nucleus and of others that developed in imitation. He accepted responsibility as secretary for more than one of these local nuclei.

In other words, if termination for the outside encourager is anticipated from the beginning and some probable date of separation set, the whole process is carried on in such a way as to make good continuation possible. The final combination of indigenous encourager, institution, and nucleus members who learn from the process, is a pattern that can be worked out over a period of several years, in the midst of both successes and disappointments.

Finally, there is the situation when an encourager hands over a process to no one who appears to be a good successor. He finds (or has trained) no adequate indigenous encourager and cannot persuade any institution to accept the responsibility. When he is an outside encourager, he must withdraw sometime. And any time for withdrawal usually proves to be a bad one. Too often he must depart for reasons beyond his control. Then what happens to the group he has nurtured and now must leave to its own devices?

Nucleus Strength for Continuation

May the group fall into the control of people unsympathetic to his hopes? Yes, it may. May it become an organization to further the careers of the ambitious? May it come to be dominated by persons who take it over permanently as their private instrument for domination? And may these dominators prove disinterested in allowing other people to grow into leadership, or in inviting other interests into participation?

All these possibilities are variants upon the theme of power, the striving to get it or the battle to hold it, when it is threatened. May not a larger nucleus become an organization devoted to power struggles? If it does, will an encourager then have inadvertently created an instrument of conflict rather than one of community? If the nucleus dominators who succeed him subvert the group to pursuit of power over other citizens, then development will have been pushed aside.

For a larger nucleus he has encouraged into being to become an instrument of struggle for power may not be wholly bad, just inadequate. If this happens, it would be better if the leaders drop the vocabulary of development and talk instead about that battle for victory which is a part of a democratic society. But will the encourager be happy at this outcome of his efforts? And will the cause of cooperative community have been served? Will the nonterminal process of ethically rational problem-solving have been strengthened for the years ahead?

There is accumulating evidence that the simple-minded conflicts of rival interests within a democracy are proving inadequate to solve the increasingly complex problems of our difficult age. Let us choose a few examples of community conflicts that need to pass beyond the stage where one interest hopes to defeat another, situations in which there is need to discover the more refined skills of cooperative thinking and acting.

One of the negative results of much effort to improve life for the poor has been that different factions of the underprivileged start to battle each other. In some cities, people of Spanish background are pitted against Negroes. This rivalry can appear in refusal to sit on the same local planning committees, or in rival campaigns when representatives of the poor are to be elected to committees, or it may even erupt in episodes of violence. One meeting of Spanish-Americans went so far as to petition the President of the United States for special treatment for their people, similar to that received by Negroes.

In certain southern states, poor whites represent the greatest block that stands in the way of progress for the poor. Some of these underprivileged whites, when they migrate to nonsouthern cities, locate themselves in ghettos that exclude other poor people. They then refuse to cooperate with others of the disinherited, as well as with the privileged.

The cause of the poor has been accepted by certain labor union interests that have sought to organize low-income people into unions of the poor. These efforts at community and self-improvement are pitted against the kind of community development set up by chambers of commerce or corporations. People at both ends of the economic scale will speak the same words of cooperation and democracy, but will expend much energy in attack upon each other's programs.

In certain smaller cities, and in "rurban" (rural plus urban) areas, can be found a rivalry between city interests and farming or rural interests that makes progress for both most difficult. This conflict is not confined to local areas merely; it extends on to legislative halls, both state and national. The conflict is especially unwise in an age when the differences between city and country living are being erased, and improvement is to be sought for the underprivileged in city and country simultaneously. One group is not to benefit at the expense of the other.

There are other examples of improvement for disadvantaged people being blocked by conflict among different factions of the poor. There is reason to suspect that opponents of such progress for disadvantaged people have welcomed the tendency of citizen groups of the underprivileged to fight each other or the privileged. The tactics of Roman emperors to divide and rule are still useful. If the opponents of improvement can paralyze progress by welcoming conflict amongst the proposers of development, they can guarantee a delay in the solution of problems.

An encourager's thinking should be clear on the matter of progress through conflict. As a believer in democracy he welcomes clashing points of view in the population he serves. But as an encourager he is committed to a more constructive and difficult search for all-inclusive community. His is a more healing and creative responsibility that represents the next great step in local democracy, beyond promotion of conflict.

But when he surrenders a larger nucleus to some people he does not know too well, there is always the possibility that citizen participants will succumb to time-honored temptations to enjoy fighting. They may tend to substitute for the constructive correcting of their own mistakes an enthusiasm to heap blame upon their antagonists.

Since a larger nucleus is an instrument of influence, it can be used to serve destructive as well as constructive purposes. During the time an encourager has been active, he should throw his influence on the side of rational and ethical approaches to progress. He should put faith in the process he can encourage in people's lives to carry on into the period of continuation.

He should operate with the hope that he will succeed enough with people to encourage them into satisfaction with cooperative development. If their experience is vital enough, they will want to continue this type of activity after his departure. We have seen nucleus groups which found the continuation of the process so gratifying that they resisted the influence of persons that tried to subvert them. He needs to hope that people are capable of taking the next steps into intelligently cooperative democracy, carrying on after his period of encouragement.

The Nature of the Continuing Process

A larger nucleus with strength to carry on the process should not become a partisan in the political wars of democracy. Yet it is the social instrument which will strengthen political democracy. This is a paradox which numerous spokesmen for community development have pointed out.

The success of large-scale democratic government rests upon vigorous, independent, and public-serving citizens in thousands of local neighborhood scenes. These citizens cannot be assumed to be available already; they must be developed by processes that accept controversy as essential to freedom, but press on to seek that reconciliation of clashing interests that serves a good community life.

The processes of community-seeking conciliation an encourager expedites provide the seedbed of growth for independent and self-motivated citizens. Some of these citizens may properly become active in partisan politics and this is good. But those who are associated with the reconciling processes can contribute more basically to the neighborhood atmosphere that nurtures democracy. They can seek community service without accusation of selfish advantage. If an encourager has done his work well, he starts a larger nucleus on its way to carrying this nonpartisan role so necessary to political health.

The community-seeking experiences which once occurred automatically now must be cultivated. An encourager has the opportunity to do that cultivating, either as an outsider who brings the process up to the point of vigor for continuation, or as an indigenous leader who takes part in the continuation.

When the process has reached a vigor to continue after an encourager's departure, there are numerous satisfactions that come to him from the evidences of continuation. He may hear of the ongoing work, even though it may deal with problems beyond his knowledge, even though the citizens may neglect to give public credit to him. When he goes back to visit, however, he will often find former associates who will welcome him with enthusiasm, who will recall the good days when he and they worked together—and they may even ascribe to him wisdom and triumphs he no longer remembers.

A more specific satisfaction comes out of letters sent that tell of his influence and ideas that linger on. They may even mention specific indigenous leaders who carry on his good work. Sometimes these letters (or phone calls) become even more specific in extending invitations to visit the scene of his former encouraging. Or they may ask for advice in undertaking some new problem. Or, most gratifying of all, they may ask him to return for specific time periods to counsel with them further.

Some Conclusions about Continuation

A larger nucleus is the key social entity an encourager builds up for continuation. This may arise from a basic nucleus that broadens its functions, or from a coalition of several smaller nuclei, or may be created independently as an instrument of community-seeking conciliation. In any case, this is the organization he builds up for flexibility of method and commitment to ethical service that expands people's concepts of all-inclusive community.

He encourages a larger nucleus to become a flexible voice of community conscience. It is flexible when it remains free to address attention to problems both traditional and unexpected, but also when citizen participants expand and refine the values by which they evaluate service to everyone. Such a nucleus can be encouraged to build up a tradition, gradually, that this citizen group is composed of members who study, plan, and take action in an unself-serving spirit. They truly seek improvement that serves community good. They tend to encourage the growth of other citizens of public serving good will.

When some of these citizens become involved in partisan politics, they should be encouraged to do so. But an encourager should urge the citizens who become thus involved to dissociate themselves from the nucleus group and act as individuals. And he should urge the nucleus as a whole to remain apart from such partisanship.

A large nucleus that serves one neighborhood can join with other such groups from other neighborhoods to build up a voice of conscience for an entire city or metropolitan area. Such a coalition will achieve the influence it should have if it speaks with the persuasiveness of conscience rather than the force of political power.

At the neighborhood level, however, an encourager should help a larger nucleus to become a focus of community good, to provide the atmosphere that makes democracy work at the local grass roots. This achievement is the greatest assurance he can have of continuation after he must depart.

To encourage citizens to believe they can create a voice of community conscience is hazardous, however. They will be tempted to succumb to the self-righteousness that threatens the usefulness of all idealists. Such self-righteousness is especially to be feared when a citizen group finds itself passing judgment upon fellow citizens or upon public policies. A larger nucleus should not make public moral condemnations very often, and then only after careful assessment of the probable consequences.

All working with people is hazardous; the dangers can be minimized, not eliminated. There are three ways to minimize the danger of self-righteousness. These have been mentioned already, but can bear repeating. First, members of a citizen group should develop a sense of humor about themselves and about the positions they take. Second, its members should keep reminding themselves that they may be mistaken; other persons and groups may be more right than they. There must be room for honest difference of opinion among idealists. And finally, they must avoid seeking the power to enforce their ideas of right upon other people. Their statements of conscience must stand upon their own merit, in competition with other statements of conscience. In the time an encourager has to build up a large nucleus for continuation, he should stress these safeguards against self-righteousness.

An encourager has the opportunity to help citizens create a social instrument of flexible stability for an era of unprecedented and unpredictable change. He has the opportunity to introduce into this continuing association a determination to make the changes that are guided by an unselfish community interest. He should consider himself successful if he can help citizens create such an instrument, even though they make decisions he does not like, both while he is with them and after he departs.

ADDENDUM FOR SOCIAL SCIENCE STUDENTS

There have been numerous writings by historians and others pointing to the fact of accelerating speed of social change. No proof of rapid change is needed for individuals who have lived through the coming of the automobile age, the air age, the atomic age, and the space age, to mention a few. What new ages are to come within the lifetimes of people now alive?

Some of the clearest statements of accelerating change can be found in political science writings. As early as the 1950's, two books that document changes in political opinion and habits were available: *Incredible Tale,*[1] by Gerald W. Johnson and *The Big Change,*[2] by Frederick Lewis Allen. Both trace out changes upon the national and international scene which have their inevitable effects upon the local neighborhood where people live.

More recently some analyses of change from an economic point of view are noteworthy. One is especially to be read for its attempts to predict the direction in which economic trends are taking human beings, *Landmarks of Tomorrow,*[3] by Peter F. Drucker. The author, in common with most economists, thinks in terms of large-scale forces and trends that can, however, be translated into meaning for local development of people.

Another book, written for the World Bank, also leans heavily upon economic contributions to change. This is *The Road to Huddersfield,*[4] by James Morris. Huddersfield is a small British town in which, according to the author, the "technical revolution" which is sweeping over the rest of the world began, with consequences as yet unpredictable. Like Drucker, Morris sees many changes beyond the economic which will stimulate and effect the future development of human beings.

A discussion by an anthropologist is found in *Traditional Cultures and the Impact of Technological Change,*[5] by George M. Foster. This presents a wide-ranging world picture, giving principles which can guide the encourager of planned development.

---

[1] Gerald W. Johnson, *Incredible Tale* (New York: Harper & Row, Publishers, 1950).
[2] Frederick Lewis Allen, *The Big Change* (New York: Harper & Row, Publishers, 1952).
[3] Peter F. Drucker, *Landmarks of Tomorrow* (New York: Harper & Row, Publishers, 1959).
[4] James Morris, *The Road to Huddersfield* (New York: Pantheon Books, Inc., 1963).
[5] George M. Foster, *Traditional Cultures and the Impact of Technological Change* (New York: Harper & Row, Publishers, 1962).

Chapter 16

What Is the Future for Volunteers?

In this last chapter we turn attention again to the volunteer who has become an encourager of human development. What will his future be as a result of working with people? Will he spend a limited amount of time at a volunteer assignment and then return to his normal way of living? Or should he look forward to some changed responsibilities in life as a result of his experience? Specifically, will his time spent developing citizens in communities prove to be an introduction to a career of service in a new helping profession?

The answer depends upon a number of factors. Age is important. If he is older, perhaps even beyond the years of active earning, yet eager to give the latter years to service, he probably will not be interested in establishing a new career. If he is young and has volunteered before having selected a field of life work—or even before having completed his education—he may be looking for experience that will guide him into a career.

A volunteer's expectations are important. He undoubtedly had certain expectations at the time he volunteered. These probably will have been revised by the experience of service. The expectations he had about life and about his usefulness will have been affected by the amount and kind of satisfaction he found in his experience as a volunteer. Will working with people have proven so interesting that he will want to go permanently into a profession of service?

The probability of his entering such a profession will depend also upon the availability of paying jobs. Various helping professions are asking for young people, and even for some older people, to take the necessary training. Among these are teaching, nursing, social welfare work, medicine, and the religious ministry. There are also a number of careers open in fields that should have a large helping emphasis, such as city and regional planning, social science research, and various kinds of government service. Many of these opportunities for a life's work require special training, usually at a university graduate level, usually after volunteer experience.

What about entering a career as an encourager of community development? Will funds be made available from federal and other sources to make such careers possible? If they are, will an encourager be called upon to take further academic training? Or will persons go into such work directly from volunteer assignments with only a minimum of further formal training, if that?

Does it make any difference whether he is an outside or an indigenous encourager? Possibly more outside encouragers will want to go into life careers of service, simply because indigenous encouragers are prone to look upon themselves as citizen amateurs who live with people and with the development process. But we should not be too sure of this conclusion. Already certain indigenous encouragers are being challenged to enter a possible newly emerging professional field. Many who respond are not necessarily persons with traditional formal educational backgrounds. So some kinds of training other than the academic are needed. Already there is an increase of training programs addressed to indigenous encouragers, but often including graduate level trainees as well. These latter, as well as indigenous amateurs need the practical field experience of encouraging citizens into processes of development.

There is a final most significant answer to the question as to whether volunteer experience will turn into a new helping profession. This answer will depend upon the volunteer. It will depend upon how successful he is with citizens, and upon how much the process brings about favorable changes in him.

National Commitment to Development

The obligations volunteers accept come as a response to a major change in the national conscience. There is an apparently permanent commitment to development, as national policy. The commitment is expressed in two types of programs. It is found overseas in development of underprivileged nations. It is found also in domestic programs that improve life for our own underprivileged. Appropriations of funds for both of these has tended toward emphasizing the growth of persons. Earlier the emphasis was upon relief, then upon construction of facilities, then upon raising of economic levels and improving of social life. In the more recently evolved programs, the shift of emphasis from the tangibles of material help to the intangibles of citizen development have become more prominent.

The clearest expression of concern for improvement of persons is found in the Peace Corps overseas, and in VISTA and other educational phases of antipoverty programs at home. But other federally financed programs exhibit this same trend, in changed emphases exhibited by the Department of Agriculture, in aid to schools, and in various vocational and adult educational programs. These all carry the implication that the nation, through its national government, is committed to development of citizens in a way that will persuade nongovernmental agencies and institutions also to become active.

As the federal government and cooperating organizations move more into development activities, there has been plenty of criticism. But the criticism is directed more at the way the work is done than at the idea of doing it. There is, therefore, every indication that such programs will continue in some form, no matter which political party is in control of executive and legislative branches of government.

The commitment to development calls for an obligation to be accepted by many individuals, to perfect the art of encouraging people to develop themselves. This means that the national atmosphere is favorable to the growth of a profession of human developers.

Some of the Dangers of Development

There are dangers inherent in a national policy of development. We will not attempt to mention all of these. We will draw attention only to some that a community development encourager needs to guard against.

First, there are dangers connected with problems of control. Who is to control use of funds, and for what purposes? Whoever has the final word on allocation of funds tends to control the programs. May this also result in control of the people who benefit by the programs? The result might be that citizens become the meek followers of the persons or organizations that set policy, that they become conformers to orders, not independent deciders.

This danger becomes specific when various antipoverty programs and the funds to make them possible become political footballs. Mayors, city councilmen, governors, heads of government offices, and miscellaneous social workers and controllers of voting blocks, join in a scramble for funds. Such scrambles for control have resulted in paralysis for community action programs in numerous cities.

A second danger for the national commitment is that development programs might be taken over by experts more loyal to established professions than to the needs of people. Social workers, educators, church workers, and social scientists are often so determined to honor the prescribed techniques and purposes of their professional employment that they become indifferent to citizen-motivated development. Various leaders of federal funding agencies have denounced such restrictions upon antipoverty and Peace Corps activities. But, if an insufficient number of workers devoted to development are available, these federal programs must fall back upon the agencies, institutions, and individuals they have denounced.

A third danger for development programs is found in the activities of naive believers in democracy. These are the simple-minded people who underestimate the complexity and difficulty of making democracy work in an age of accelerating change and increasing complexity. The clearest example of this naiveté is found in the holding of elections to choose representatives of the poor on community policy-making committees. Such poorly thought-out elections have been held in more than one American city, with unhappy results that dismayed the idealistic promoters of such naive democracy. The only comment an experienced community development worker could make is, "Well, what did they expect? Of course poor people were uninterested. They who suffer so much from the alienation of our time can be brought into community participation only after a process of encouraged development."

In one large metropolitan area, the experts estimated that some 400,000 poor citizens were qualified to vote (by having incomes below an agreed upon figure). Of this eligible number, only 2659 came to the pooling places to vote—less than one percent. (Some 54 of these votes were challenged and discarded). And this number turned out after a block-by-block campaign to stir interest, after loudspeaker trucks toured the poverty areas urging people to vote. The total effort cost some $61,000, and included a group of representatives who could scarcely claim to represent the poor. Worst of all, funds and energy that could have expedited the development process had been diverted into an election that respects the forms but not the substance of democracy.

These various dangers argue strongly for emergence of a profession of workers trained to start those processes of development which people shall choose for themselves. Volunteers are at present the most promising persons available for this assignment. But if volunteers are just amateurs, will they have the necessary skill and stamina to contend with politicians, entrenched professionals, and the naive folk who think democratic gestures will solve complicated problems? They will need training for a responsibility that extends over the years. Should this training be suitable for a new profession, at the graduate-school level? Or should a more informal and shorter training for on-the-job encouragers be worked out? Or should both kinds be used?

What Is Happening to Volunteers?

It is too early to speak with assurance as to what will happen to the new breed of volunteers. All we can do is make guesses on the basis of experience in organizations that have been employing this new kind of worker-with-people in the past. The work of the American Friends Service Committee and other privately financed idealistic endeavors is instructive, but throws little light upon large-scale publicly supported programs. The Peace Corps experience is the most helpful.

Many volunteers from Peace Corps experience go into already established helping professions, education, health and social work, religious work, and so on. Others return to become administrators of Peace Corps or Office of Economic Opportunity programs on a more or less permanent assignment. Still others have become teachers in colleges and universities that prepare new generations of volunteers. Many have prepared for these various responsibilities by taking further graduate study to qualify themselves.

It should be clear by now that the job for the volunteer, which we have been outlining throughout this book, is complicated, intricate, and delicate. Are volunteers helping to create a new profession of human relations, one devoted to encouragement of local development? Yes, perhaps. The answer depends upon what is meant by a profession, and upon the understanding we all have of the intermediary role between people and presently existing professionals.

If professionalization means training that limits flexibility to respond to people's needs, if it means a fixed procedure one must follow in order to prove competent, if it means competition with other helping professions, then let us not professionalize. But if it calls for training in the delicate skills to respond to human need in the social situations where people are found, if it means a methodology that stresses experimentation, with minimum fear of condemnation for innovation, if it means an intermediary role that strengthens other helping professions while calling upon them tactfully to be more human, then let the new profession come.

We should recognize, however, that we are calling for a new breed of professional. He is a highly skilled person who finds his satisfaction in the growth of citizens and in allowing the institutions that operate in his area to claim credit for the development that occurs. His assignment is one of relating people who need help to organizations that can help them. It is also to stir people into the initiative that seeks help in a way that increases their independent dignity.

If a volunteer can be satisfied with such a skilled but modest role, he will help to define a new profession and may even become part of it. He will cooperate in creating this profession, if he can be flexible to learn from the people he would help, and can adapt his methods of work to their needs.

Encouragers of local human development can afford to make flexibility central to their emerging profession because they believe in the potentials for good that can be cultivated in people. Other helping professions have given first loyalty to knowledge and services believed to be good for people. Community development, if it becomes a profession, can be unique in centering upon the skills to encourage people into discovery of their needs, and to cultivate cooperatively directed processes of growth in their lives. A profession of flexibility would place reliance upon people and upon the expected favorable outcomes of encouraged development.

Some Tentative Predictions

Whether future Congresses, social agencies, churches, schools, universities, and charitable foundations will take the steps to make such a profession financially possible is difficult to predict. The need is there. Will it be met by people with funds?

Whatever the answer, the following modest predictions can be made:

1. Compensated volunteerism (both abroad and at home) will continue and increase as a part of American life—and of the life of a number of other industrially advanced nations.
2. Many individuals who benefit from this experience will find themselves in program-planning, supervisory, and training responsibilities after some term of volunteer duty.
3. Training programs for new volunteers and for those who go on to advanced professional-type responsibilities will increase. These will take the form of both informal field plus seminar experience and formal instruction that leads to some kind of academic degree.
4. The continuation and expansion of development programs will depend upon many factors, some of which are beyond present antici-

pation. Among these, a very important one to think about is how effectively present and future volunteers carry out their assignments as encouragers.

ADDENDUM FOR SOCIAL SCIENCE STUDENTS

The serious student who wishes to pursue the possible profession of community development further, will find a very extensive, annotated bibliography in the Appendix of *The Community Development Process,*[1] pages 308 to 324. He might also study the pamphlet by Arthur Dunham, *Types of Jobs in Community Development.*[2] This gives a summary and classification of the kinds of jobs then available (1964).

Two other sources of information can be recommended. One is the magazine already mentioned, *The Community Development Journal.*[3] The other is the United Nations Department of Economic and Social Affairs. This Department publishes community development materials from time to time. One of the best is *Study Kit on Training for Community Development.*[4] Each of these, in its own way, will keep a student informed of developments as they occur.

---

[1] William W. Biddle and Loureide J. Biddle, *The Community Development Process* (New York: Holt, Rinehart and Winston, Inc., 1965).

[2] Arthur Dunham, *Types of Jobs in Community Development* (Columbia, Mo.: University of Missouri, School of Social and Community Services, 1964).

[3] *Community Development Journal* (22 Kingston Road, Didsbury, Manchester 20, England).

[4] *Study Kit on Training for Community Development* (New York: United Nations Department of Economic and Social Affairs, 1957).

Index